JEET KUNE DO
THE SYSTEM WITHOUT A SYSTEM®

By George Hajnasr

Bloomington, IN Milton Keynes, UK

AuthorHouse™
1663 Liberty Drive, Suite 200
Bloomington, IN 47403
www.authorhouse.com
Phone: 1-800-839-8640

AuthorHouse™ *UK Ltd.*
500 Avebury Boulevard
Central Milton Keynes, MK9 2BE
www.authorhouse.co.uk
Phone: 08001974150

© George Hajnasr. All rights reserved.

No part of this book may be reproduced, stored in a retrieval system, or transmitted by any means without the written permission of the author.

First published by AuthorHouse 5/22/2007

ISBN: 1-4208-3215-8 (sc)

Printed in the United States of America
Bloomington, Indiana

This book is printed on acid-free paper.

JEET KUNE DO "The System Without A System®"
WWW.JKDUS.COM

This step-by-step instructional book is a one of a kind. It gives you an in-depth look at JKD with its detailed teachings and over 3200 demonstrational photos, having over 450 pages of 8 1/2 x 11 size, keeping the art of Jeet Kune Do alive. This book is intended for the mere beginner to the highly skilled martial artist or JKD practitioner. George Hajnasr's "The System Without a System"®, all rights reserved. No part of this material may be reproduced or utilized in any form or by any means .The material in this Book is only to help you improve yourself.

Disclaimer:The adoption and application of the material offered in this book is at the reader's discretion and sole responsibility. The author and publisher of this book are not responsible in any manner whatsoever for any injuries that may occur indirectly or directly from the use of this Book, since the physical activities described herein maybe too strenuous in nature for some readers to engage in safely. Exercise is not without its risks and this or any other Martial Arts program may result in injury. To reduce the risk of injury in your case, consult your doctor before beginning this exercise or the study of this book. The instructor and advice presented are in no way intended as a substitute for medical consultation, the instructor disclaims any liability from and in connection with this book. As with any Martial Arts program, if at any point during your training you begin to feel faint, dizzy, or have physical discomfort, you should stop immediately and consult a physician. The specific self-defense practices illustrated in this book may not be justified in every particular situation or under applicable federal, state or local law. Neither the author or the publisher make any warranty or representation regarding the legality or appropriateness of any techniques mentioned in this book.

Table of Contents

Part 1: THE FUNDAMENTALS OF JEET KUNE DO
Experience   13
JKD The System Without A System ®   14-15
In My Own Expression?   15-16
Jeet Kune Do Rank   16
JKD (Terminology)   16
Essence of Jeet Kune Do   17-18
The Three Stages – Cultivations of learning Jeet Kune Do   19-22
The Immovable Elbow Moving Line   23
Targets, Gates and Weapons   24
JKD Nine Weapons of Attack   25
Centerline (Joan Seen)   26-28
Jeet Kune Do - Five Ways of Attack   29-30
Jeet Kune Do Yum /Yeung (Yin Yang) Symbol   31-32
Internal and External Development   33
Speed, Rhythm, Distance and Timing   34-35
By-Jon -Pyramids Structure for Offense and Defense   36-37
By-Jon   38
By-Jon Stance Positions   39
By-Jon's Root   40-43
Other Martial Arts Stances   44
Orthodox Fighting Stance - Southpaw Fighting Stance   45
Jeet Kune Do - Right Lead   46
Why Do We Use the Vertical Punch and Not the Horizontal Punch?   47-48
Jeet Kune Do 1 Inch Punch (Choon Goon Kune)   49-52
The 1 inch Kick   53-55
The 1 inch kick against a person   56-57
Mechanics of JKD   58-59
The Eye Flick   60-64
Warming Up- Stretching Exercises   65-73

PART 2: THE BASIS OF JEET KUNE
JKD Foundation and Development/ Siu Leem Tau   76-104

PART 3: BASIC STAGES
JKD Bow -Ging Lie Salutation   106-109
Footwork-Moving Stances   110-117
Eight Basic Defense Positions from a By-Jon   118-120
Yin/Yang -Blocks and Strikes   121
Yin and Yang Blocks Definitions   122
Strikes   123-126
Hands Blocks   127-130
Palm Strikes   131-133
Elbows Strikes   133-134
Jeet Kune Do Right Lead Punch   135-140
Jeet Kune Do Hammer Principle/Straight Blast   141-143
Hip Rotation and Body Alignment   144
Jeet Kune Do Kicking   145-147
It's Not Just A Kick- It is A Jeet Kune Do Kick   148-152
JKD Advanced Hook Kick   153
Burning Foot Sidekick   154
JKD Five Corner Kicking   155-156
JKD Kicking Drill   157-168
Basic Punching and Kicking Combinations   169-173

PART 4: JKD EMOTIONAL CAPACITIES
Sensitivity Drills 176
Chee Don Sow 178-180
Chee Sow 181-184

PART 5: JKD VIGOROUS CAPACITIES
Energy Drills 185
Gock Ing Sing (Five Star Blocking) 185-186
JKD Ten (10) Blocks With a Partner 186-192
Teet Sa Jan (Iron Palm Training) 193-196
Pock Sow /Gwa Choy Drill 197
Kune Sue Kune /Pock Sow Kune Sue Kune Drill 198
Tun Lop Sow Drill 199-200
Fon Sow (Trapping Hands) Drill 201-202
Lop Sow (Grabbing or Pulling) Gwa Choy (Back Hand) Drills 202-204
Pock Sow Gwa Choy/Bong Lop Gwa Choy Drills 205-206
Pock Tun /Da pock Drill 207-208
Pock Da (Slap Hit) Drill 209-211

PART 6: TRAPPING STRATEGIES
WINDOWS OF ATTACK
The Gates 212-241
Trapping Reversals - Stupid Traps 242-247
FIA (Foot Immobilization Attack) 248-249

PART 7: THE CLASSICAL STAGE
The Wooden Dummy Form 250-316

PART 8: CONTROLLING STRATEGIES
Small Joints Lock Manipulations 317-325

PART 9: SCIENTIFIC STREET FIGHTING
Scientific Street Self Defense 328-348
Hand to Hand Combat 349-374
Club Defense 375-386
Knife Defense 387-407
Gun Defense 408-419

PART 10: NON-SPORT STAGE
Ground Fighting 420-435

PART 11: SHARPENING THE TOOLS
Nunchaku 436-451
Sparring & Sport VS. Street Fighting 452-454

PART 12: EXPRESSING YOUR SELF
Jeet Kune Do - Street Combat 455-464

Jeet Kune Do Terminology Index 465-481

DEDICATION

With Love,
To my wife, Marissa
And children, Gaby, Hannah and Noah

Once upon a time there was a man named Lee, who founded a Martial Art known as JKD.
No one had a smile brighter than this awesome fighter.
As a warrior, there was no mightier.
His words were philosophical, his technique was first rate, even to this day he's referred to as the "**Great**". His passing made us sad, but his teachings are not gone, his legacy was not to follow, but to "*Walk On.*"

George Hajnasr

Acknowledgement

Special Thanks to all of my friends and students that helped me put this book together.

Wadih Maalouf
Brian Wilson
Paul Redlon
Noel Debois
Robert Ball Senior
Robert Ball JR
Andy Kasimatis
Gregory Gesek
Mark Wilson
James Manning
Mike Redlon
Tony Fiory
Justin Ditito
John Basler
Joseph Bellabona
Brian Verkaart
Chris Baker
Dan Haidar
Jaima Nazarian
Lauren Schier
Kathy Bearse
Liz Pratt
Alisa Conway
Wendy Orwig
Darlene Vaughn
Jane Piper
Debra Dooley

Great thanks to a great **JKD Historian** Mr. Paul Bax for his knowledge and Ideas.
Great thanks to master Augustine Fong of Tucson Arizona, for giving me a permission to use his Wing Chun glossary of terms.
Great thank to Century Martial Art Supply for giving me permission to use their equipment in this book.

Last but not least, special thanks to the world kick boxing champions
Hamid Larizi
Mohammad Hadifi
Jose Lobo
Waseem Saad

Special thanks to the man who made me who I am today in Martial Arts, **Shihan Paul Curtin,** founder of **Eclectic Karate** ® I highly salute you.

My goal is to help anyone that has an "Empty Cup" and an open mind, (from beginners, to advanced black belts, or even (World Kickboxing champions) how to express themselves.

Special thanks to Sifu Steve Golden.
His thoughts and ideas helped me become a better JKD practitioner.

Sifu Golden's thoughts on JKD:

JKD is a method or methods based on sound and provable principles. What Bruce Lee did was pull together principles and truths that have been around for hundreds or thousands of years. He then used them "his way" to make a combat system that used universal truths in a way that best fit his skills and personality. That is Bruce Lee's expression of JKD.

The information that Bruce Lee gathered, documented, and left in his notes gives us hints on how to put those truths and principles together into a usable and effective method for our own use. When that is done JKD becomes your own personal use and expression of those principles. JKD is alive and well in each of us when we follow these principles of combat. That does NOT mean that we must execute those principles in the same way that Bruce Lee did. It also doesn't mean that we can't do it the way he did.

The beauty of JKD is that it gives you the tools and lets you build what you personally need to gain effectiveness and excellence.

So, is it JKD if you deviate from these principles? Maybe. It's very important to understand that the principles are not laws. They are guidelines. There are times when you should break the "rules" because the situation dictates it. But you should also know and understand the implications of doing so. Do I stand strong side forward? Sometimes. Do I use the "Bi Jong" stance? Rarely. Am I doing JKD? Hmmm. I'm not sure I can answer that one. But, am I using the principles that Bruce Lee united? You bet I am! Does it work? Of course it does.

I've asked people and I've also been asked to define JKD. If you make the mistake of defining it you have destroyed its very spirit. That's because any definition is restrictive. It forces the method into artificial bounds and structures. If you want to understand JKD, then understand its principles but don't be bound by them. My description, not definition, of JKD should give you the spirit of JKD but not lock it into restrictive bounds.

Personally, I do not like using the term JKD because of the restrictions the term generates. I do say JKD, just as I have here, but that's only a matter of convenience so we know what subject we're discussing.

Steve Golden
June 17, 2004

(The Taoist Wu Wei and Wei Wu Wei)
"which he considered to be the highest levels of martial art"

Sifu Patrick Strong

Special Thanks to a Great Teacher and Mentor for his thoughts and ideas and who paved a better way for my JKD Journey.....

Preface

To the reader:

Thank you for the opportunity to spread the art of Jeet Kune Do, as developed by the late founder of Jeet Kune Do (JKD), my idol and inspiration. My skills **are not** by any means compared to the skills of **Sijo** (the founder) or any other JKD instructors in any way, shape, or form. This book is based on my own interpretation, which is a complete **"System Without a System®."** My practice of Jeet Kune Do is a combination of other martial arts skills based on the Founder of Jeet Kune Do's fighting methods, principles, and philosophy, in which I have learned over the years and compiled into one detailed book. Many people suggested I call my book "The Encyclopedia of JKD," because of its in-depth explanation. This book demonstrates Jeet Kune Do step-by-step, which is something that has not been done before, though many have claimed to have authored such a work. As such, I urge you to compare knowledge, talent and skills and I am sure you will see the difference.

My main reason for writing this book is that, not having previous knowledge about JKD and having purchased many books on the subject, as a beginner I had a very hard time understanding the whole theory behind JKD. I wanted to learn badly, but couldn't fully understand from the books due to the lack of detailed pictures. Too many books before mine describe the art of JKD through explanations and concepts, but so few of them actually demonstrate. As the old adage goes, **"a picture is worth a thousand words."** My goal is to teach non-JKD students and help JKD practitioners to fully understand the methods and theories of JKD through both text and detailed pictures. After studying classical martial arts for ten years, and learning and researching JKD through many of the original students of the founder, I have come to the conclusion that each of his students had their own way of teaching JKD, based on how they had learned it at the time. Each one also had his own way of practicing JKD, due to the fact that the founder had different schools in Seattle, Oakland, and L.A. Each school taught a slightly different approach. I have compiled everything that the followers of JKD had to offer, as well as everything that I learned from classical martial arts, and refined it into my own system. This is not to say that what you see is exactly what other masters have shown me, but it is a combination of their techniques. The best of JKD that they had mastered, along with my own way of practicing JKD. Thus, here you have it--a complete **System Without a System®**.

After two years of organizing my book, hours of typing and taking over 20,000 photos to give you the best, the truth now lies before you. My objective is to make JKD simple for you to understand the art and what lies behind it. After you have learned from this book and understand the theories, then you can start hacking away at my interpretation. Use this book and its teachings to express yourself and create the way that best fits you as an individual. Even though this book teaches a system, do not become the product of this book. Simply be yourself. That way, you don't create a rigid system, and the name Jeet Kune Do remains only in the heart, as the Founder of Jeet Kune Do originally intended.

The truth, behind my way of Jeet Kune Do, The System Without A System®

Learn The Basics   **Applying The Basics**   **Dissolving The Basics**   **Become The Basics...**

Step by step process to the **Emptiness** stage. This is when your mind and body become one.

FOREWORD

By Dr. Ellyn Robinson

      The study of Martial arts is very diverse. *"Jeet Kune Do"* is the only non-classical Chinese martial art available today and it is also known as **"Scientific Street fighting."** Sifu George Hajnasr brings passion, expertise, science, and extreme dedication to his new book "JKD the System without a System®".
      If you are a martial artist or a true fitness enthusiast, then you must read "JKD The System Without a System®". This new work by Sifu George Hajnasr is extraordinary. It is a step by step method of both teaching the art of Jeet Kune Do, as well as teaching the philosophy and theory behind the technique. With over 3000 action photos and step by step descriptions, diagrams, and foot work pathways, anyone new to this sport can easily enhance their technique.
      I have been teaching physical education at the college level for over a decade, and I have NEVER seen a martial arts book this completely organized, and orientated toward the reader.

Dr. Ellyn Robinson, CSCS, CPT is a professor of exercise science at Bridgewater State College, in Bridgewater, Massachusetts. She has been teaching physical education for 14 years, and was a nationally ranked swimmer, bodybuilder, and runner. She has competed in Taekwondo and Tang-Soo-Do .styles of martial arts, and is now beginning her study of Jeet Kune Do.

The Biography & Fundamentals of
Jeet Kune Do The System Without A System®

Experience
In My Own Expression?
"It Is what it Is"
Jeet Kune Do Rank
JKD (Terminology)
Essence of Jeet Kune Do
The Three Stages – Cultivations of learning Jeet Kune Do
The Immovable Elbow Moving Line
Targets, Gates and Weapons
JKD Nine Weapons of Attack
Centerline (Joan Seen)
Jeet Kune Do - Five Ways of Attack
Jeet Kune Do Yum /Yeung (Yin Yang) Symbol
Internal and External Development
Speed, Rhythm, Distance and Timing

By-Jon -Pyramids Structure for Offense and Defense
By-Jon
By-Jon Stance Positions
By-Jon's Root
Other Martial Arts Stances
Orthodox Fighting Stance - Southpaw Fighting Stance
Jeet Kune Do - Right Lead
Why Do We Use the Vertical Punch and Not the Horizontal Punch?
Jeet Kune Do 1 Inch Punch (Choon Goon Kune)
The 1 inch Kick
Mechanics of JKD
The Eye Flick
Warming Up- Stretching Exercises

About the Practitioner

I Don't Kick - "It" Kicks

George Hajnasr, proud, devoted husband, father of three beautiful children and successful businessman was born February 11, 1966. He is the youngest of eight siblings and resides in Kingston, Massachusetts. In this book you will read about the experiences that led George to where he is today. You'll also gain some of his knowledge of the martial art Jeet Kune Do The System Without A System®.

A Sifu / Sensei/ founder of Jeet Kune Do The System Without A System®. Black belt holder and over **30 years** experience in various styles of Martial Arts, and a dedicated practitioner of Jeet Kune Do. George Hajnasr's disciplines are drawn from: Eclectic Karate®, Wing Chun Gung Fu, Ju-Jitsu, Aikido Western Boxing, Kickboxing, Ground Fighting, and anything else that works.

Keeping the authentic teachings of the Original Jeet Kune Do alive. Whether it's through Karate or any style of Martial Arts, as long as we remain united. You will be a much better martial artist.

Experiences!

Ever since seeing the film, "The Big Boss" aka "Fist of Fury," I have been a die-hard fan of the Founder of Jeet Kune Do. Watching him on film had a big impact on my life. I loved watching him move on screen. It was like nothing I had ever seen before.

As fast as the Founder of Jeet Kune Do's moves were, his life was over even faster. I was around eight years old when the news spread that Founder of Jeet Kune Do had died. He was truly my idol and I had always wanted to be just like him. Now I would never have the chance to meet him. Growing up with the passion to be "Founder of Jeet Kune Do," I decided to purchase my first book on martial arts. Not having enough money to take an actual martial arts class, I gathered all the books and information that I could get my hands on. I applied the knowledge I learned from these books and began to practice on my own. I even went as far as to make my own nunchaku. At the age of 16, I was finally able to sign up for Kung Fu. I had no idea what form of martial arts the Founder of Jeet Kune Do had practiced, although I thought he had done Kung Fu. I did not acquire the knowledge that I was yearning for in that class, so I started going from one school to another. Every teacher had a different view on what form of martial arts Founder of Jeet Kune Do developed, never teaching the true aspect of it. I once again decided to read everything and anything on Founder of Jeet Kune Do, and again began practicing on my own. One day, by chance, I met a a local instructor by the name of **Shihan Paul Curtin**. He had created his own style of martial arts. I was very impressed by his moves and decided to study under him, taking private lessons for about twelve years. Even though I enjoyed taking the classes, in the back of my mind I still wanted to be like Founder of Jeet Kune Do.

Around 1993, I finally started getting a grasp on the form of martial arts that Founder of Jeet Kune Do had developed, called **Jeet Kune Do.** He also studied a system called Wing Chun Gung Fu. I started attending seminars with many of Bruce Lee's original students. I would partake in any class or seminar that had something to do with Founder of Jeet Kune Do.

I started training in Wing Chun Gung Fu through private lessons and remained studying **Eclectic Karate®** with Shihan Curtin. I began to incorporate everything I had learned from Master Curtin; books, videos, seminars and private lessons, along with the 20 years of martial arts research. This resulted in my own expression of **"Jeet Kune Do."** Just as Founder of Jeet Kune Do intended, I absorbed what was useful, rejected what was useless, and added what was essentially my own.

Today many Jeet Kune Do practitioners might do what Founder of Jeet Kune Do did and some might do what Founder of Jeet Kune Do said. Some might believe in teaching someone, **"how to fish or give them a fish,"** but I truly believe in showing them how to work the boat first. Then they can catch much bigger fish. To truly understand Founder of Jeet Kune Do, you have to train like him and work as hard as he did. I try my very best to follow his teachings and his way of life. I truly believe, as Founder of Jeet Kune Do did, that you should have a foundation in martial arts and in life. As for my life, Jeet Kune Do has a very deep meaning for me, as you will learn in this book. You will also learn the base system of **Wing Chun** as Founder of Jeet Kune Do did. You will be able to flow from one system to another without being limited to one. You will get to feel the beauty and effectiveness of other martial arts and how well they go together. Remember, nothing in this book is etched in stone; you can change it, add to it, and modify it to fit your process of continuing growth. In my many years of martial arts, people have asked me what kind of karate I do? In reply I tell them, **"I study Jeet Kune Do and Karate."** Since very few people have ever heard of Jeet Kune Do, I clarify by telling them that this is the type of martial arts Founder of Jeet Kune Do developed. Many martial art teachers do not think much of Jeet Kune Do because it is not a system of martial arts. Founder of Jeet Kune Do developed it personally for his own training. To me, Jeet Kune Do is a way of life; it is more than just a form and much more effective than any one individual style. Jeet Kune Do allows the artist to be free from all **classical** forms of martial arts. Showing the essence of Jeet Kune Do is one of the main reasons I began writing this book. This is not a Founder of Jeet Kune Do biography; nor is it a concept; it is an example of the proof that Jeet Kune Do is more than what most martial artists believe. Within this book, you will find the complete Jeet Kune Do system without the basis of an actual system, which I created, including its foundations; **Wing Chun, Fencing, and Western Boxing**. In addition, you will find illustrations from Eclectic Karate®, Shotokan and Kenpo Karate, Ju Jitsu, Aikido, Judo, Kickboxing, and Ground Fighting. All of these techniques will work in an actual fight. When you are through studying my teachings, I hope that you will have gained a better understanding of what Jeet Kune Do is all about. I will show you the way, but it is up to you to find your freedom. You will also notice that my Jeet Kune Do might be a little different from other Jeet Kune Do practitioners. It doesn't mean that either practitioner is wrong, as long as the essence of Jeet Kune Do is present.

Jeet Kune Do: The System Without A System®
It Is What It Is: Just a Name!

Jeet Kune Do: The System Without A System® is my own interpretation of the original Jeet Kune Do (scientific street fighting). My art is based ONLY on my own experiences, years of research, private lessons and seminar training, which led me to create my own ideas and full understanding of Jeet Kune Do as a fighting art. **Jeet Kune Do:** The System Without A System® is **NOT** as a style, system or a method of fighting based on someone else's interpretation of JKD.

Since the death of Jeet Kune Do's founder, many interpretations of the art have surfaced which has created massive confusion in regards to exactly what Jeet Kune Do is. Prospective practitioners are confused as to why there is so many different instructors teaching so many different interpretations of the same art. Why is this?

The founder of Jeet Kune Do developed the most aggressive fighting art to date because he uses all arts yet he was not bound by any of them. A JKD practitioner can adapt and fit into any situation at any given time. That's what makes JKD unique and different. JKD is not a style, a system or a set way of practicing a technique. The art is not based merely on technique, but on theoretical principles, philosophies and actual applications that fit in real life street situations. The unfortunate passing of JKD's founder left such a big legacy behind that many of his original students never got to learn the complete art, since he was changing his method continually over time. Many of the first generation students spread his art the way it was presented to them through the three schools where he taught (Seattle, Oakland and Los Angeles). Some followed his original teachings, which in its early stage required the study of Wing Chun Gung Fu, and later as he progressed he changed his art to Jeet Kune Do.

So why do many practitioners call it different names such as **Jun Fan**, **Jeet Kune Do**, **Jeet Kune Do Concept** or **Jun Fan Jeet Kune Do**? What is the difference? There is no real difference. The only difference I personally see is that most are not **UNITED**. In other words, some took a different approach to how they should apply JKD. Some decided to add different arts to it, improve on it or just stick to the original teachings of the Jun Fan Gung Fu years, which consist of a very strong base and foundation of Wing Chun Gung Fu as I have. I have absorbed all of the founder's principles, methods and theories, and taken from anyone who has ever taught me JKD (which includes first and second generation students of the founder) and other martial arts the best way they knew how, and created my own expression of Jeet Kune Do, which is called **Jeet Kune Do: The System Without a System®.**

Does that make it a wrong or different way of applying JKD? Absolutely not. Am I teaching and practicing JKD? Definitely! Just like the founder said, "How can I express myself totally and completely?" He further commented, "You think a fight is just one kick, one blow?"

So my personal feeling is that JKD practitioners don't need to stick to one particular way of doing a technique or movement. In addition, my system is not based on any one person's set way of doing JKD. What makes **Jeet Kune Do: The System Without a System®**, unique? The art is NOT unique. The label is just another name, which can be wiped out at any giving time and it is not bound by any particular way. Unfortunately, because of **politics**, the name of what I teach is simply different. Also, what gives me knowledge to express myself? What is JKD and what is not JKD? My skills were compiled by learning from over ten of the top original students of the founder of Jeet Kune Do, and hours of private classes along with over 30 years of martial arts experience. As a black belt in various styles of martial arts, I have experienced what works and what doesn't work. My enthusiasm for Jeet Kune Do has driven me to write a book with over 460 pages on the art. In addition, I have produced a complete DVD series on JKD.

Just as the founder of Jeet Kune Do intended, I absorbed what is useful, rejected what is useless, and added what is essentially my own. I have a very informative website dedicated to Jeet Kune Do **(WWW.JKDUS.COM)** which is packed with everything I have learned and absorbed over the years from others who have a love for JKD.

So my advice to anyone wanting to learn JKD is that you don't need to stick to one particular way of doing a technique or movement, nor should you base your training on any one person's set ways of doing JKD. To look and move like the founder of Jeet Kune Do, you must follow the art step by step just like any other art, even though you have to go back and learn that rehearsed routine, learn what is behind it, take few punches and learn to fight on the ground. That way, you are not limited to just punching and kicking and you are not a fish out of water should a grappling situation ever arise. To walk the same path that he walked you must follow his principles, methods and theory that he left behind. Once you understand and absorb these principles, then you liberate yourself from any particular way of doing JKD.

As long as the essence of JKD is presented in an honorable and respectful manner, then it should not make a difference as to what people call it. Jeet Kune Do was not meant to have a label because its founder never believed in styles or systems. **It is what it is**: Jeet Kune Do. So we can refer only to whether you've learned it from different instructors or from the founder himself. This should not change the true meaning or what lies behind Jeet Kune Do, which is to simply express one's self honestly. **"If people say Jeet Kune Do is different from "this" or "that," then let the name of Jeet Kune Do be wiped out, for that is all it is, just a name. Please don't fuss over it"** (Bruce Lee Tao of Jeet Kune Do).

Peace, Love, Jkd

Sifu George Hajnasr
"I do not believe in systems or methods of fighting"

What Is "Jeet Kune Do" In My Own Expression?

Jeet Kune Do is the only non-classical Chinese martial art available today. The art is also known as **"Scientific Street Fighting."** Jeet Kune Do translates from Cantonese to **"The Way Of The Intercepting Fist." Jeet** means to stop or intercept, **Kune** means fist or style, and **Do** means the way. It was founded by the late Bruce Lee around 1965, and was accepted and recognized around the world. Unfortunately with his passing on July 20th, 1973, he left an enormous legacy behind. Jeet Kune Do, the martial art is very direct. The art does not and cannot remain the same. JKD must change as time changes. It is not rigid but is fluid; also it favors **simplicity** and **directness.**

Jeet Kune Do can be changed and improved upon as time proceeds. Some moves used thousands of years ago might not work in today's society. People used horses to travel and they used knives and swords in combat. Fortunately in this day and age the use of these weapons legal are impractical. Jeet Kune Do is a process of growing and constantly improving. The art takes the form of whatever works, no matter what style the practitioner draws his or her chosen tactics from. JKD does not become that style because style tends to separate people from each other. They might think their style is the only answer for combat, but every style has its strong and weak points. In Jeet Kune Do, we take the stronger points out of that style and use whatever works from it but we are not bound by it.

Jeet Kune Do does not beat around the bush. Instead JKD gets directly to the point. Jeet Kune Do is a 'chiseling away process'. A diamond cutter cuts away at the rough, losing almost half of it until the beauty and brilliance of a diamond is revealed. Jeet Kune Do is one's self-expression outside all fixed patterns. It is a system with no system. You express the technique. You don't simply perform the technique-you become the technique. Don't become the product of that technique - you don't hit. Let "it" hit without even thinking of hitting. Don't concentrate on just one thing. If you do, you are going to miss all the glorious things around you. Jeet Kune Do takes the easy way out with the least amount of energy. Jeet Kune Do doesn't use any fancy or unnecessary stances, because in real fighting none of the fancy stances work. It might look good, but looking good will not help in a life-threatening situation. Just simply express yourself through any unsophisticated movement.

Other martial artists are limited to one style or method of fighting. The students are performing the system through themselves. They are copying everything the instructor shows them. They, in return, are the products of that style. Perform, practice and apply the art according to the styles defined techniques and applications. The art cannot be changed. Heaven forbid the student changes or modifies their particular style. By that I mean practitioners of most traditional arts are very limited. Jeet Kune Do (JKD) uses no way as way because "when ever there is a way there lies the limitation." JKD practitioners use what works in a real fight.

You can change, modify, and add to it, and so "that way it is a continuous growth of knowledge." Always keep an open mind and absorb whatever works with the least amount of energy.

However, that doesn't mean that Jeet Kune Do is all over the place like some people may believe. What this means is that you are free in your martial art to train in different styles or cross train, as I will demonstrate in this book. Don't be surprised if a good Jeet Kune Do practitioner will flow from one system to another system. If someone wishes to lean towards one system then that's they're prerogative, but you're limiting yourself. Some fight situations might be in kicking range; others might be in punching range, and some in trapping range or even ground range. If you lack one of these ranges you will lose no matter how skillful you are in one style of martial arts. A good JKD practitioner uses everything. You name it - you should grasp it! The student must still learn the basics and fundamentals so they have a good foundation to build upon.

Jeet Kune Do: The System Without A System ® *Rank!*

The way I teach is by promoting ranks or sashes. The students, however, are not required to wear their sash in class. The sash is only for personal achievement and recognition, and nothing more. You do not need to wrap yourself with a belt or sash to show how skillful you are (**"belts only hold your pants up"**). Originally, the founder of Jeet Kune Do had a very unique ranking system that consisted of different colored Yin and Yang. The seven sashes represent the way the students should progress through my way of teaching, in which is a very strong foundation from Wing Chun Gung Fu. Once the students completes the seven ranks to Black sash level, the student has to complete the three levels of training, Partiality, Fluidity and Emptiness. That is when the student receives full certification in the level they have fully completed with hard work and years of commitment and full knowledge of the art. **I DO NOT** hand over these last three levels very lightly. The students must be able to defend themselves under any conditions and circumstances without any hesitation or prearrangements. The mind and the body must be one and the thinking level no longer exists. All moves should be executed without thinking.

JKD (TERMINOLOGY)

I tried my very best to describe the words the way they should be pronounced in Chinese Cantonese the way I have learned from my instructors. The way they are written is not necessarily the right way they are spelled. I tried the best way that I can to make it easy for the reader to be able to pronounce the words in English **PHONETIC** fashion." Note" all Cantonese words are in bold lettering, with the English pronunciation in parentheses. ( )

Essence of Jeet Kune Do

"Research Your Own Experience"

"Absorb What Is Useful"

"Reject What Is Useless"

"Add What Is Essentially Your Own"

"Using No Way As Way"

"Having No Limitation As Limitation"

"Simplicity, Directness, And Non-Classical"

Research Your Own Experience: To really appreciate the art of JKD, it is important to first research other styles of martial arts. This will allow you to see the true differences and decide what will make you a better practitioner. For example:

Paul Curtin's Eclectic Karate®: possesses a strong base of street fighting; mixes traditional ways with new ways, linear shotokan with circular kenpo karate, joint manipulations with jujitsu; the practitioner develops internal strength from within, becoming competent in the required movements from the three different disciplines.
Fencing: offers good mobility, straight lines, and the shortest distance between two points, with the strong side forward.
Wing Chun Gung Fu: features good centerline defense, the economy of the straight line, and sensitivity reaction in trapping, as well as the economy of motion.
Kickboxing: possesses a very strong kicking base in straight or curved, high or low lines.
Judo: offers good balance, in throws, foot sweeps, and joint locks.
Western boxing: features rapid footwork, speed, power, accuracy, and combination of physical and mental abilities.
Aikido: possesses continuity in flowing movements.
Grappling: features body tackling, surprise attacks to take downs, joints and choke locks, and stamina improvement.

Absorb What Is Useful: Take anything that works from the above martial arts (combative arts) and make them useful for you as an individual. Some techniques that are useful for another person might not be useful for you in real life situations.

Reject What Is Useless: After you have understood the whole theory behind a particular art or technique, and you find that it doesn't suit you or work for you, simply reject it, because there is no reason why you should learn something that is of no use to you.

Add What Is Essentially Your Own: Making a technique work for you in a threatening situation is the most effective way. You start creating simple ways to practice better, faster, and more effectively. Because people are tall and short, big and small; you should make the technique work in the way that is most effective for you, not using an instructor's way of doing it.

Using No Way As Way: You will not create a particular set way of applying movements or techniques. One individual style or method of fighting doesn't have all the answers. If you create a set way, you have created a weakness in your open mind, body and spirit, and have filled your cup to the top, leaving no room for other ways, even when you feel that someone else's way might be more effective then your set way.

Having No Limitation As Limitation: This fits hand and hand with the previous belief, because once you have created a set way, making that technique the only answer for all individuals, you have created limitations in your training. When you are limited, you are sure to be defeated.

You might ask, "Isn't the essence of JKD to use no way as the way, and to have no limitations? It all sounds very confusing. There *is* a set way in JKD, whether it is the right lead or strong side forward or rear heel up-- isn't that a way and a limitation? This question came to my mind, and I asked and searched for the answer. I came to realize that it is not a set way or a limitation. It is the best proven way to reach your opponent without any restrictions or limitations, compared to a traditional fighting method. There are many ways to get from point *A* to point *B*, but one way--JKD--is shorter and paved. The other ways are long and rocky. Which road should you take?

Simplicity: Keep your movements simple. This does not mean you should add more; as well as it does not mean just one hit, because different attacks are treated differently. They can be a straight or curved line because some might require more than just one motion. Make your moves very natural. Don't get into any fancy moves because you might block a hit or take down at the same time. Respond to it like it is a normal every day action. Every Jeet Kune Do practitioner tries to be very simple in his or her technique but this does not mean he or she lacks technique in real situations. You are only allowed one punch or kick before the other person grapples you and you both end up on the ground. All the fancy movements do not work in real life situations unless your opponent is a robot. Every Jeet Kune Do practitioner tries to be as soft as water, yet flexible as a bamboo stick. No matter what the situation is, you flow around it like water and take shape to fit the situation at that moment.

Directness: (Fits hand-in-hand with simplicity) Do what comes naturally. If an opponent strikes you, do not step back with your right foot, tight fists by your side, blocking with your left hand, pulling your left leg back into a cat stance. If you do, you will get knocked out. In Jeet Kune Do, just block, punch. If someone jumps in front of your car you would do what comes naturally to you, and slam on the brakes. Do not indulge in any unnecessary sophisticated moves. If someone pins you against the wall, don't try to do fancy Ju-Jitsu moves, it might work but it also might not. Why pin the wrist? Circle the wrist and elbow, then lock the wrist, then hit. You are not fighting a corpse. If you try to do that, things might not go your way and you will be opening yourself up to bigger trouble. In Jeet Kune Do, simply pin hit, or pin knee the groin, or just hit. It's very direct and you have a much better guarantee against your attacker.

Non-Classical: Traditionally classical forms, katas, and efficiency are all equally important. They do give you a good base and foundation. You do not need 20 forms and 20 katas to have a good base. The economy of form and katas is very important, but efficiency is anything that works in reality. In Jeet Kune Do, a student does not need to wear fancy
uniforms. He or she can be as comfortable as they want. They are coming to me to teach them, not to look pretty, but to learn how to defend themselves. Some classical practitioners might argue that it shows discipline, respect, and integrity. That might be true, but on the street you are not walking with your uniform on. So why not leave it for the student to decide what to wear during training? Some instructors might make it a rule that you must wear a uniform or you can't train if it doesn't fit the school curriculum. To me that is not right. A good student is anyone that has an "empty cup." A good martial arts instructor should leave the door open to anyone that is willing to learn regardless of forms.

There Are Three Stages Or – Cultivations Of Learning In Jeet Kune Do The System Without a System ®

A step by step process of learning, just like any other combative martial arts!

STAGE ONE (1)

STAGE TWO (2)

STAGE THREE (3)

PARTIALITY
The Basic Stage!

STAGE 1: PARTIALITY, SHARPENING THE TOOL - STICKING TO THE NUCLEUS: The student must learn the basics; this is where the practitioner gets introduced to **Siu Leem Tau** (little idea) Wing Chun form.

Now you're thinking to yourself, I am doing a form where Jeet Kune Do is supposed to be formless? I trained in many forms like **Siu Leem Tau, Chum-Q–Biu-Jee** and the **Wooden Dummy forms** and in over **25 karate katas**. However, what I did not do is make them the center of my training and was never bound by them as some other classical martial artist might be. Because in real life situations, you are not fighting in a pattern and rehearsed routines don't work in a real fight. Your opponent is not standing still, nor is he a robot. What the forms and katas will give you is a good foundation. It toughens the student's legs by having him or her stand still for a long time or stepping forward or backwards with leaning stands or keeping low to the ground. It is also a very good exercise. What it also teaches you is to fight multiple opponents in different directions and helps develop power. Forms/kata have you in stances, moving, stepping, shuffling, turning, twisting, blocking, striking, grabbing, leaping, throwing, hacking, locking, breaking, choking, snapping, and torqueing. Should one face an adversary one should be better equipped to deal with the uncertainty of physical combat due to the diligent training.

From the performance of forms/katas, Diligence in training means understanding that might be useful if you choose to train in forms and katas, which I highly recommend. What you shouldn't do is put all your emphasis, heart and soul into forms or katas. As I said before, you are not fighting in a pattern. You should apply these techniques in the forms and katas as you learn them to real life situations; otherwise it is useless for you to train in them unless you fully understand what lies behind them. Besides, if Founder of Jeet Kune Do trained in **Siu Leem Tau**, why not follow in his footsteps?

I feel that you have to have a form to hack away from, and you must have a form to be formless. Because it is very easy to take someone and say, here are a few punches and kicks, raise the heel, that's a **By-Jon**, and here are a few hand traps, add some footwork to it and there you have it, JKD. That's fine if the practitioner had previous training and he or she knows how to punch, kick, and add power to movement. But if you don't, to me, that's just chop suey. Let me assure you, it's much deeper than that.

First, you must have a good, **solid foundation,** and you need to practice few forms and katas to help you develop a stronger base. Second you must have **commitment**, and a lot of hard work and an open mind, and then you might achieve your goal. The student must learn how to place their hand correctly and execute the punch and blocks from any position not necessarily from a fighting stance, that is why for another reason, I felt that this form should be shown. A practitioner must also learn how to use their weapon to its maximum potential, in real situations if you ever need to. Then you might be able to call it **JKD**. I know Founder of Jeet Kune Do said **"its only a name, don't fuss over it,"** but to me, its more than just a name. I am very proud of saying that I train in JKD, so when I demonstrate or talk about JKD I give it my very best so that I represent it the best way that I know how.

Another major reason is because of my many years of research and finding out what works and what doesn't. I came to realize that the economy of **Siu Leem Tau** is very important and many of the techniques that are extremely effective and have been used and practiced in JKD, were founded and generated from this form. These include the JKD vertical punch, hammer principle, corkscrew, shovel hook, and the straight blast. They all rely heavily on the **Immovable Elbow Moving Line.** It doesn't mean that the elbow doesn't move. What it means is that your arm moves forward and backward in a straight line when it's extended from the body without exposing the elbow. This will help you develop much more powerful blocks and strikes. By practicing this form, it will help you develop the immovable elbow moving line. I strongly believe in building a very strong foundation in a practitioner by taking from any style, even if I have to practice forms, to develop it, and hopefully you will "**find the cores of your ignorance**" like I did.

FLUIDITY
The Application Stage!

STAGE 2 – FLUIDITY, UTILIZING THE TOOL: LIBERATING FROM THE NUCLEUS: This is where the practitioner begins by putting the technique together. The techniques are generated into applications like blocking, striking, and counter attacks, in order to start generating actual applications in street situations. **Now the journey to Jeet kune Do begins**, and it's a long journey.

You will be introduced to JKD fighting stance (**By-Jon**) the only fighting stance you need to master; that's why **JKD is** so simple. No cat stances, no leaning stances, no horse stance, and no unnecessary fancy stances. After you master your fighting stance and understand the pyramid structure and why it's so effective. You will move on to **Footwork,** which is the back bone and the foundation of JKD. After you apply different strikes, blocks, and kicks, you will get introduced to **JKD terminology**. I feel that if a practitioner is learning JKD he or she must learn every basic block, kick, palm strikes, knee, elbow, and yin and yang block in Cantonese.

After you start understanding what lies behind the blocks and strikes, you will start applying some of the blocks to toughen up your hands and forearms by practicing **Five Star Blocking,** which will prepare you for much more advanced drills, like **JKD 10 blocks** with a partner that will help you develop faster reaction in blocking against any attack.

Iron Palm, will help you develop and build stronger and tougher hands so that your block becomes a strike. Every part of your hands will be developed; the inside, the outside, the edge, and the knuckles. After developing hand blocks and strikes now you will move on to basic kicking, and then add foot work to your kicks by practicing **Five Corner Kicking and Kicking Drill.**

Now the student is ready to start combining the punching and kicking together into actual combinations by being introduced to **Western Boxing and kickboxing.** You will have an unlimited number of combinations that you can apply and generate from and use in different **broken rhythm** applications (i.e. not repeating the same technique twice in the same attack.) After feeling very confident about what you have learned, and starting to generate power from your blocks and strikes, you are ready to move on to much more advanced drills. You will be introduced to **Energy Drills.** Their purpose is to have a much faster reaction time when blocking and striking. After these drills are mastered you will move on to **Sensitivity Drill,** which will help you develop feeling and reaction - as soon as you get touched by an opponent your reaction will be instant. At this stage of training you are ready to develop your **Hand Trapping (Gates)** range and in fighting. This is the most devastating range of fighting known in JKD and it helps the practitioner to trap your opponent's hand blocks and strikes and convert them into useless weapons. Before the student starts applying the techniques that you've grasped from all the drills and hand traps you must first apply them on the **Wooden Dummy,** which will help you in your trapping, blocking and striking simultaneously and toughen up your hands and feet.

Scientific street combat is then ready to be applied in actual street situations. You will take everything that you have learned and apply them into street **Self-Defense, Hand to Hand Combat, Club, Knife, and Gun Defense** and you will not be limited into any type of block or strike - everything starts coming together as one. **Ground fighting** is the end of your journey because you're not a complete fighter unless you possess ground range and are able to take care of yourself if the fight ever went to the ground.

EMPTINESS

The Non-Thinking Stage!

STAGE 3 - EMPTINESS, DISSOLVING THE TOOL: RETURNING TO THE ORIGINAL FREEDOM: This is the highest level of training where the practitioner responds to any attack without even thinking of the move or how to attack. This is where **"IT"** responds with a technique from any style at the time of attack. Your mind and body become one, and you are no longer thinking of what to do in threatening situations. This is a level that is very hard to achieve and it takes years of practice. You hit, block, kick without even thinking. You must train and practice heavily, so **"when you need it, it is there."** This is where you return to the original freedom. You start hacking away everything that is unessential and make it very simple. You absorb what works and are not afraid to reject what doesn't work.

At this level of training, you go back and take every movement, every technique, and every punch and kick, and ask yourself, "How can I make it much more effective and extremely useful for me as a person?" Some techniques are applied against a tall person, some against a short person. Every person is built differently, so how can I use my skills to their highest level, but keep it very simple and effective against any attacker?

What is "IT"?

"IT" is extremely important in JKD, in that your fist hits, your leg kicks, and your hand blocks as part of natural reactions and movements. Every tool in your body is used to its fullest, without thinking. IT attacks back because your body and mind physically and mentally become **ONE**... you don't respond for the sake of responding; you execute the techniques with purpose and accuracy, and with the proper timing and correct structure. IT does the most effective interception with the simplest and most direct techniques available against any attack without any wasted movement s or unnecessary pre-arrangements....

The Immovable Elbow Moving Line

The Immovable Elbow Moving Line, Where it is not necessary to have the elbow at a stand still. The elbow moves back and forth on a straight line in a very deceiving way. Without having to expose the elbow, release the power outward from the body in a straight line, which will give maximum support to bones in blocking and striking. By maintaining a straight line and proper elbow positioning, this will create a cutting angle of 45°, which will help in blocking by deflecting blows in a powerful way, and intercepting blocks instead of parrying or pushing. By intercepting at a 45° angle instead of just pushing his block away, your force will shake the opponent's whole structure; he will feel your block throughout his whole body, not only at the target area.

The Straight front lead, moves back and forth in a straight line to the target, the elbow will move, but the line doesn't.

In trapping or blocking at a 45-degree angle, the front lead strikes in a straight line. When trapping especially if you don't attack on a straight line, by trying to retract the hand for reloaded power, your opponent would have taken you out. There is no time for reloading. From the blocking position, the strike is executed in a direct line.

The same elbow line principle is applied in retracting the opponent's arm on a straight line.

Targets, Gates And Weapons

There are many primary and secondary targets a practitioner should consider. All of your weapons can be used against your attacker, in self-defense situations. Some of the targets can be very vital if struck precisely, and should not be taken lightly. You can attack through three main channels, also called "gates",(upper, middle, and lower). The same principles of attack through your own gates can be used against you as well, that is why its important to maintain a good By-Jon position in order to protect your self from any real damage. (Refer to the By-Jon stance)

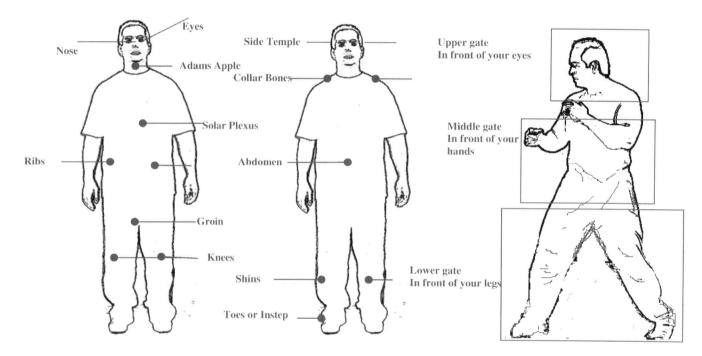

Jkd Nine Weapons Of Attack

Centerline (Joang Seen)

In Jeet Kune Do, there are many imaginary lines that a fighter should be aware of (see diagrams below). The most commonly used tactic is a **Straight Line,** this being for defense or offense. The reason why the straight line is favored in JKD is because it is the shortest distance between two points and you reach your opponent much faster. The Basic Line or straight line is the most common line. Wherever you look, that should be your target, allowing you to reach your opponent faster and with more power. By being in a JKD **By-Jon** (fighting stance) or front lead, this allows you to be one step further and closer to the target. By being an orthodox fighter, the attacks will come from the rear, which might be a straight line, but not always the shortest line between A and B. Using the shortest distance will also be non-telegraphic and this will offer you the advantage of the **Inside Center Line**. You will be able to hit him by blocking his attack, but he cannot hit you because you have the advantage of his inside centerline, which is the line between the **Blocking Line** and the **Center Line.** By taking the inside centerline, this will give a big target area on which you can strike your opponent and cause much more damage. Meanwhile, all of your vital organs are on the centerline, which is a good reason that your rear hand should always protect your centerline.

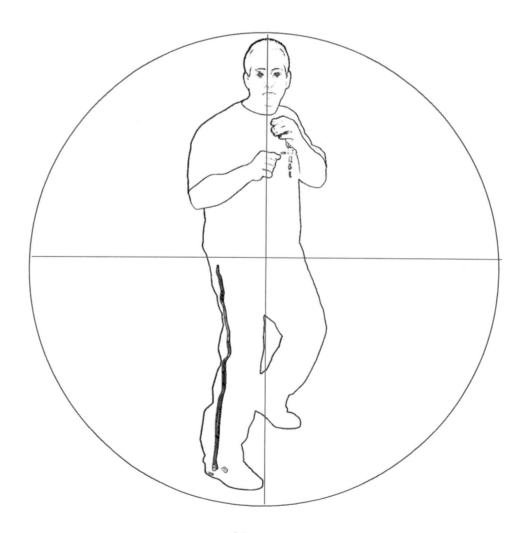

Imaginary Lines

Front lead Straight Line

Where you look you strike

Inside Center Line- and inside Center Line advantage

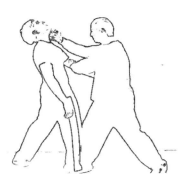

    Another line called the **Mother Line** goes from the top of your head, passing through your body, down to the floor. It's the core axis of rotation. It is in you. The Mother Line is the attack line. It's the target area; you take advantage of it while executing the techniques. Next is the **Self Center Line**. This is a vertical line painted down the center of your face to your feet, dividing your body into two equal parts. The Self Center Line moves with you, no matter what angle you turn. It is painted down the middle. When you move, it moves. This is the line you follow during practice when no opponent is present and it is mainly used to help you execute techniques correctly. All blocks and attacks should be in reference to the Self Center Line. You are protecting your Self Centerline, while trying to target your opponent's Line. A **Center Line Plane** allows the core of your Mother Line to be connected with the core of your opponent's Mother Line, no matter which way either opponent moves, shifts or circles. The Center Line Plane always connects the two fighters. The outside curve line is called a **Blocking Line.** This line goes from the outside from any blocking motion and connects to the Center Line. A Jeet Kune Do fighter or practitioner takes advantage of the area inside the Center Line.

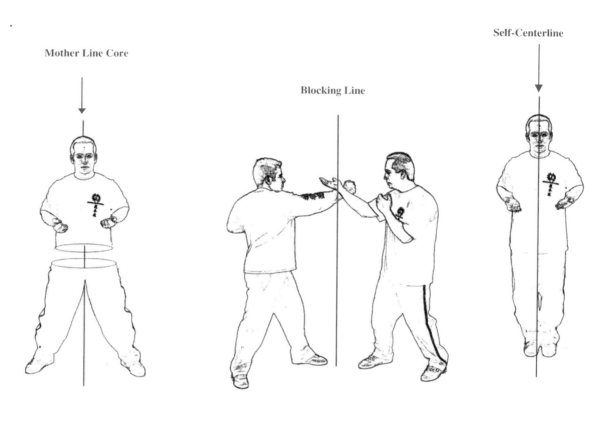

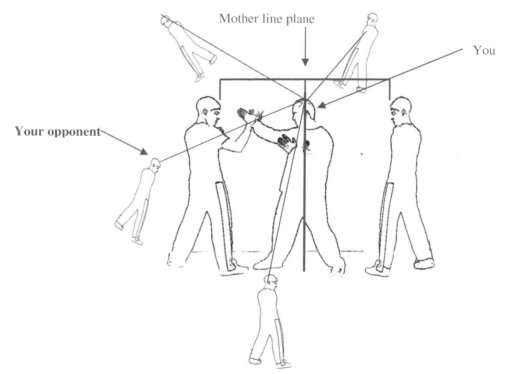

Jeet Kune Do - Five Ways of Attack

SDA: Single Direct Attack - A single blow can be **Choon Choy** (a JKD devastating punch), or **Gwa Choy** (backhand), or it can be compared to a boxers jab or cross. It can be **Jick Teck** (straight kick), **Ow Teck** (hook kick), and **Juck Teck** (sidekick), or some other attack, as long as the attack is single, one motion and direct. It can be executed with footwork to add more power to the attack. The practitioner must be in the JKD **By-Jon** (ready fighting stance). Hands and wrists must be very relaxed and delivering the clenched punch only about **2"** in front of its target or at its moment of impact. You must put your hip behind it, snap it, and put your energy and power into your fist making it into a weapon.

One   Two

ABC: Attack by Combination- This can be a boxer's jab, cross, hook, or upper cut. Hands combination, hand and feet combination, or vice versa, etc. The two motions must be part of one motion delivered with **broken rhythm**, and it can be executed with more than just one attack-ie- **Jik Teck** (front kick), **Choon kune** (punch), **Gwa Choy** (back hand), **Pie Jon** (inward elbow) "**using every part of your body.**"

HIA: Hand Immobilization Attack- *Fon* Sow, this is also known as 'trapping hands.' When you completely immobilize your opponent's hands using several different techniques, **Gum Sow** (pressing hand), **Pock Sow** (slapping hand), and **Lop Sow** (grabbing hand), just to name a few. If done properly, this will give you the opportunity to strike without a counter strike from your opponent. This can also be **FIA**: FOOT IMMOBILIZATION ATTACK. You intercept anything that is put in front of you by taking his power, bringing it to a dead stop, and eliminating all of the opponent's weapons, leaving him without any recourse.

PIA: Progressive Indirect Attack - Distance and timing are the keys to **PIA**. The key is to fake out your opponent, to open him up for an attack no matter how well he is guarded. By using for instance, **Chop Choy** (low hammer) for a fake, not connecting the hit to the lower gate, or fake to the eyes with the rear hand, but land with a **Gwa Choy** (back hand) to his head. Or it can be fake low with a **Jick Teck** (front kick) but land high with a **Ow Teck** (hook kick, round house).

ABD: Attack by Drawing - Deceptive fighting. The object is to deceive your opponent (this is done intentionally to set up your opponent) so when your opponent strikes at the opening you are ready to attack with a counter attack. Just simply invite your opponent in, let him think he's welcome by giving him an opening for an attack but sure enough surprise him with an attack. For instance "for an opponent to reach you, he must move towards you". That should offer you an opportunity to intercept him by using your longest weapon against his nearest target, his knee cap. For example, deliver a massive **Jeet Teck** (stop kick), or side kick him to the head. You can also simply intercept his thought and emotion before he even scores by delivering a JKD punch **(Choon Choy)**.

Yum /Yeung (Yin / Yang) Symbol

The JKD symbol is the **Yum/Yeung** (pronounced **Yin /Yang** in Mandarin dialect). It consists of two colors, **RED** and **GOLD**. The red part represents **Yin** motion - anything that is negative. The gold part represents **Yang** motion - anything that is positive. They are complete opposites but compliment one another. **Yin** represents the feminine, anything soft or passive, yang is anything that is masculine, hard. **Yin/Yang**, dark and light, male and female, negative and positive, hard and soft etc….also surrounded by 10 arrows representing the flow of energy and my ranking system, in which consists of **SEVEN** sashes and **THREE** certification levels…. The colors of the **Yin** and **Yang** are **gold** and **red** and have no significant meaning compared to black and white. I just simply tried to stay away from tradition by using different colors. The red and gold arrows represent the flow of energy of **Yin** and **Yang**, a non-stopping learning process of continuing growth. The little circles inside **Yin** and **Yang** represent connectivity. No matter how tough a male can be, if he loses someone very close he will cry. In addition, no matter how soft a female is, if you hurt someone very close to her, she will become very strong. What it means is every person has a little negative and positive in them, or femininity or masculinity, and life in itself. The outer Gold and **Red** frames and the inside black area of the logo represents the stages of learning My The System Without A System®. The **Gold Frame** is the first stage, the **Red frame** is the second stage, and the **Black area** is the third stage. They also compliment each being incomplete without the other. It also reads in English **PHONETIC**

(Mow 無) (Jeah 招) (Sing 勝) (Yaow 有) (Jeah 招)

You might ask yourself, is JKD The System Without A System®. Hard or Soft? From all the years of my experience, I have found it to be both.

YIN AND YANG

Yin/Yang. Total opposites, but they compliment each other. Either fighter should be both yin and yang to be a complete fighter. Therefore, it doesn't matter what style of martial arts you choose to practice, as long as it helps you if you ever need it. By that I mean if you don't have an "**empty cup**" then you are not going to be either yin or yang. You must learn from a yin style and a yang style. Combine the two so that way you will have a complete circle energy flow of yin and yang. A common mistake that most martial artists make is that some might favor yin soft style and some might favor yang hard style. They think these are separate entities but yin and yang are inseparable. They are both a complete flow of movement that compliment one another.

The **Yin** and **Yang** in Jeet Kune Do can be developed and identified as it is developed in the Wing Chun Gung Fu system, where JKD has a very strong base from Wing Chun Gung Fu. A JKD practitioner can also develop the same internal and external elements including four internal: Emptiness, Stillness, Sinking and Softness and four external: Technique, Timing, Angle structure, and Power. These are also known as the **Eight Elements Of Internal And External Development.** Once a Jeet kune do practitioner develops both internal and external powers, he or she has reached and developed the art of "**IT**" which is the art of Emptiness - the last level of training in JKD. This is when you react naturally to your environment, without thinking and ready for what ever may come.

Internal and External Development

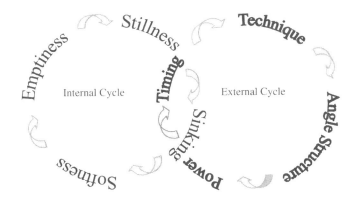

This cycle is also known as the **"Primary Cycle Of Development"**

This cycle will help a JKD practitioner discover and develop the difference between **Hard** and **Soft** by combining both qualities together.

The Eight Elements

Internal

Emptiness - the art of Emptiness is the last level of training in JKD. This is when you react naturally to your environment, without thinking.
Stillness – the art of Stillness occurs when you are aware of your surroundings and not charging your opponent blindly. You are not distracted by anything.
Sinking – the art of Sinking occurs when all of your energy is focused into your middle, the center of your gravity. This enables your strikes to be well grounded and most forceful.
Softness – the art of Softness means your moves are "fluid" and concise. Your strikes will be forceful without exerting unnecessary energy.

External

Technique – the art of Technique is when you have mastered the movements of JKD. They are second nature to you and you know when to apply the proper technique in real life situation.
Timing – the art of Timing is most essential and it fits hand and hand with technique. Knowing when to apply the technique at the right time. Even if your technique is the best, without proper timing the technique is useless, and your distance, speed, and rhythm will be misjudged.
Angle Structure – the art of the angle structure is accuracy. In order for your angle structure to be effective your moves must not be sloppy and must be well focused.
Power – the art of Power will develop as your technique, timing, and angle structure come together. Without technique, timing, and angle structure, power is useless.

Speed, Rhythm, Distance and Timing

Speed and Rhythm depend on the individual. Some people are very fast, some medium fast, and some are slow, but sometimes a slow technique can be fast--this depends on the situation. Timing can make all the difference, because it compliments both speed and rhythm.

If an opponent punches me with a slow punch, and I time my block at the correct slow speed at that exact rhythm, I'll block it. If he hits slowly, I block slowly. So, I follow his rhythm to be accurate with my counter attack. One must figure out his opponent's speed, and then match his speed to the opponent's. Practice, repetition, and drills--especially the paper drill--help to achieve this ability. To build speed timing and rhythm, begin by taking an 8.5 X 11 piece of paper (thicker quality paper or an old magazine will do) and letting it hang from a short string at the same height as your head (maybe off of a door jam). Move around the paper; treat it like a speed bag. If you miss it, it might be because you hit too soon. This enforces finding the right moment to strike. It is realistic because the paper will seem to flow around you. All types of punches and angles can be used against the paper. Your timing must become perfect for it to work well. Speed and timing must be accurate and perfect. A broken rhythm repetition becomes crucial in this exercise. You should watch how the paper moves, and use the broken rhythm on it. Mix it up.

Using a real speed bag and working with rhythm builds hand speed, but using paper is preferable due to its low cost and silence. However, the best practice is to work with a partner on actual strikes, as it teaches when to really block and when to punch. The main point is that you must make the most of your individual skills--if you are slow, your timing can still be correct.

Distance is a very difficult subject, taking years of practice and personal experience to judge correctly. Also, distance is always preferential. With these drills, you can learn when to and when not to attack, and the opponent can move in different directions. Results come through a lot of sparring practice, and different levels of sparring can help. Applying correct timing is essential to getting proper distance. While both timing and distance can help your skill, if your speed is poor then the attack can fail. Therefore, the three main points to consider here are <u>speed</u>, <u>timing</u>, and <u>distance</u>. I don't agree with people who say you can be 'taught distance.' Learning to judge distance is entirely up to the individual. All that matters is that you stop the attack. How can one know an opponent's stance and attack combos? One simply cannot. The ability to judge distance can be improved on the counterattack. With JKD, defense is also offense. Advancing is always better because then the opponent is backpedaling and has less power.

Speed training with weights can help develop speed. Use 2-3 pound weights in each hand. Make sure you follow through with your punches. If you stop and pull back, it will damage your elbows. Then, after using the weights, do the same exercises without the weights.

Neither timing, speed, nor distance can actually be taught--these skills are all self-taught. Ideas and hints can be given as to how to improve in these areas. However, the decision of when to execute is up to you. JKD timing is much faster than that of other martial art forms. Once a practitioner has developed his or her own way of judging speed, distance, and rhythm, then the **Economy of Motion** is developed, which is non-tenseness, posture relaxation, and physical focus. It's getting from point one to point three without dealing with point two. It's never wasting a technique; it's getting to the point. There's never a need to show body language before executing a technique, and never any wasted movements. It's all one motion.

Timing (See Gon): Timing plays a big part. There are six varieties of timing: self-timing, regular timing, created timing, breaking timing, delayed timing, and double timing.

SELF-TIMING: Self-timing is a part of you. It relies heavily on body unity. All techniques are to be executed at the same time. For example, you can block and punch at the same time. You can block, pivot, and strike simultaneously. This is why I teach with the Wooden Dummy. It teaches you all these things and allows everything to be timed right. Good coordination is self-timing.

REGULAR TIMING (SEE GON SING): Regular timing is similar to self-timing, with a slight difference. You have to time the attack just right. You can strike either before he strikes or when the door is opening or closing (retreating). You borrow the opponent's power so that when you intercept, you are using his power plus your own power, giving you double power.

CREATED TIMING (JAY JO SEE GON): In created timing, you must initiate the attack. Strike him before he strikes you. It is like making time to spend with the wife and kids--if you do not do it, someone else will be living in your house. You must strike at any opening before your opponent does. Intercept his emotions. Initiate the first attack by creating timing. It is like forcing him to open the door but knocking first. As he opens the door, he will be facing a strike.

BREAKING TIMING (DA PO SEE GON): In breaking timing, there is a delay between a block and a strike. You hold your opponent's attack, so you can strike before he closes the door or retreats back to position. If he strikes at you, then you hold his strike before the counter. This way, you are breaking his timing by delaying.

DELAYED TIMING (TOE YIN SEE GON): Delayed timing is done intentionally to delay the block or strike. For example, you would feed a light strike while waiting for a better opening to make a more powerful strike. It is deception.

DOUBLE TIMING (SEUNG CHOONG SEE GON): Double timing is any two timings put together.

To practice your speed, rhythm, and timing, use a speed bag, or you can also puncture a hole in an 8 1/2 x 11 piece of paper or an old magazine, and let it hang off a small rope at head height, which works just as well.

BY-JON
PYRAMIDS STRUCTURE
FOR OFFENSE AND DEFENSE

 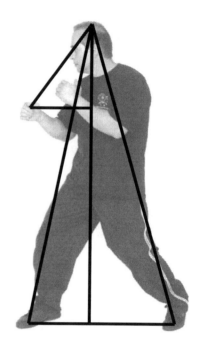

JKD By-Jon on- guard position (semi- crouch stance) is the only, and the most effective fighting stance for attacking and defense. It is the **backbone** of JKD, and combined with front lead, it is the most well structured fighting stance. It is geometrically designed into imaginary pyramids and triangles in relation to the **Self-Center Line.** Using the JKD
By-Jon is unlike other Martial Arts fighting stances, they don't concentrate on the centerline. Some do, but many don't. They leave it open, therefore, your vital organs, which are on the centerline, are exposed. Some even leave the lower part of the body unprotected. Some do not have any mobility, and some are too rigid. From all my years of training and research, I have found that a JKD fighting stance is so well plugged. It is almost like a cage of little pyramids surrounds you. This is very difficult for an opponent to penetrate it. Combined with proper footwork and training, it is unlikely to be touched. Geometric structure of JKD by-Jon is well designed so that your blocks and attacks are designed of little Pyramids, which are also the most powerful structure known. Every angle of JKD block fits in a geometric Pyramid in relation with a centerline. Whether it is an attack or block, it all fits in the Pyramid structure that has a very strong base, flowing all of your energy into a single most direct point with the fastest and most powerful path into your opponent. Every JKD stance footwork attack or defense has a pyramid structure. It could be a block or an attack like **Choon Choy** (straight punch) or **Tun Sow** (showing hand block) etc. Or it can be a block hit and you will generate much more power by maintaining it. The on guard position allows the practitioner to be very mobile, by taking small steps or big steps. Whether the attack or defense is on a straight or curved line, it allows both a very good balance when bridging the gap between you and your opponents, and a very smooth path without any restrictions to your movements, or feet repositioning.

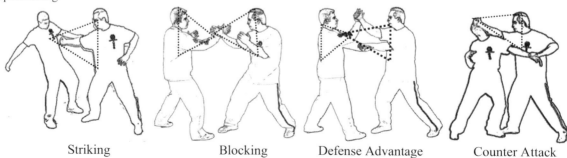

Striking   Blocking   Defense Advantage   Counter Attack

When a JKD fighter is in a fighting stance position (by –Jon), imaginary pyramids are created. When a JKD fighter extends the arm for an attack or a block, all the imaginary pyramids are created geometrically.

1 highest point top or tip (apex) **A** each angular point of polygon (minimum of three sides) **B** meeting point of lines that forms an angle, these pyramids are created from the tip of your **Mother Line Core** to the tip of the block or an attack in relation with **Self Center Line** and the **shoulder.**

BY-JON

ON GUARD POSITION /READY FIGHTING STANCE- RIGHT OR LEFT LEAD

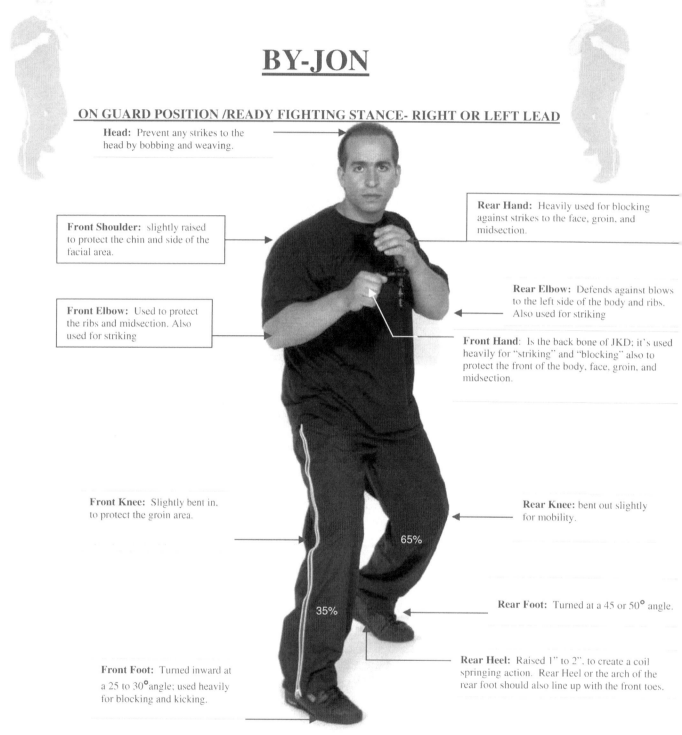

Head: Prevent any strikes to the head by bobbing and weaving.

Front Shoulder: slightly raised to protect the chin and side of the facial area.

Front Elbow: Used to protect the ribs and midsection. Also used for striking

Rear Hand: Heavily used for blocking against strikes to the face, groin, and midsection.

Rear Elbow: Defends against blows to the left side of the body and ribs. Also used for striking

Front Hand: Is the back bone of JKD; it's used heavily for "striking" and "blocking" also to protect the front of the body, face, groin, and midsection.

Front Knee: Slightly bent in, to protect the groin area.

Rear Knee: bent out slightly for mobility.

65%

35%

Rear Foot: Turned at a 45 or 50° angle.

Front Foot: Turned inward at a 25 to 30° angle; used heavily for blocking and kicking.

Rear Heel: Raised 1" to 2", to create a coil springing action. Rear Heel or the arch of the rear foot should also line up with the front toes.

By-Jon Stance Positions

The posture is very relaxed, still, sunk, and ready for any attack and defense. It is like a cobra ready to strike at any moment.

The Head: Chin slightly bent forward to avoid any under blows. This will also help to bob and weave much faster.

Rear Hand: This is heavily used for blocking against any oncoming straight punches, hooks, upper cuts, or kicks. It is also used for striking and hand immobilization.

Rear Elbow: Mainly used to protect against any round kicks against the ribs or the side of the body.

Rear Knee: Slightly bent out for faster mobile and springing action.

Rear Foot: *Turned* outward at a 45 to 50 degree angle.

Rear Heel: Raised 1" to 2" off the ground creating a coiled spring action. By raising the heel up, it offers better mobility for footwork and sprinting to reach the opponent much faster, and with much more power. It forces your whole body weight behind the punch. Also the rear heel or the arch of the foot should line up with the front toes to allow free path from rear kicking. If your front foot is in too much, then the rear foot cannot attack on a straight line. You would have to adjust your structure to score a proper invisible kick.

Front Hand: Is the **backbone** of JKD, used heavily for striking. In addition, it is used against front blocking, any straight line punches, or curved line.

The **front hand** protects against any attacks, whether a front kick to the groin, or round kicks, or any type of kick.

Front Elbow: Used mainly to protect against any round kicks, hooks to the body, or midsection, and also used for power strikes.

Front Knee: Slightly bent and turned inward to protect against any blows to the groin area.

Front Foot: Turned inward at a 25-30 degree angle used heavily for kicking and stop blocking like (**Jeet Teck**).

Rear and Front Foot: Approximately two feet apart from each other, wider then the shoulders, and the weight distribution is 35% on the front leg and 65% on the rear leg to a total of 100%. "**Note** "weight distribution may vary among practitioners.

There is more then one way to get to a **By-Jon**. You can do it from a Wing Chun stance position while practicing Siu Leem Tau, or you can just simply do it from a very natural position.

Yee Jee Kim Yin Ma (Goat restraining stance or character 2 pigeon toe horse stance).

The Yee Jee Kim Yin Ma is a Wing Chun stance. By itself it is not a fighting stance but its purpose is to build a very good base for a **JKD By-Jon** (ready fighting stance).

(1)

By-Jon's ROOT
First choice

The **Yee Jee Kim Yin Ma** (goat-restraining stance, or charters 2 pigeon toe horse stance), plays a big part in building a very strong **By-Jon**. Unlike other styles of martial arts, this is the only fighting stance you need to learn in JKD. That is one very good reason why JKD is so simple the **Yee Jee Kim Yin Ma** will also give the proper and the exact distance between the two feet for a proper **By-Jon** stance.

(2) (3) (4)

From a **Yee Jee Kim Yin Ma** stance pivot out to your right **Cho –Ma** (pivot stance), to approx a 30-degree angle. That will give the proper distance between the two feet. Raise the rear heal approximately **1-2"** off the ground. Left hand on centerline guarding it.

(5A)   (5B)

Get posture all sunk down and ready. Sit back slightly and remain in a very relaxed posture. Rear hand on center line, front hand waist height, front hands slightly clenched but not fully closed or open dangling very loose and relaxed ready to fire at any time.

On Guard Position!

Second Choice

Distance between the two feet, for a proper **By-Jon.**

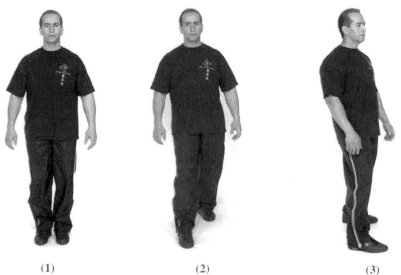

(1) (2) (3)

At a natural stance, step forward with your right foot approx 2 feet. Pivot to your left approx 30 degrees so your feet are parallel to each other.

On Guard Position!

(4) Front and back view By-Jon

5) Side view By-Jon

It is extremely important that the rear heel is raised approx **1-2"** off the ground. That will create the springing coil action and you will have much faster mobility.

Example of Other Stances Of Martial Arts

I am sure you can find something wrong with every fighting stance, even a JKD stance. To me, I have found it to be the most proper stance for sparring and real life situations.

(1) (2) (3) (4) (5)

(6)

(7)

1) Toes are pointed in, has no mobility, and lower gate is exposed.
2) Too much weight on one foot will easily get knocked off balance.
3) Too low to the ground, no mobility, and too rigid.
4) Lower half of the body is too exposed and no centerline defense.
5) Very good centerline defense. However, no mobility.
6) Good defense line, but the lower gate is exposed.
7) **JKD Stance,** good center line defense, upper, middle, and lower gates are protected and good mobility.

Orthodox Fighting Stance   **Southpaw Fighting Stance**

The orthodox fighting stance is the most commonly used stance in most fighting styles. Most of the power is generated from the rear .The southpaw fighting stance is heavily used in Jeet kune do, because it is based on fencing. Whether you are righty or lefty you have to lead with the strong side forward, generating all the power from the front lead and by bringing all the power forward. Your front and the rear hands become the power hands. That way you have two weapons that you can use to their fullest. The orthodox rear kick is a very powerful kick if you are an orthodox fighter, but the southpaw rear kick is rarely used from the right lead in JKD. Usually it is used from the rear left kick about 5% of the time to strike the knees low for take downs. This is because you want to reach the target without telegraphing the kick, so the front leg is used heavily.

Telegraph (i.e. all the strikes are executed from the rear) an orthodox kick or punch can be noticed before or on its way to the target, so it is very easily blocked or countered.

The leading straight right is the bread and butter punch in JKD.

Techniques are drawn from the following:
Wing Chun Gung Fu
Western Boxing
Fencing
Kick Boxing
Paul Curtin's Eclectic Karate®
Kenpo Karate
Shotokan Karate
Jiu-Jitsu
Aikido
Grappling
" Absorb What's Useful"

Jeet Kune Do - Right Lead

Right Lead And The Right Hand Are The **Backbone** Of JKD

The right lead, unorthodox fighting stance is not limited. It is the fastest, shortest, and most direct line between you and your opponent without telegraphing the attack. It is unlikely to get blocked and there will be less damage to one's hand. You put all your power forward. If you are left handed, you lead with your left. It's like **Fencing,** but you take out the sword and screw on a fist. A Jeet Kune Do punch should whip and should be executed without any effort. A JKD punch is very scientific because of looseness and its whip power. A punch must come from the hips, never tense and only clenched at moment of impact. Every punch should be backed up with a guarding hand protecting your Center Line.

Fencing

Jeet kune Do fighting stance is based on the **On-uard** position of a fencer.

Why Do We Use The Vertical Punch and Not The Horizontal Punch?

YUT (SUN)   JEE (character) CHOON (thrusting) KUNE (fist)

Intensive study has proven that a Jeet Kune Do punch is much more powerful and effective than a karate punch, whereas the karate **Seikin Zukie** punch showed more effectiveness as far as exercises and muscle development is concerned. The vertical punch is the most natural position to release the power equally to the target, and your wrist and elbow will not bend when the punch connects with the target. In addition, you are not open for any injuries; your whole bone structure, alignment, and every muscle in the arm is used to its maximum equally, like the forearm, biceps, triceps and the shoulder. Also we use the last three knuckles instead of the first two knuckles, so it's like hitting someone with a 2x4. By rotating the hand when executing the horizontal punch and adjusting the wrist to line up the bone with the fist you are not distributing the power equally. Some muscles will be used more then others, that is why you might be injured. Some techniques might require a horizontal punch, but it is executed differently from the karate horizontal punch – in Jeet Kune Do it uses the same exact principle as the vertical punch. This way you still have your whole bone structure and alignment behind it. Just simply turn the wrist inward without adjusting the knuckles so they can line up with the target.

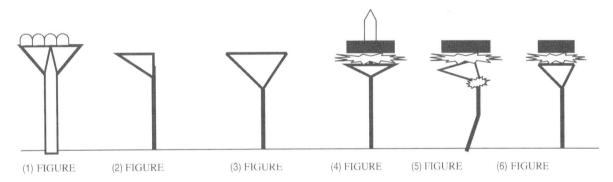

(1) FIGURE   (2) FIGURE   (3) FIGURE   (4) FIGURE   (5) FIGURE   (6) FIGURE

FIGURE (1-4) The vertical punch is compared to a nail supported by a little spring around the fingers. When it impacts with the subject it will collapse equally, and the fingers will get pushed down as the knuckles stick up impacting the target with the whole bone structure behind it for full power.

FIGURE (2-5) The horizontal punch. When it impacts with the target it can cause wrist injury and the elbow to bend, resulting in lack of bone alignment.

FIGURE (3-6) The JKD horizontal punch it is executed the same way as the vertical punch using only the last three knuckles, not the first two knuckles. When its impacts with the target it will have the same amount of power and bone alignment behind it.

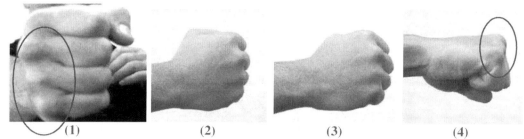

(1) The JKD vertical punch uses the last three knuckles. (2-3-4) As you rotate the wrist to a horizontal position, the hand should have the same bone and muscle structure behind it by still using the last three knuckles.

Testing The Power Behind The Vertical Punch

If you smash your hand into your partner's vertical punch, you will see that like smashing against a 2x4, the whole arm is extremely strong from the shoulder all the way up to the fist in very good alignment as well as a good locked position.

Testing the power behind incorrect horizontal punch. By smashing your hand against your partner's fist you will realize that the wrist will bend down and the elbow will kick out on impact. Most people assume a horizontal punch is the correct punch to execute, because they have seen boxers use it. However boxers wrap up their wrists to prevent injury.

JKD horizontal punch uses the last three knuckles, in a very natural way. **(1)** Karate horizontal punch uses the first two knuckles by adjusting the wrist side ways to line up the bone behind it. Another test is to place the fist in either position in a very natural way against the wall. **Figure (1)** you will realize that the first two knuckles don't even connect with the surface, only the last three knuckles do.

Jeet Kune Do 1 Inch Punch (Choon Goon kune)

"IF I AM GONNA PUNCH I AM GOING TO DO IT"
"You've got to put your whole hip into it, then snap it, and let all your energy out."

The Jeet Kune Do **1 Inch** Punch is one of the most popular, and powerful punches that Founder of Jeet Kune Do ever demonstrated. It will knock a person who is over 200 lbs back 5 feet from just a single blow. This punch is not for show. It is extremely effective and is used in Jeet Kune Do training from every aspect of fighting. When you are in close quarters, you can deliver the **1"** punch without having to retract the hand in order to reload the power. The power is released from the tip of the toes all the way up through the front knuckles of the right lead hand.

To execute the **1"** punch with power and effectiveness, the lower gate from the hips down must be very relaxed. The rear heel is raised approx 2" to 3" off of the ground, ready to trigger the punch. The rear knee is bent. The upper gate is very relaxed at the moment. When releasing the power you must push up with the ball of the foot as you come up, rotating the hips, and keeping the rear foot at a 90-degree angle. Your arms and shoulder should be in a straight line/lock position. This punch goes right through the target. You should focus on what is on the other side of the target. **"Don't think, feel"**, means that you should not think about getting hurt in this process, because you will be holding back your power, and you will be blinded by your tenseness. When punching, you must punch approximately 5" beyond the target - that is the only way that the 1" punch will have power and force behind it.

Rotation Of The Hips And Pivoting Of The Rear Foot

(1)　　　(2)　　　(3)

1) Lower gate down, rear heel up 2". 2) Push up with rear ball of the foot. 3) Rotate the hips and pivot the rear foot at a 90° angle.

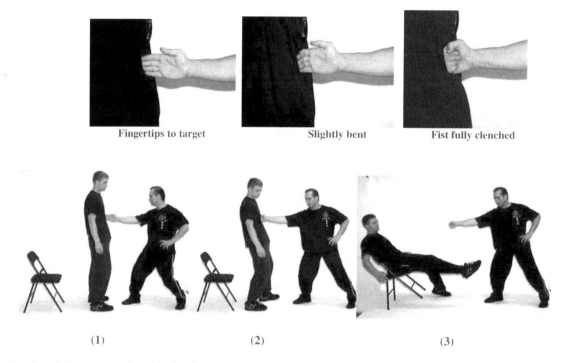

Fingertips to target | Slightly bent | Fist fully clenched

(1) (2) (3)

Place the tip of fingers against his body. Lower gate is down, rear heel up, rear knee bent, front knee slightly bent, other hand on your hips. Concentrate all of your energy into one point. Clench the fist into a vertical punch as you rotate with the hips and push with the ball of rear foot into the target knocking him back into the chair.

Using A Phone Book For Practice

Follow the same movements as above, but have your partner hold a phone book against his chest. Repeat the 1" punch many times until you are very comfortable and you feel that you are generating enough power without telegraphing the punch or retracting it. You can also practice against a punching bag or a sand bag.

Re-Breakable Board

This is a re-breakable board, which can be used after you feel that you're ready to connect with something harder than a phonebook, but softer than wood. It comes in many levels of difficulty, which I highly recommend prior to breaking wood, it is also less costly. It's made of high strength plastic which allows the board to be broken time after time, where the wooden board allows you to only break it once.

#1044 (Century Martial Art Supply) approx cost $45.00 US

 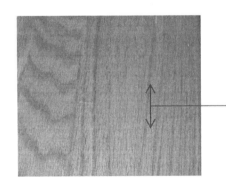

Breaking Grain Direction

Practice on the real thing when you feel ready. I recommend ¾" pine at first
Do not punch against the grain of the wood. –To avoid breaking against the grain of the wood you must follow the direction of the grain not across.

Place the tips of the fingers against the wooden board, sit back slightly, push up with the rear ball of the foot as you rotate the hips. By driving the punch into the target, all three motions must be part of one motion… at first it will feel like **1-2-3.** With practice, your hit should be fluid.

Results of 20 minutes of shooting the photos for the 1" punch.

The One (1") Inch kick

The one-inch kick is a very effective kick and it is not merely for demonstration purposes only. The power that is being generated from just a short distance can be very easily applied in close quarters fighting. If a person understands the principles, application and theory behind the kick and learns to generate power from this short distance, they will have no problem delivering power from a long distance. Therefore, the kick can be used during tight grabs, clinches and ground attacks. It can even be utilized while standing still and can be executed with power snap from as little as 1".

Hip Rotation: It is very important that the hip rotates at the moment of impact and line up with the target. The power from the hip is what makes the kick so effective and powerful. Without having to rotate the hips a few things will happen: 1) you will have no snap during delivery and 2) you will not penetrate the target due to the lack of power that is being generated from the snap.

Rear Heel: The starting position of the rear heel is at a 90°-degree angle. The rear knee is fully locked. The right or front leg is fully extended against the target with the heel about 1" away and with toes touching the target. Execute the kick by rotating the rear foot until it is fully facing the target. Again, two things must happen: one, you have to rotate the rear heel and snap the front heel into the target simultaneously with speed and snap. Otherwise you will not cause much damage while penetrating the target. Two, it is very important that you rotate and snap the front heel without reloading. You must push all the energy forward that is being generated from your hip and rear heel rotation.

When do you use this Kick?

This kick is used in many demonstrations to showcase the power behind it. However, do not place your foot against someone's chest or any other target to execute it. This kick is used in short, close quarter distances. For example: a short one inch kick snap can be delivered against someone's shins or instep during a bear hug, clinch, or even a head lock. It can also be executed against a charging attack while you are flat on your back and the other person is rushing into the attack. You can then use this kick to deliver power instead of pushing off.

Velocity and Alignment: Applying all of one's body weight into the target generates the force from this kick. Therefore, the rear heel and the hips will line up perfectly after the quick rotation of the rear heel and the shoulders. The kick is executed in one fluid motion, forcing body power and velocity and perfect alignment, including the leg, being fully extended and perpendicular to the floor.

(A) Face your target (B) Start to lean back

Make sure that you maintain full balance as you lean back for execution of the kick. Focus on the target.

(C) Place the front toes against the board (D) Snap the heel into the board. Make sure that you lean back and rotate the hip and rear heel to it's fullest so that the rear heel lines up with the target.

(A) (B)

Outside View
Adhere to the same principles as described in the previous set of photos.

Full body and hip rotation is a must!

(A) Place the toes against the board

(B) Drop the heel into the target with full hip and body rotation into the board

Full execution of the kick, will cause full penetration of the target.

The 1" kick against an opponent!

Applying the kick against an opponent can very easily be done. You first have to consider that your opponent is not going to stand still and simply let you execute the kick. NO real fighter will stand still! However, this is how this kick should be used.
During a side kick impact against a moving target this kick can be executed with full power and impact. At the end of the side kick, you then release all the power from the last 1" away from the target, in which it will impact against the moving target with power and speed. All the power from the side kick will impact with that extra power and velocity from the 1" kick and the results are complete penetration and no loss of energy.

In Demonstration Only

(A) Face your opponent   **(B)** Start to lean back

Make sure that you maintain full balance as you lean back for execution of the kick. Focus on the target.

(C) Place the front toes against the torso   **(D)** Snap the heel into the mid section. Make sure that you lean back and rotate the hip and rear heel to it's fullest so that the rear heel lines up with the target.

Foot Positioning & Rotation!

(1) Ready Stance **(2)** Rotate the rear heel at a 90 °angle **(3) Full** rotation until it lines up with the target…

OUTSIDE VIEW

From a READY stance. Rotate the rear heel at a 90 °angle counter clock to a full rotation to generate power from the kick.

FULL HEEL AND BODY ROTATION IS A **MUST!**

Mechanics of Jkd
The Half Beat Kick!

In this section I am going to discuss how to apply the mechanics of JKD. We are going to apply what is called **"half beat mechanics"**. Most practitioners assume that confrontations start from squared off positions. However, that is not the case in this scenario. From **long range**, it is very easy to deliver a non-telegraphic kick so there would be no need for half beat kick. But what happens when a person is up close to you? What if I need to kick my opponent from a **close range** while at the same time delivering power with speed and snap without getting jammed? My intentions are only to kick not to punch. I just want to hurt them and drop them where they stand within a 12-inch distance. There are two ways to do it. If the person is standing right in front of you within that range and I execute a round-house kick to the opponent's lower gate without applying the half beat kick, I will get jammed and be unable to generate any significant power. There will be no rotation of the hips or snap when executing such a kick. When applying the half beat kick, you must move in a lateral motion, front to rear, toe to toe, to a rotated rear heal position. That forces your body to gain distance and give you full extension of the front leg and full body and hip rotation. This kick should be applied simultaneously with speed and snap. Launch the kick as soon as the rear foot lands. This half beat kick can also be applied using the knee as well. Many other attacks can also be applied using this technique, such as front kicks, sidekicks and stop kicks. The half beat kick can also be applied from a By-Jon **long-range** position, which will not only help the delivery of your kick, but also will increase the kicks power and deceptiveness. Kicks are much more devastating using the half beat kick, due to the power generated from the gain of distance, hip, body rotation, and snap.

(1)   (2)   (3)

From a By-Jon position **SHORT RANGE**. Rock your body in a lateral motion like ,toe to toe ,as you rotate you hips and body into a pivoted body alignment and execute a kick to the closest target .The rocking motion must be done as One motion, and simultaneously into the target guaranteeing full explosiveness snap and power and gain of distance.

(1) (2) (3) (4) (5)

From a **LONG RANGE** By- Jon –position, same principles as the SHORT RANGE should be applied, where in the Long Range when these principle are applied you close the gap to a closer distance or it can also be executed to target more out of range opponent.

The Eye Flick!

The eye Flick is a maneuver used to target an opponent's mouth and eyes. This strike can also target both the ribcage and groin. While the Eye Flick appears to be similar to a backhand, this strike is much more deceptive and faster in delivery in actual motion against any of the aforementioned targets. The Eye Flick is somewhat of a sneak attack. This technique is being demonstrated book form for the first time and was previously only shown to my students and viewers of my website. Since I have received a lot of questions about this technique, I have reluctantly decided to share this devastating move in print. As mentioned before, the Eye Flick initially appears to be very similar to the backhand, but the difference in execution is the necessary flick of the hand from the wrist. In order to execute correctly, your hand must remain extremely loose and dangly at all times. Thus, one would not begin by standing very tight and clenching the fist as with the backhand. Instead, you must completely loosen the hand and the wrist. In order to test the body parts and experience how loose the hand and wrist should be, begin by dangling the hand in a very loose position. Then, flick the hand in midair. When flicked the hand should make a flapping sound, similar to the noise produced by a bird's moving wings in the air. This sound is actually the wind moving through the fingers as a result of the speed in delivery with which the move is executed. If this sound does not occur, this means that the maneuver is not being executed with enough speed and will not be as effective. As a result, the flick will resemble a backhand and be slow and telegraphic. Be sure that the hand and the wrist are very loose at all times to execute an Eye Flick.

Why the Eye Flick Not the Backhand?

As previously mentioned, the eye flick is very deceptive because the strike appears to be a backhand but you can use it much more frequently in half the amount of time then you can with the backhand. Due to the speed in which it is executed, the eye flick is difficult for the opponent to even see coming. Thus, your opponent will have a very hard time defending it, because the strike can repeatedly be delivered with such tremendous speed, along with the same amount of snap every single time, as opposed to the back fist which can be very easily detected and stopped because of lack of speed and snap during execution and delivery.

Which causes more damage? The backhand can cause more damage because it is executed with body weight and hip rotation behind the hit. Therefore, the impact is much more devastating and the results can be a knockout. The Eye Flick is compared to a bee sting that stings and causes swelling to the targeted area and the opponent will only feel its impact seconds after the impact. The result is total lack of vision, along with a stinging effect and internal, long lasting pain.

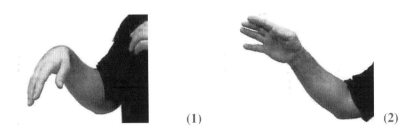

Inside View

(1) Very relaxed wrist and hand position **(2)** release the power from the wrist using the back of the fingers.

Outside View

(A) The back hand TOO tense **(1)** The Eye Flick is very relaxed attack and it can be executed with speed and lots of power and snap. It can also be delivered from any position.

(2) Fold the hand in a inward motion **(3)** Release the power from the wrist into the eye, mouth or the groin, using the back of the fingers for proper contact.

JKD's *Five Ways of Attack can be applied during delivery!*

Don't just limit your self to just one hit. JKD's Five Ways of Attack can be applied and executed effectively. Example: In the photos below the Hand Immobilization Attack (HIA) is being used to pin the opponents hand to secure full delivery without counter attacks.

Be sure to rotate the hip as you release the power from the snap of the wrist and the hip rotation. Also make sure that you control or immobilize the lead hand for a free delivery. A few things you should consider when delivering the eye flick from a close range attack: the rear hand should protect the face while delivering the attack to stop any counter attack to your own face. When the eye flick is being delivered from a fighting position long range, make sure that you use the push shuffle footwork for a fast, non-telegraphic strike.

(1) Remain very relaxed   **(2)** From a close range, pin and hit the target with that back of the fingers and maintain full control of the lead hand.

(3) From a long range, use push shuffle footwork to get closer to the targeted areas on the face.

From a long range, no footwork is needed. Only a single direct attack, hip rotation and slight body lean is all that is needed to deliver the eye flick with speed and power. The eye flick can be delivered with lightning speed in a straight line.

The back hand moves on the same line of attack as the eye flick, but the difference is that the back hand moves back and forth much slower.

Practice and sharpening the fingers!

Like any weapon the fingers should be toughened up against a bag or focus mitt. Experiment with different types of delivery and how much speed is lost during execution of the backhand instead of the eye flick. The back hand is much slower.

Use the back of the fingers to build elastic delivery like motion and to toughen up the back of the fingers.

Warming Up- Stretching Exercises

Warming up is very import before each class or training session. You must be fully warmed up and stretched. In addition, it will prevent any injuries during training, and you will be able to train to your maximum potential. Warming up can be done with or without a partner.

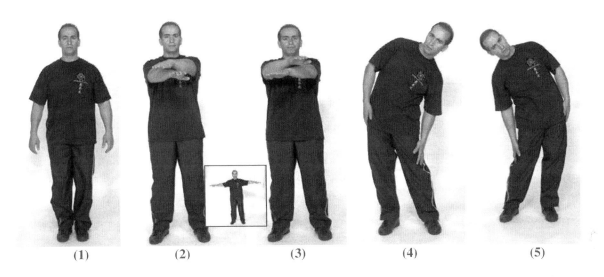

Feet together - place left over right, right over left, hands on your hips, bend side to side, repeat many times.

Both Hands On The Hips, twist to the right and the left. Place both hands on your knee and lean forward as you lock the rear leg for an extra stretch, and do it on both sides. **Butterflies-** both feet together grab the toes and push your knees down with your elbows for extra stretch of the groin area.

Pull out the left leg and reach for your toes, repeat on the right side also. If you cannot reach for your toes reach for your ankle, do both sides. Bring **both feet together, and reach for your toes**. Keep the knees down. **Open up both feet and bend forward** as far as you can and reach for the center.

Balance yourself on one leg, grab the foot, and pull the leg up as far as you can to stretch the hips. **Pivot to your right and left** as you grab the top of your foot and pull it up as you lean forward as much as you can.

(20)   (21)

Maintain balance, **grab the bottom of the foot and raise the leg** as far as you can to stretch the groin area on both sides.

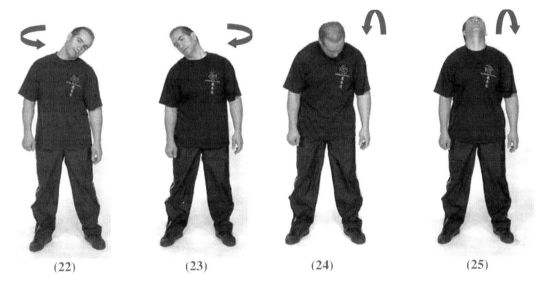

(22)   (23)   (24)   (25)

Rotate the head and neck side-to-side circle back and front.

(26A)   (26B)   (26C)   (26D)

(26E)   (26F)   LEFT SIDE. REPEAT IN A CIRCULAR MOTION

Place the right elbow inside of the left elbow and circle forward, down and up to loosen up the shoulders. Repeat on both sides.

(27) NORMAL HAND POSITION   (28) DIAMONDS   (29) KNUCKLES

(30)   (31)

Push-Ups - hands apart, shoulder width, back straight, knuckles, and diamond push up. Pump as many as you can, do all the way up, and all the way down, don't rest the chest on the floor.

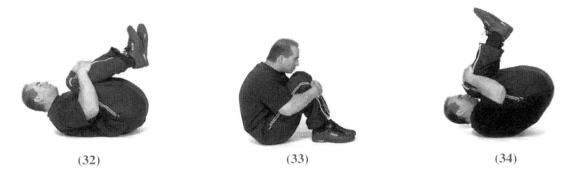

In A Sitting Position, hands by your knees, curl up into a ball, and rock from the shoulders to your feet to loosen up the spine.

Leg Raises - place both hands behind your back, straighten the legs out, heels are not touching the floor; head also is not touching the floor. Bring the knees all the way back to your chest, and shoot them back out straight. Repeat many times.

Place the hands behind your back and raise the legs in a upward position as far as you can to stretch the lower back.

Crunches - both hands behind your neck, back and feet completely flat on the floor, crunch forward and relax back, do it as many as you can.

(41)   (42)   (43)

Side hip stretching - one arm on the hips or in a cross-position, grab the knee and pull it in as far as you can to stretch the hips and the lower back while maintaining the cross position. +

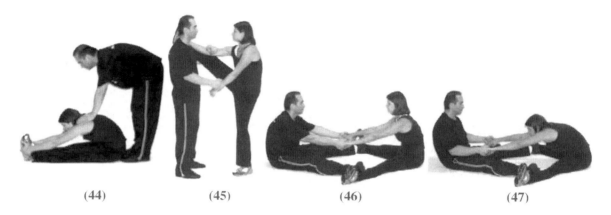

(44)   (45)   (46)   (47)

Partner Stretching - simply push down on the shoulders to allow your partner to get a full stretch. In a standup position, either partner places the leg on the shoulder, as the other partner wraps the hands around the knee to maintain the locked position, and stretch up the leg. **Inside leg stretching**- either partner places the feet on the inside of the other partner's ankle area, both hands locked, pull in as you push out the legs.

(48)   (49)   (50)

Side Sit-Ups With A Partner - grab each other's hands, knee-to-knee, pull back flat as you maintain the grip. Other partner remains in a seated position, then the cycle continues. ****

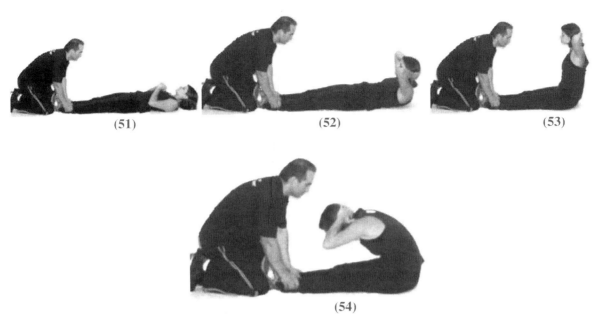

Partner (**A**) in a flat position as partner **B**) holds down both of partner (**A**)'s feet. Partner (**A**) sits all the way up and all the way back as many times as she can until results are achieved.

Stretching with a Bo staff or a broomstick. Stretch side-to-side, or front-to-front.

RESULTS, OF HARD WORK

Many martial artists neglect the most important tools which are developed muscles. Too much time spent on developing skills and sharpening techniques, but so little time spent on building **natural** physical condition. It is important for a martial artist to maintain both. By helping better the technique to generate more power and add more stamina to your body, a better physique will result in fewer injuries when training.

You must train and keep in good shape so when you want it, it's there. When you train, it doesn't matter what in kind of martial arts, you must give it 110 % and maintain a good physique. Trying your very best will always pay off in the end.

OTHER EXERCISES, NOT SHOWN CAN BE DONE TO BETTER YOUR SELF

<u>Walking</u>
<u>Running</u>
<u>Bicycling</u>
<u>Speed Bag</u>
<u>Leather Medicine Ball</u>
<u>Weight Lifting</u>
<u>Jump Rope</u>
<u>Sports Activities</u>
<u>Healthy Diet</u>

　Jeet Kune Do

The Path To Your Journey!

JKD Foundation and Development / Siu Leem Tau

JKD Bow -Ging Lie Salutation

Footwork-Moving Stances

Eight Basic Defense Positions from a By-Jon
Yin/Yang -Blocks and Strikes
Yin and Yang Blocks Definitions

Strikes
Hands Blocks
Palm Strikes
Elbows Strikes

Jeet Kune Do Right Lead Punch

Jeet Kune Do Hammer Principle/Straight Blast

Hip Rotation and Body Alignment

Jeet Kune Do Kicking

It's Not Just A Kick- It is A Jeet Kune Do Kick
JKD Advanced Hook Kick
Burning Foot Sidekick
JKD Five Corner Kicking
JKD Kicking Drill
Basic Punching and Kicking Combinations

PARTIALITY

The Basic Stage!

This Is The Most Important Stage Of Development!

"A House Can NOT Be Built Without A Foundation"

Jkd Foundation and Development - Siu Leem Tau

Siu Leem Tau (the little idea) - before we start, it is good to understand the origins and development of Jeet Kune Do. While there may be many explanations, the best way to explain it is to say that JKD is **formless,** meaning no katas or forms are performed; they are classical martial arts. I try to follow every aspect of the teachings of JKD, but in order to follow someone in their footsteps; we must go back to their origins. We must understand what he trained in and what he studied. In addition, we must understand how he became so skillful. As we all know, Bruce Lee trained in Wing Chun Gung Fu, from which his foundation originated. We also know that he knew **Siu Leem Tau** (the little idea), and the **Wooden Dummy**. I am sure he learned many forms before realizing that not all forms work in real life situations. This is when he changed to Jeet Kune Do, in which many train diligently, following his teachings as he intended. By performing this form, you are not a bad JKD practitioner, since even the founder of the system has done it. After many years of practice and research, I came to realize that the way to build a very strong student is by teaching them proper structure as well as a good, solid foundation. Otherwise, all the techniques will be sloppy, and there will be no power generated from your movements. After developing the proper structure by performing **Siu Leem Tau** for a long time, and feeling confident with your technique, you can start to pull away from this form, because it is then that you will have developed the internal and external powers.

Wing Chun Gung Fu - First Form
Siu Leem Tau (The Little Idea)

The **Siu Leem Tau** form consists of **108 motions**. Like other forms in Wing Chun Gung Fu, the Wooden Dummy, Chum-Q, and Biu-Jee, all consist of exactly 108 motions. The number 108 represents 108 little ideas. Because it has significance in the Chinese lunar/stars, mathematics, superstitions, and religion, the Chinese people also prefer it. The 108 motions are divided into three parts. The first part must be performed very slowly to build internal energy or **Hay Gong**. By performing the first part very slowly, the proper timing, and structure are developed. The combination of the two will develop power. This will also promote a relaxed atmosphere, having the practitioner's mind clear, and feeling a source of power flowing through the body. The practitioner must keep the lower body sunk throughout this form, remaining in a calm state for the entirety. The second and third parts will develop external powers by executing the techniques with speed, power, and snap. You must maintain proper position in relation to the centerline. The practitioner must remain in the **Yee Jee keem Yin Ma**, the mother stance of Wing Chun, or the goat-restraining stance. This is not a fighting stance, but a foundation stance. It builds a very good base and foundation from standing still in the same position for a long time. The completion of this depends entirely on the practitioner; it can last as long as one hour or as little as one minute. By combining internal and external powers, the completion of this form will generate speed, as well as growing the ability for blocking, striking, and whipping from a short distance. This form also consists of **Three Family** blocks, the **Bong Family**, the **Tun Family**, and the **Fook Family**. They're also known as the three poisons of Wing Chun Gung Fu. The Bong family blocks use the outer edge of the arm, the Tun family blocks use the outside of the hand, and the Fook family blocks use the inside of the hand. The economy of this form is very important. It teaches the student to learn almost every hand block and strike, and to maintain the centerline, which is crucial in JKD. It also teaches
The Immovable Elbow Moving Line. In the end, this teaches the student every aspect of correct structure and gives a good, solid foundation.

Hoy Sick Sequence
Stance Opening Sequence

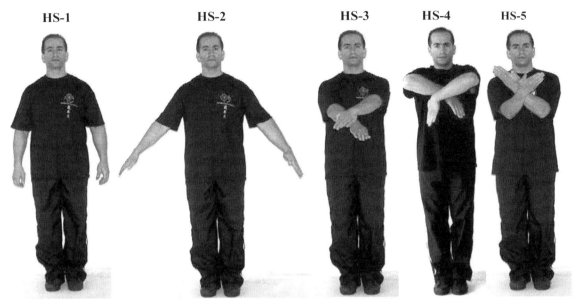

NATURAL STANCE **SUP JEE SOW** (CHARACTER 10) the **X**, START ROLLING **KWAN SOW** (rolling hands)
SUP MEANS (TEN) **JEE** (character) **SOW** (hand)

Straight posture, feet together, hands by your sides, and very relaxed. Place the left hand over the right hand, keeping hands at a distance of two fingers away. Hands and wrists should not be touching. Start rolling your hands from the outside to the inside in a downward motion, without letting your hands touch your chest. In doing this, your hands should be at an upward angle so you are looking at your palms.

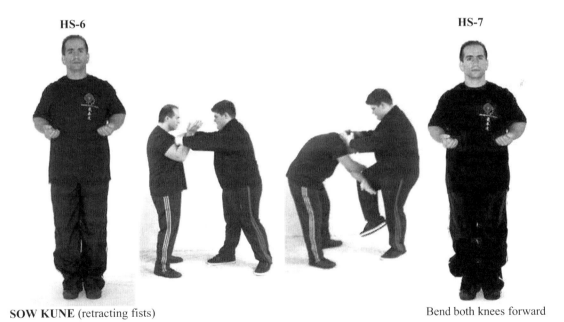

SOW KUNE (retracting fists)   Bend both knees forward

Retract your fists without touching the body; keep your elbows in about one fist distance from the ribs, and fists a distance of 2 fingers from your sides. Start the opening of the horse sequence by bending the knees forward and maintaining your upper body in an upright position. Do not lean forward.

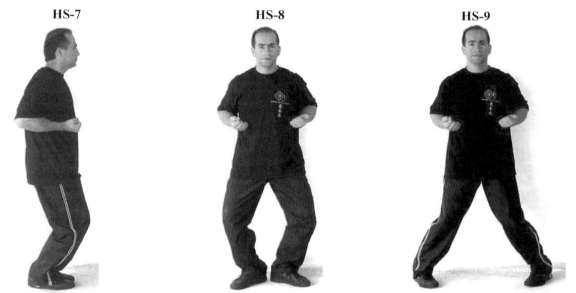

SIDE VIEW (ONLY) HOY- MA (open the horse)   **YEE JEE KIM YIN MA** (character 2, pigeon toe horse stance)

Open the horse stance by pointing toes outward and keeping heels together. Keep back straight, and turn heels out by pivoting at the toes into a **Yee Jee Kim Yin Ma** (character 2, pigeon toe horse stance or goat restraining stance).

First part

SUP JEE SOW (CHARACTER 10) X   START ROLLING   KWAN SOW (rolling hands)

From the **Yee Jee Kim Yin Ma** position, shoot out hands with snap and power in a downward angle into an "**X**", block position simultaneously. Keep hands a distance of two fingers away from each other. Hands and wrists should not be touching. Start rolling your hands from the outside to the inside in a downward motion, without letting your hands touch your chest. In doing this, your hands should be at an upward angle so that you are looking at your palms.

Sow Kune (retracting fists) (left) place the fist on center **Yut Jee Choon Kune** (**Character Sun**) (Thrusting punch vertical punch)

With fists retracted, and in the **Yee Jee Kim Yin Ma** position, place the left fist on the center of the body with the knuckles facing outward. Thrust fist forward in a straight line by extending the arm at the elbow into a locked position and towards center mass at a 45° angle in relation with your own centerline.

Tun Sow (showing hand) ———— **Huen Sow** (circling hand) ———— **Chop Kune** (horizontal punch)

The hand must flip up to **Tun Sow** facing the sky, and snap with two fingers pinched, three closed.
Circle **Huen Sow** with the index finger and thumb pinched together, pointing at the centerline. Continue circling inward and downward pointing the two fingers to the floor. Close the fist slowly, without tension. As you retract the fist back, immediately thrust the right punch forward in a straight line with **Chey Kune** (extension retraction punch), with no delay. By doing so, you are creating a pulling, punching motion.

Chey Kune (extension retracting punch) **Tun Sow** (showing hand) **Huen Sow** (circling hand)

The vertical punching hand must flip up to **Tun Sow** facing the sky, and snap with two fingers pinched, three closed. Circle **Huen Sow** in an inward and downward circular motion. The index finger and thumb should be pointing at the floor, with the back of the hand facing the ceiling at the end or completion of the motion.

TUN SOW TO HUEN SOW CIRCULAR MOTION

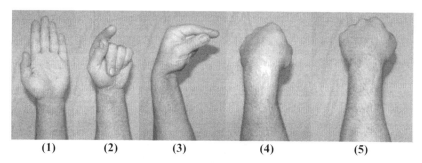

(1)   (2)   (3)   (4)   (5)

1) **Tun Sow** (palm up block/showing hand) **2-3) Index finger and thumb** are pinched together **-4) Circle inward and downward 5) Fist close.**

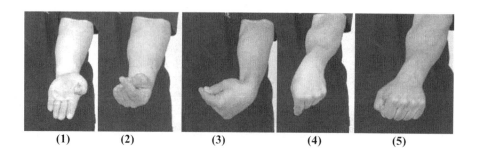

(1)   (2)   (3)   (4)   (5)

Close the fist without tension. **Chop Kune** (horizontal punch)

The next sequences are the **Three Family Blocks**. The **Tun Family** uses the outside edge of the hand and wrist like **Tun Sow** (showing hand), **Noy Jut Sow** (outside jerking hand), and **Ding Sow** (J-hand/raising hand), also called **/Hay Sow** or **Tie Sow**. The **Bong Family** uses the outside edge of forearm like **Bong Sow (wing arm deflection), Fack Sow (high block), Biu Jon Sow** (thrusting hand), **Jom Sow** (chopping hand), **Tuet Sow** (freeing hand), **Fun Sow** (horizontal chop), **Lon Sow** (l-bar arm)**,** and **Woo Sow** (guarding hand). The **Fook Family** uses the inside palm and the fingers of the hand. For example, **Fook Sow** (bridging hand), **Pock Sow** (slapping hand)**, Gum Sow** (pressing hand)**, Cow Sow** (catching hand), **Huen Sow** (circling hand), **and Loy Jut Sow** (inside jerking hand). The three family blocks **(Tun, Bong,** and **Fook)** are also known as the three poisons of wing Chun, this is why they are overly repeated.

Tun Sow (palm up block/showing hand)

As you retract the fist, immediately open the left hand in **Tun Sow**.
Very slowly move up with Tun Sow, **and start the** Hay Gong. **Breathing normally from the original** Tun Sow **position, your hand extends forward and away from your body, along the same path of** The Immovable Elbow Moving Line, **until the motion is completed and the arm fully extended. Inhale and exhale** 4 times **per motion. This will give you the proper timing to switch to the next move.**

Huen Sow (circling hand)   **Woo Sow** (guarding hand)

Snap the wrist inward, with two fingers pinched and three closed pointing at your chest. Start circling inward and downward with **Huen Sow** pointing down at the floor. Flip up to **Woo Sow** (guarding hand), and very slowly pull back with **Woo Sow** on the centerline. Maintain natural breathing, inhaling and exhaling **three times** per motion. This will give the proper timing to switch to the next move. It is called **4-3** breathing, with four out and three in. As you pull back with **Woo (11C),** make sure the hand stops about one fist distance away from your chest.

Fook Sow (Bridging hand)   **Tun Sow** (Showing hand)

1) With the index finger and thumb pinched, and the other three fingers closed, snap the wrist inward pointing at your chest with **Fook Sow.** Slowly move up with **Fook** as you inhale and exhale **4 times;** then with full extension of the arm flip up to **Tun Sow**, palm up.

From a fook position, circle **Huen Sow** with two fingers pinched and three closed pointing at the floor. Flip up to **Woo Sow** and pull back slowly with **Woo Sow** on the center. Then inhale and exhale **3 times maintaining the** elbow in.

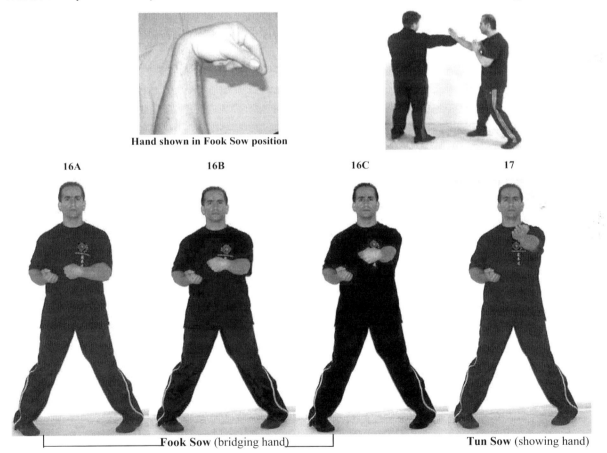

2) With two fingers pinched and three closed, snap the wrist inward to **Fook Sow** (bridging hand position). Then very slowly move up with **Fook,** full extension of the arm, and flip up to **Tun Sow**. Inhale and exhale **4 times per motion.**

Huen Sow (circling hand) — Woo Sow (guarding hand)

Circle **Huen Sow** with two fingers pinched and three closed, flip up to **Woo Sow** (guarding hand), and pull back slowly with **Woo Sow** on the center. Inhale and exhale **3 times** per motion.

Fook Sow (bridging hand) — Tun Sow (showing hand)

3) With two fingers pinched and three closed, snap the wrist inward to **Fook Sow** (bridging hand), then very slowly move up with **Fook**, and flip up to **Tun Sow**. Inhale and exhale **4 times** per motion.

Huen Sow (circling hand)   Woo Sow (guarding hand)

Circle **Huen Sow** with two fingers pinched and three closed, flip up to **Woo Sow** (guarding hand) pulling back slowly with **Woo Sow.**

Inhale and exhale **3 times per motion.**

Pock Sow (slapping hand)   Jing Jan (vertical palm heel strike)   Tun Sow (showing hand)

4) Push **Pock Sow** at 15°, followed with **Jing Jan** forward striking at centerline, then open to **Tun Sow**, palm up.

Huen Sow (circling hand)   Chop Kune (horizontal punch)

Circle **Huen Sow** two fingers pinched, three-closed, and rotate the hand inward and downward with two fingers pointing at the floor. Close the fist without tension.

Tun Sow (showing hand)

As the left hand retracts back, immediately open the right hand in **Tun Sow** position. Note: Execute the same moves for the right side as you did on the left side. Proceed slowly with the right hand for the first part. Extend slowly forward, with **Tun Sow** away from your body along the **Immovable Elbow Moving Line.**

Proceeding slowly with **Tun Sow**, breath normally (i.e. inhale and exhale **4 times** per motion). This will give you the proper timing to switch to the next move.

| Huen Sow (circling hand) | Woo Sow (guarding hand) |

Switch to **Huen Sow** inward and downward, flip up to **Woo Sow**, move slowly back with **Woo Sow** in a straight line to front of chest, and stop at one fist worth of distance. Inhale and exhale **3 times per motion**.

| Fook Sow | Tun Sow |

1) With two fingers pinched and three closed, snap the wrist inward to **Fook Sow** (bridging hand). Very slowly move up with **Fook**, and flip up to **Tun Sow** (showing hand). Maintain normal breathing (i.e. inhale and exhale **4 times** per motion).

Circle **Huen Sow** (circling hand) inward and downward with two fingers pinched and three closed. Then flip up to **Woo Sow** (guarding hand), and pull back slowly with **Woo Sow**.

2) With two fingers pinched and three closed, snap the wrist inward to **Fook Sow** (bridging hand). Very slowly move up with **Fook,** and flip up to **Tun Sow** (showing hand).

Circle **Huen Sow** (circling hand) inward and downward, and with two fingers pinched and three closed, flip up to **Woo Sow** (guarding hand). Pull back slowly with **Woo Sow**.

3) With two fingers pinched and three closed, snap the wrist inward to **Fook Sow** (bridging hand). Very slowly move up with **Fook** and flip up to **Tun Sow** (showing hand).

| Huen Sow | | | Woo Sow | |

Circle **Huen Sow** with (circling hand), two fingers pinched and three closed. Flip up to **Woo Sow** (guarding hand), and pull back slowly with **Woo Sow**.

Pock Sow (slapping hand)   **Jing Jan** (vertical palm heel strike)   **Tun Sow** (showing hand)

4) Push **Pock Sow** at a 15° angle, followed with a **Jing Jan** strike straight on the centerline. With the arm and elbow fully extended, open **Tun Sow** palm up.

Huen Sow **Chop Kune** (horizontal punch) **Sow Kune** (retracting fist)

Snap the wrist inward as you circle downward with **Huen Sow**, with two fingers pinched and three closed. Rotate all the way down until the index finger and the thumb are pointing to the floor. Close the fist, without tension, as you pull it back by your side. Both fists should be about two fingers' distance from your sides and elbows, about one fist distance from your ribs.

SECOND AND THIRD PART SHOULD BE DONE WITH SPEED, SNAP, AND WHIP POWER
Second part

Left **Gum Sow** or **Gum Jan** (pressing hand) right **Gum Sow** **Soong How Gum Jan** (double rear pressing hand) **Cheen Soong Gum Sow** (front double pressing hands)

From a retracted fist position, open with left palm up; rotate hand and snap down into a fully-locked arm position. As the motion is fully completed, repeat the same motion on the right side. With your hands positioned palm down, resting on your lower back, simultaneously snap down into a fully-locked arm position. Follow it with a front snap with both hands, and have arms extended and fully locked.

Left over right   **Soong Fun Sow** or **Wong Jan** (double horizontal chopping)   Right over left   Turn the hands

Fold both arms in, to chest level. Proceed to extend the arms, as in a side-chopping motion. Return to original position, with hand folded in at chest level. Place the left hand palm down over the right arm elbow joint at about 2" distance from one another. Chop out, and bring back the left hand under the right arm elbow joint, palm down **Lon Sow** (L -bar arm).

Soong Jom Sow (double chopping hands)   **Soong Tun Sow** (double showing hands)   **Soong Loy Jut Sow** (double inside jerking hands)

(Remember to execute these moves with speed and whip power, and to be being relaxed and not tense.)

Chop down with both hands simultaneously, having elbows remain at your side. Twist hands outwards in a scooping motion, with palms raised upwards. Rotating the position of the hands, pull inward, stopping one fist-distance from solar plexus. Fingers should be clinched together and pointing forward, not out to the side.

Soong Biu Sow (double thrusting hands)   **Soong loy Jut Sow** (double inside jerking hands)

From a **Jut** position, shoot both hands forward, into a fully-locked arm position at throat level. Pull back both hands towards solar plexus and repeat movement as illustrated in movement **#58.**

Left over right **Soong Chey Kune** right over left (double straight thrusting punches)

Retract both fists, having knuckles face outwards. Thrust forward both fists on the centerline with left fist over the right fist at chest height, both fists fully clenched, and both arms fully extended. Retract both fists backward, stopping one fist-distance from self. Reload the power and repeat the same motion by thrusting both fists forward on the center, with right fist over left fist and with both arms fully extended.

Soong Hung Sow (double strolling hands) **Soong Ding Sow** (double raising hands) **J** hand or chicken neck **Sow Kune** (retracting fists)

From a punching position and without retracting the hands, drop down with both heels of the hand and with palms facing down at an angular position. Raise both hands upward with the index and the thumb pinched together and pointing at the floor, and the elbow and arm should be fully locked. Retract both fists to your side, to their original position.

THIRD PART
SPEED, SNAP AND WHIP POWER

Cow Sow (hooking hand or catching)   **Noy Jut Sow** (outside jerking hand) **Chung Jan** (spade palm strike)

From original position, pass the left hand across the centerline in a whipping motion, with left fingers slightly bent. Stop two fists' distance in front of the right shoulder. From **Cow Sow** position, rotate the palm upward and inward at a 45° angle, whipping across the centerline, and stopping in front of the left shoulder. Both motions (the inward and the outward motions) should be done as a wiper motion, as if the elbow is pinned down against your side and only the arm wipes back and forth. Thrust the palm forward at a 45° angle, using the elbow and shoulder as the source of power.

|____ **Huen Sow** (circling hand) __| **Chop Kune** (horizontal punch)

Snap the wrist inward as you circle downward with **Huen Sow**, with two fingers pinched and three closed. Rotate all the way down until the index finger and the thumb are pointing to the floor. Close the fist fully without tension, and with knuckles facing up.

|____ **Cow Sow** (hooking hand or catching) __| **Noy Jut Sow** (outside jerking hand)   **Chung Jan** (spade palm strike)

As you close the fist, execute the **Cow Sow** across the centerline, repeating the motion as illustrated in movements **66A** thru **68**. Use the elbow and shoulder as the source of power.

| Huen Sow (circling hand) | Chop Kune (horizontal punch)

Snap the wrist inward as you circle downward with **Huen Sow**, with two fingers pinched and three closed. Rotate all the way down until the index finger and the thumb are pointing to the floor. Close the fist fully without tension, and with knuckles facing upward.

Tun Sow (showing hand)   **Gung Sow** (low sweep block)

As you retract your fist back, immediately thrust your palm up in the **Tun Sow** position along **The Immovable Elbow Moving Line.** Then fold your hand down near the right shoulder to generate power, and sweep the arm down in a chopping motion at the center line, using your elbow and shoulder as the source of power.

Tun Sow (showing hand) or **Low Sow** (scooping hand) | **Huen Sow** (circling hand) | **Chung Die Jan** (low spade palm)

Without moving your elbow, scoop and twist your hand upward with palm facing up, generating power from the wrist and elbow. Snap your wrist inward with two fingers pinched and three closed. Rotate your wrist fully to generate power, and strike out, with your palm open at the center and your arm and elbow fully extended at waist level.

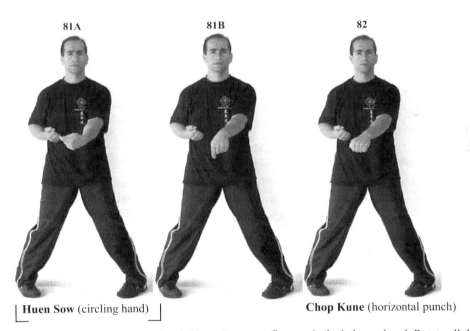

Huen Sow (circling hand) | **Chop Kune** (horizontal punch)

Snap your wrist inward as you circle downward with **Huen Sow,** two fingers pinched, three-closed. Rotate all the way down until your index finger and the thumb point to the floor. Close your fist fully, without tension, your knuckles facing up.

Tun Sow (showing hand) Gung Sow (low sweep block) Tun Sow or Low Sow (scooping hand)

Repeat the same exact movement on the right hand side, as illustrated on the left side in movements 76 thru 82, using snap and power.

Circle Huen Sow Chung Die Jan (low spade palm strike)

88A **88B** **89A** **89B**

Huen Sow (circling hand)   **Chop Kune** (horizontal punch)   **Sow Kune** (retracting fist)

Snap the wrist inward as you circle downward with **Huen Sow,** two fingers pinched and three-closed. Rotate all the way down until your index finger and thumb point to the floor. Close your fist fully, without tension, your knuckles facing up. Pull your hand back by your side, fists fully clenched. Retract your fists, without touching your body, until your elbows are about one fist's distance from your ribs and your fists are two fingers' distance from your sides.

90A **90B** **91A** **91B**

Bong Sow (wing arm deflection)   circle from the inside out **Tun Sow** (showing hand)

From a retracted fist position, drive your arm forward on the centerline by rotating your elbow and shoulder. Your finger must face straight ahead at throat level. Circle your hand into your chest but do not touch it. To generate power, flip the **Tun** with your palm up, at waist level, parallel to the floor.

Pow Jan (lifting palm) | **Huen Sow** (circling hand) | **Chop Kune** (horizontal punch) | **Sow Kune** (retracting fists)

Without retracting your hand, hit, with palm up, to throat level. Snap your wrist inward as you circle downward with **Huen Sow.** With two fingers pinched and three closed, rotate all the way down until your index finger and thumb point to the floor. Close your fist fully, without tension, with knuckles facing up. Pull your hand back by your side, fists fully clenched. Then retract your fists, without touching your body, until your elbows are in about one fist's distance from your ribs and your fists are two fingers' distance from your sides.

Bong Sow (wing arm deflection)   circle from the inside out   **Tun Sow** (showing hand)

Repeat the same exact movement on the right hand side (as demonstrated in **90A THRU 95B**).
From a retracted fist position, drive your arm forward on the centerline by rotating your elbow and shoulder. Your finger must face straight ahead at throat level. Circle your hand into your chest but do not touch it. Generate power by flipping the **Tun** with palm up, at waist level, parallel to the floor.

Pow Jan (lifting palm) | **Huen Sow** (circling hand) | **Chop Kune** (horizontal punch) **Sow Kune** (retracting fist)

Without retracting your hand, lift it, with palm up, to throat level. Snap your wrist inward as you circle downward with **Huen Sow.** With two fingers pinched and three closed, rotate all the way down until your index finger and thumb point to the floor. Close your fist fully, without tension, with knuckles facing up. Pull your hand back by your side, fists fully clenched. Retract your fists, without touching the body, with elbows in about one fist's distance from your ribs and with your fists two fingers' distance from your sides.

Tuet Sow (freeing hand)

Place the edge of your right hand at a 45° angle inside the crease of your elbow, and scrape the back of your hand along the left forearm, past the left hand. Rotate the left hand up, with palm up, as your right hand passes over it. Note that you must twist your palm up and scrape it along the forearm simultaneously. You should hear a scraping or whipping sound from the friction of the hand and the forearm being rubbed together. The sound comes from the speed and the power of this motion.
This sequence is repeated three times.

Tuet Sow (freeing hand)

<u>**Repeat the same motion as above.**</u>

Place the edge of your left hand at a 45° angle inside the crease of your elbow, and scrape the back of your hand along the right forearm past the left hand. Rotate your right hand up, with palm up, as your left hand passes over it. Note that you must twist your palm up and scrape it along your forearm simultaneously. You should hear a scraping or whipping sound from the friction of your hand and forearm being rubbed together. The sound comes from the speed and the power of this motion.

Tuet Sow (freeing hand) | **Gung Sow** (low sweep block) | **Yut Jee** (Choon Kune)

<u>**Repeat the same motion as above.**</u>

Place the edge of your right hand at a 45° angle inside the crease of your elbow, and scrape the back of your hand along the left forearm, past the left hand. Rotate your left hand up, with palm up, as your right hand passes over it. Note that you must twist your palm up and scrape it along your forearm simultaneously. You should hear a scraping or whipping sound from the friction of your hand and the forearm being rubbed together. The sound comes from the speed and the power of this motion. At the completion of the third motion, retract your left hand, stopping against the center of your chest, knuckles facing forward.

Lynn Why Kune (continuous chain of punching) **Straight Blast**

Thrust out your left fist with **Chey Kune** (retraction extension punch) as your right hand fully retracts to the centerline. Using the same motion, thrust out **Chey Kune** with your right hand as your left hand pulls back, making a tight fist by your side without touching your ribs. All three motions are **The Straight Blast (ORIGINATED from this part of the form) Lynn Why Kune** (continuous chain of punching).

Flip your hand up to **Tun Sow,** facing the sky, and snap two fingers pinched and three closed.
Circle **Huen Sow** with your index finger and thumb pinched together, pointing at the centerline, and continue circling inward until the two fingers point to the floor. Close your fist slowly, without tension, and retract your left hand back to the original position as you bring both feet together into a natural stance.

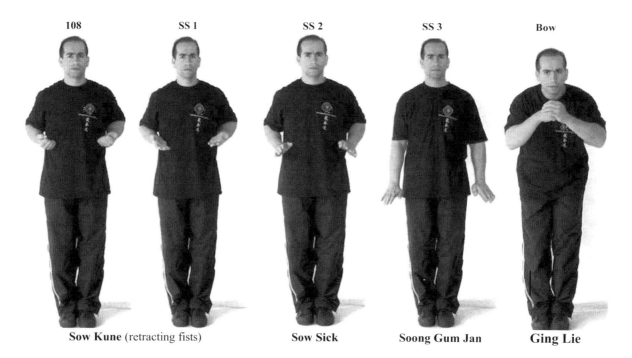

Stand with **Sow Kune** (retracting fists), both feet together, back straight, and open very slowly into **Soong Gum Jan** (double pressing hands) and **Sow Sick** (closing the stance). Note that the **Soong Gum Jan** are not done in the manner of a strike. In a relaxed and very slow movement, bring both hands to your chest and twist down very slowly.

Every movement in this form is based on an actual technique that you can apply to self-defense or hand-to-hand combat. It is not necessary to take a **Yee Jee Kim Yin Ma** position, but rather a **By-Jon**, or natural, stance. The primary reason I teach this form is to help my students to block or strike from either side, left or right lead. It also helps to build a very good foundation, as I mentioned before.

截拳道

The Journey Begins
Ging Lie

Jkd Bow /Salutation

Natural Stance

THE OPENING BEFORE AND AFTER EACH TRAINING SESSION
"Never take your eyes off your opponent"

The **JKD** bow **(Ging Lie)** should be done before and after each training session. The primary reason for the bow is to show respect for **all styles of martial arts** and appreciation for what you are learning. It is also used to show respect for the instructor, Jeet kune do, and each other (just in case someone gets hurt during training). My bow is a little different because I like to include the **Hoy Sick** (stance opening) sequence of **Wing Chun Gung Fu**, my base system, the foundation of my training, and my love for **JKD**. Each movement in the bow represents an actual combative technique. Extra movements are also shown, because the different instructors that I have trained with have all had unique bows. I combined all of their movements into my own bow, which consequently has deep meaning. If you do not wish to do the whole bow then you can start with photo **4-A** and exclude photos **8** and **9**. You may also just do movement # **8**.

1) SUP JEE SOW (character (10) x hand)   **2-A) Start** rolling **out / in**   **2-B) QWAN SOW** (Rolling hands)

1) Stand with feet about 3" apart, both hands open. Place your left hand at right waist height, not touching, at one finger's distance. **2-A)** Start rolling from the outside/in, but do not touch your chest. **2-B)** Snap both hands out, facing the ceiling, with elbows in.

Application: This form represents peace and love for **JKD**, but it can also be low **X** block against any low kicks or straight attacks, since taking away one hand gives you a low sweep block. **Gung Sow** and the rolling hand can be a **Tun Sow** (showing hand) block.

3) SOW KUNE (retracting fists **4-A)** LEFT HAND COVERING THE RIGHT HAND FULLY CLENCHED   **4-B) GING GYEUK**
(Front kick)

3) Retract both hands back, fully clenched, but not touching the sides of your feet together. **4-A)** Cover your right hand with your left hand at shoulder height, with your left hand in **Lon Sow** (bar arm) position at chest height.
4-B) Step forward, with the right leg kicking forward about 1' off the ground, keeping your fist covered.

Application: You can elbow someone behind you, or you can elbow and kick low to someone's shin in order to close the gap for more attacks.

4-C) step with right leg **5) SUP JEE SOW** (character 10) left foot stepping forward **6-A)** Start rolling out / in as you pull back the left leg.

4-C) Land with the right foot at a 45° angle. **5)** Step forward with the left foot as you simultaneously **Sup Jee Sow** at shoulder height. **6-A)** Drag your left foot back foot as you start rolling inward, but do not touch your chest.

Application: An **X** block high, finger jab, or block.

6-B) QWAN SOW (rolling hands) feet together **7) SOW KUNE** (Retracting FISTS) **8) GING LIE** (BOW) SALUTE

6-B) Place both feet together in the original position and snap the **Qwan Sow** elbows in about two fingers' distance from your ribs. **7)** - Retract both fists back, fully clenched, but do not touch your sides. **8)** With your feet about 3" apart, place your left hand over your fully clenched right hand and bow. Always keep your eyes forward.

9) SOONG KUNE (Double fists)   **9-A) SOW KUNE** (Retracting FISTS)   **10-A) SOONG TUN SOW** (double showing hands)   **10-B) SOONG GUM JAN** (double pressing palms)

9) –Stand with both feet at shoulder width apart and show both fists, fully clenched, with elbows one fist's distance. **9-A Retract** both fists back, fully clenched, but do not touch your sides. **10-A)** Slide your left foot into your right foot to the original position, placing both hands near the waistline, barely touching. Keep palms up, posture straight, and elbows one fist's distance from your ribs. **10-B)** Exhale very slowly, lower both hands, palms down, and finish.

Application: Pressing hand block from a standing still position, or a strike to the groin.

Footwork Moving Stances (Ma-Boo Or Jow Ma/Gyeuk Ma)
The Delivery System !

Footwork is the foundation of **JKD**. Almost every movement is executed with footwork, and all the power and energy must come from it. Whether pivoting, advancing, retreating, sidestepping, or circling, you are not going anywhere without your feet. I personally depend heavily on footwork. Having no footwork is like driving a racecar with 450 horsepower but no wheels. You will not go anywhere. Your footwork is your wheels--you cannot execute a technique to its full potential without it, and you will not get far in your practice. You can know all the moves and be the best puncher or kicker, but without footwork, you are not going to cause much damage.

As a **JKD** fighter, it is extremely important to practice foot work. It must be practiced periodically to achieve flowing results. It must become part of you. There are many martial arts that do not use much footwork. Their techniques are based on torque and power from a standing still position. Also, many techniques are done either with overly exaggerated steps or with no mobility. Many focus on only linear or circular movements. This is not the case in **JKD**. A good **JKD** practitioner adapts to any position and flows in any direction.

To achieve flowing movement in footwork, you must place extreme importance on the fact that to reach your opponent, you must move to him. Without movement there is no attack, and without attack there is no scoring. To reach your opponent with speed and power, you must use footwork. To close the gap between you and your opponent during trapping, blocking, or counter attack, you must use footwork.
To build strong and flowing footwork, first you must be in a **By-Jon** stance, remaining very loose, with your whole posture fully relaxed, and feet wider apart than your shoulders. Also, no matter how far or how fast the front foot moves, the rear foot must follow in the same direction. It is important that you maintain good balance, especially when moving forward or side-to-side. You should check your feet and make sure that the rear heel always lines up with the front toes, in a good, solid **By-Jon**. Do not end up with your feet the same width apart as your shoulders, because your attack or technique will be very weak, and you will be very easily pushed back and off balance, no matter in which direction you are moving.

Many students I have witnessed are too busy focusing on how well the hands are moving, but they forget about their 'wheels,' which are the most important part of executing the technique. You don't want to end up with your feet too close or out of alignment, or with the groin area fully exposed, which many practitioners (including myself) have done. If you do not fully train yourself to the point where every movement in **JKD** is being executed simultaneously with some kind of footwork or motion, then you will learn the hard way.

Note: In circling, for teaching purposes only, you can move around clockwise in slow motion. Otherwise, do not move around clockwise like a robot--be alive, add a little hop every time you circle. Not only that will break the rhythm and confuse your opponent, but it also helps with your flow and helps execute any technique with full speed and power.

"ALL MOTIONS ARE PART OF ONE MOTION DURING DELIVERY"

1) **(TOH MA)** ADVANCE SHUFFLE/STEP SLIDE.
2) **(TOY MA)** RETREAT SHUFFLE/STEP SLIDE BACK.
3) **(CHEEN FIE MA)** ADVANCE /PUSH SHUFFLE.
4) **(HOW FIE MA)** QUICK RETREAT/ PUSH SHUFFLE BACK.
5) **CHEEN SING MA (PENDULUM)** ADVANCED DISPLACEMENT/SLIDE STEP FORWARD.
6) **HOW SING MA (PENDULUM)** RETREAT DISPLACEMENT/SLIDE STEP BACK.
7) **(LOY SEEN WHY OR YOW BIN MA)** SIDE STEP TO RIGHT INSIDE FACING.
8) **(NOY SEEN WHY OR JORE BIN MA)** SIDE STEP TO LEFT OR OUTSIDE FACING.
9) **(HOW HUEN JUNE MA)** BACK CIRCLE STEP THROUGH.

1) ADVANCE SHUFFLE/STEP SLIDE (TOH MA) By-Jon stance: step with your front foot to (3) slide with your back foot to (2)

Step slide is used to meet an attack with a block or strike. You must step first and slide the rear foot. Its mainly used to close the gap between you and your opponent. "Note" if you step with the front foot 1' then you must slide the rear foot 1', if you step with the front foot 6" then the rear foot slides 6". You must maintain the pyramid structure. If you don't you will lose balance. And your block and counterattack will be sloppy. You must apply the same principle to all of the footwork.

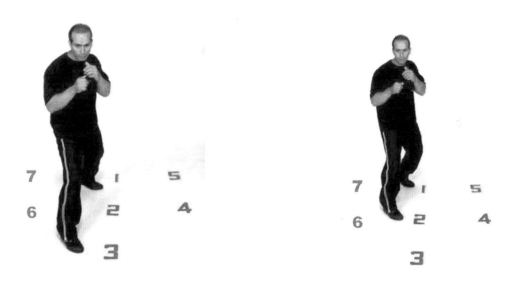

2) RETREAT SHUFFLE/STEP SLIDE BACK (TOY MA) step with your back foot to **(1)** slide back with your front foot to **(2)**

Step slide back is used to escape an attack and regain the attack line.

3) QUICK ADVANCE /PUSH SHUFFLE (CHEEN FIE MA) **By-Jon** stance push with your rear ball of the foot forward to **(3)** as you slide the rear foot to **(2)** with speed.

The push shuffle is used to lunge forward with speed from a fighting stance for kicking or punching without closing the gap just one straight line to the target with no delay.

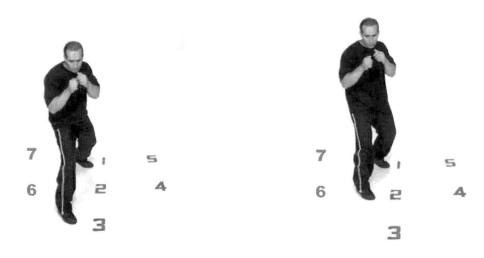

4) QUICK RETREAT/ PUSH SHUFFLE BACK (HOW FIE MA) Push with your front ball of foot back to **(1)** as you slide the front foot to **(2)**

The push shuffle footwork is used to get away from any attacks with speed.

5) ADVANCED DISPLACEMENT/SLIDE STEP FORWARD: CHEEN SING MA (PENDULUM) By-Jon stance:
Right foot forward: slide left replaces right **(2)** (right foot) advances to **(2)** both feet must pass the center every time. The rear foot always must get hidden behind the front foot to make your attack effective.

The slide step is used for rapid kicks. It helps to strike with multiple kicks without stepping with the front foot. Also its very deceiving footwork because it helps you deliver a very powerful kick without the opponent seeing the front foot move. By sliding the rear foot first it helps execute the front kick right on target with power and speed.

6) RETREAT DISPLACEMENT/SLIDE STEP BACK: HOW SING MA (PENDULUM) Right Foot Forward:
Right foot replaces left foot **(2)** left foot retreats to **(1)**

The slide step back is used to get way from any attacks with speed. It almost serves the same purpose as the push shuffle back.

7) SIDE STEP TO RIGHT INSIDE FACING (Loy Seen Why or Yow Bin Ma) **By-Jon** stance-Right foot forward right foot moves first to **(6)**
followed by left foot to **(7)** NOTE: "if left foot is forward you do the opposite move."

When right side stepping, you move the right foot first then the left foot follows. The side step is used to strike from a side angle with a hook punch or a hook kick. Also it helps to bob and weave from side to side to avoid any straight strikes.

Left foot moves back to (1) than right foot moves back to (2).

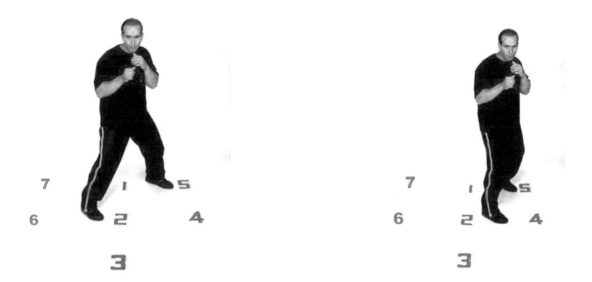

8) SIDE STEP TO LEFT OR OUTSIDE FACING (Noy Seen Why or Jore Bin Ma) **By-Jon** stance, right foot forward, left foot moves first to **(5)** followed by right foot to left **(4).**

When left side stepping the left foot always moves first and is then followed with the right foot. Left side step helps with any strikes to the outside of your target. Also it serves the same purpose as the right side step. They fit hand and hand.

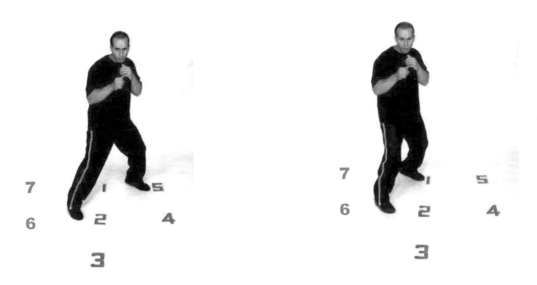

Right foot moves back to **(2)** then left foot moves back to **(1).**

9) Circling

BACK CIRCLE STEP THROUGH (HOW HUEN JUNE MA)
(Spin 360 degrees, clock wise 90 degrees at a time)

```
      6
      |
3 ---( )--- 9
      |
     12
```

    From a By-Jon position, circle the rear foot to **(4)** but the front foot remains on **(2)** then the rear foot circles to **(3)** and the front foot remains on **(2)**.

Maintaining good **By-Jon,** circle the rear foot to **(5)** and the front foot remains on center **(2)**. Return back to original position with both feet on **(1)** and) **(2)**. The circling foot work helps you to circle around your opponent in any angle without switching feet. In addition, it helps in maintaining full awareness at any direction. Repeat the same circling motion the opposite side or left lead. Note - the front foot must remain on the center when circling. It is like you nailed the front toes into the floor and you cannot move them out of position only in a circling position on the front ball of the foot. The rear foot only circles in a wide circular motion. When you get good at your foot work, you should add a little hop to your movement. Your foot work should be very alive and fluid, and you must remain very light on your feet. Do not drag your feet on the floor. The proper way to check your footwork; you should not hear your feet scrap or drag against the floor. Your footwork should be as if you walking on air.

FOOT WORK COMBINATION PATTERN WITH ADDED HAND COMBINATION

FROM A **By-Jon** POSITION (FIGHTING READY STANCE)
HALF AND FULL BEAT

Step slide advance.
Step slide retreat.
Side step to the right.
Side step to the left.
Push shuffle advance.
Push shuffle retreat.
Slide step advance.
Slide step retreat.
Double advance.
Double retreat.
Double right.
Double left.
Advance retreat one motion.
Retreat advance one motion.
Right, left one motion.
Left, right one motion.
Circle clock wise, ¼ turn at a time.

FROM A By-Jon POSITION (FIGHTING READY STANCE)

Step, slide, advance/**Choon Choy** (thrusting vertical punch), or **Gwa Choy** (back hand).
Side step to the right. Right hook.
Side step to the left. Left hook.
Push, shuffle advance. **Jick Teck** (front kick)
Slide, step advance, **Ow Teck** (hook kick)
Step, slide, advance. **Chop Choy** (low hammer punch)/**Gwa Choy** (back hand)
Double Advance. **Soong Jick Teck** (double front kicks)
Step, slide, advance. **Soong Ow Teck** (double hook kicks)
How Jick Teck (rear front kick) Step, slide, advance. **Ow Teck** (hook kick)
Rear Oblique kick step, slide, advance. **Die Ow Teck** (low hook kick)

Eight Basic Defense Positions from a By-Jon (Fighting Ready Stance)

THE EIGHT ORIGINAL JKD BLOCKS

By-Jon (Ready Position)

1) FRONT TUN SOW (showing hand)   **2) FRONT POCK SOW** (slapping hand)

3) FRONT **GUNG SOW** (low sweep block)　　**4)** FRONT **GUM SOW** (pressing hand)

5) REAR **TUN SOW** (showing hand)　　**6)** REAR **POCK SOW** (slapping hand)

7) REAR **GUNG SOW** (low sweep block)　　　　**8)** REAR **GUM SOW** (pressing hand)

OPTIONAL BLOCKS

9) FRONT **BONG SOW** (wing arm deflection)　　　　**10)** REAR **BONG SOW**

(In Wing Chun, the reverse **Bong** is never used) they feel it goes against the Yin and Yang structure, but in **JKD** there are no limitations.

Yin/Yang Blocks and Strikes

There are many **Yin** and **Yang** blocks and strikes in **JKD**. To determine which is **Yin** and which is **Yang** is very simple. Any blocks that are in reference to the centerline are **Yang** blocks. Any blocks in reference to self-centerline are **Yin**. A better way to remember this is that most of the time when blocks have been executed inward, with positive energy, they are **Yang** motions. Any blocks that are executed outward with negative energy are **Yin** motion. If your opponent is standing in front of you, then the core of the **Mother Line** is connected to his **Mother Line** core. That will be the positive energy line, directly on the plane, right in front of you. But if you happen to move, then the imaginary centerline remains on center while your **Self-Centerline** travels with you. No matter how you shift, your **Self-Centerline** moves. Then the **Yin** blocks, follows the negative power, in relationship with the self-centerline. In addition, some techniques are executed with just **Yang** powers. Like **Pock Sow Choon Choy,** (slapping hand, back fist) **Gum Sow Gwa Choy**, (pressing hand, back fist) most of the time all motions in **JKD** are **Yin** and **Yang** with all strikes finishing in **Yang** motion on the centerline.

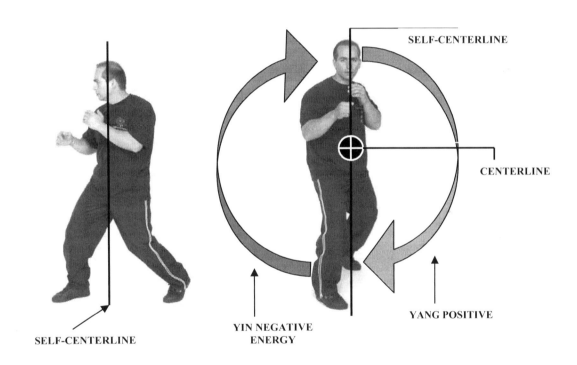

Yin and Yang Blocks Definitions

YIN MOTIONS	
1) Woo Sow	(Guarding hand)
2) Tun Sow	(Showing hand)
3) Noy Jut Sow	(Outside jerking hand)
4) Tuet Sow	(Freeing hand)
5) Huen Sow	(Circling hand)
6) Gung Sow	(Low sweep block)
7) Lon Sow	(Bar arm)
8) Lop Sow	(Grab or pull)
9) Fack Sow	(High block)
10) Ding Sow	(J-hand)

YANG MOTIONS	
1) Biu-Sow	(Finger jab)
2) Pock Sow	(Slapping hand)
3) Jom Sow	(Chopping hand at angle)
4) Fook Sow	(Bridging hand)
5) Bong Sow	(Wing arm deflection)
6) Biu Jon Sow	(Thrusting hand)
7) Jut Sow	(Jerking hand)
8) Cow Sow	(Catching hand)
9) Hung Sow	(Strolling hand)
10) Loy Jut Sow	(Inside jerking hand)
11) Jeep Sow	(Breaking block)
12) Chum-Q	(Bridging block)

YANG STRIKES	
1) Choon Choy or Choon Kune	(Straight vertical punch)
2) Cho Kune or Chop Choy	(Low hammer punch)
3) Foon Nun kune	(Phoenix punch)
4) Goon Jee Kune	(Ginger punch)
5) Chow Kune or June Kune	(Shovel hook 45° upward angle)
6) Loy Doy Gock Kune	(Inside diagonal punch/hook)
7) Chop Kune or Ping Choy	(Horizontal punch)
8) Gwa Choy	(Back hand)
9) Lynn why Kune	(Continuous chain of punching)
11) Jing Jan	(Vertical palm strike)
12) Chung Jan	(High angle spade palm strike)
13) Chung Die Jan	(Low spade palm strike)
14) Pow Jan	(Upward palm strike)
15) Fun Sow	(Chopping hand)

Strikes

JKD PUNCH: (YUT JEE CHOON KUNE) (CHARACTER SUN)
THERE ARE NINE PUNCHES ON THE YUT JEE CHUN KUNE (CHARACTER SUN) VERTICAL PUNCH

IN WING CHUN GUNG FU THERE ARE NORMALLY ONLY (8) PUNCHES

There are two more punches, the whip punch **Fon kune**, and **Tie Kune** (raised punch). The **Fon Kune** is divided into two motions inside (**Loy Fon Kune**) and outside (**Noy Fon Kune**). The only difference is that with the **Fon Kune** you start with arm extended, circle in and whip the vertical punch out on center. In outside circular motion, start with arm extended, circle out and whip the vertical punch at the center. **Tie Kune** starts low and finishes high. Neither one is shown because they are both vertical punches. Also the **back hand** and the **Lynn why kune/hammer principle** are used heavily in **JKD** therefore we use nine punches.

"Note every JKD punch or strike should be backed up with guarding hand (Woo Sow) for extra defense line."
First you should practice all of the blocks and strikes in a Yee Jee Kim Yin Ma (goat restraining stance) position to build a strong base, then you can practice them in a **By-Jon**.

1) **Choon Choy** or **Choon Kune**.
2) **Cho Kune** or **Chop Choy**.
3) **Foon Nun Kune**.
4) **Goon Jee Kune**.
5) **Chow kune** or **June kune** upward 45° angle.
6) **Loy Doy Gock Kune**.
7) **Chop kune** or **Ping Choy**.
8) **Gwa Choy**.
9) **Lynn why kune/Hammer Principle**.

THE NINE PUNCHES

"**Yut**" the Chinese character meaning" The Sun"

YUT JEE CHOON KUNE   (CHARTER SUN) vertical punch)
The straight vertical punch is the most used punch in JKD.

- 123 -

2) Strike downward on the centerline it is mainly used in feinting (PIA).

1) Thrust forward away from the center of your chest using shoulder and elbow power with knuckles facing forward.

(1) Yang motion - **Choon Choy** or **Choon Kune** (vertical punch)

(2) Yang motion- **Cho Kune** or **Chop Choy** (hammer punch)

(A)

3) The thumb is pressed down against the index finger in a trigger like position. Other three fingers are fully clenched. This punch is not heavily used, but its uses are to dig that one knuckle deeper into the opponent's face. Example: the three knuckles will meet flat with the face as the finger digs deeper into the eye.

(3) Yang motion **Foon Nun Kune** (phoenix punch)

4) It resembles an uncut ginger root (A) its main use is to strike the throat and get in tight places.

(4) Yang motion **Goon Jee Kune** (ginger fist)

5) It resembles boxer's upper cut. It is used heavily in close quarters and it is executed at a 45° angle.

6) It resembles a boxer's hook but it is executed with knuckles facing up.

(5) Yang motion **chow kune** or **June Kune 45° angle** (shovel hook punch)

(6) Yang motion **Loy Doy Gock Kune** (inside diagonal/ cork screw)

(7) Yang motion -**Chop Kun**e or **Ping Choy** (horizontal punch)

(8) **Yang** motion- **Gwa Choy** (back hand)

7) It resembles the karate Seikin Zuky punch, except we use the last three knuckles instead of the first two. It is used heavily to strike (leak an attack) to the abdomen in trapping.

8) It is used heavily in JKD almost as much as the vertical straight punch, using the back of the hand and knuckles.

(1)   (2)   (3)   (4)   (5)

(9) Yang motion -**Lynn Why Kune/Hammer Principle.** (Straight blast) continuous chain of punching. Retract the fist after each strike and maintain the elbows in. As you strike the hand drops down in a pedaling circular motion as the other hand shoots forward.

Hammer Principle

Note: The Hammer Principal that I teach is NOT the same as what other JKD practitioners may demonstrate. The "Hammer Principle" taught in my system is based on the form, Siu Leem Tau.

(1)　　　(2)　　　(3)　　　(4)　　　(5)

This punch is done in the same circular motion as the straight blast except with **one hand**. It launches forward from your body and retracts in a circular motion back to the center.

"Hammer Principle /Lynn Why Kune " punches are done in a circular motion without exposing the elbow. **The Immovable Elbow Moving Line** root (**Siu Leem Tau**) are the most popular punches in **JKD**. Also they are used to break down a very good defense line.

The hammer principle is executed in a deceiving way.

Hands Blocks

1) POCK SOW	9) WOO SOW	17) BIU SOW or BIU JEE
2) TUN SOW	10) TUET SOW	18) FACK SOW
3) BONG SOW	11) LOP SOW	19) GWAT SOW
4) HUEN SOW	12) GUM SOW	20) JEEP SOW
5) GUNG SOW	13) LON SOW	21) FOOK SOW
6) LOY JUT SOW	14) COW SOW	22) CHUM-Q
7) NOY JUT SOW	15) HUNG SOW	
8) JOM SOW	16) DING SOW	

1) Yang motion- block **Pock Sow** (slapping hand)

2) Yin motion - **Tun Sow** (showing hand)

1) Either Perry the punch or just clamp on.

2) The open hand must remain on angle because if you don't he can slip up, and continue with his attack.

3) Yang motion **Bong Sow** (wing arm deflection)

4) Huen Sow (circling hand)

3) The tip of the front fingers should be on the same level as your partner's throat to get proper **Bong Sow**. If you don't then his strike will hit your head and the block is useless. When executing **4) Huen Sow** the index finger and thumb should be pinched and the other three fingers should hook on his hand, wrist, or elbow acting like a little trap so you can always maintain sensitivity as you circle the hand outwards to open him up for more attacks.

5) Yin motion **Gung Sow** (low sweep block)   **6) Yang** motion **Loy Jut Sow** (inside pulling block or jerking hand)

5) Is executed either with hand open or hand closed, blocking on the centerline or pass through. **6)** You can either push down with the heel of the hand or simply grab and jerk back.

7) Yin motion **Noy Jut Sow** (outside pulling or jerking hand).   **8) Yang** motion **Jom Sow** (chopping hand).

7) Using the edge of the wrist, with palms up pass outward. 8) It can be used to strike or block cutting at a **45°** angle.

9) Yin motion – **Woo Sow** (guarding hand block) note: "every **JKD** block or attack should be guarded with this block.

It can be done either dead ahead in front of your nose or with a little twist out to deflect any blocks.

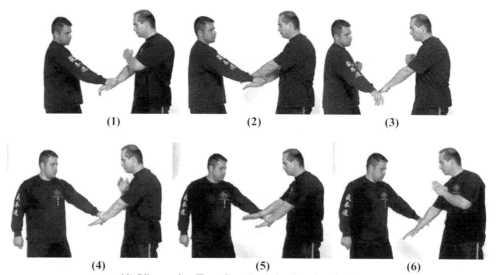

(1)   (2)   (3)

(4)   (5)   (6)

10) Yin motion **Tuet Sow** (swiping hand or freeing).
This is mostly used to free a wrist grab from either side for self-defense situation. Strike down with **Gung** motion, to release his grab. Repeat it on each side.

11) Yin motion – **Lop Sow** (pulling hand or grabbing).   **12) Yang** motion – **Gum Sow** (pressing hand).
11) Its main uses are pulling out and trapping. **12)** Either press down the fist or pin down during trapping at the wrist or elbow.

13) Yin motion – **Lon Sow** (low pulling hand waist level **L-bar arm**).   **14) Yang** motion – **Cow Sow** (catching or hooking hand).

13) Pull out, it resembles the regular **Lop Sow** but it's executed at lower level. **14)** Simply clamp on his elbow or wrist and jerk back. Its main use is trapping.

15) Yang motion – **Hung Sow** (strolling hand or heel).   **16) Yang** motion – **Chum – Q** (bridge block).

15) Looks like **Jut Sow** but it is not. **Jut** pulls inward, **(Hung)** straight down.
16) Both strikes are executed inward. At the same time the rear hand strikes the inside of the wrist, the front hand strikes the outside of the elbow joint.

17) Yin motion – **Ding Sow/Hay Sow or Tie Sow (J** –hand raising hand) or chicken neck. **18) Yang** motion – **Biu Sow (or Biu Jee)** or **Biu Jon Sow (**thrusting hand /finger jab or shooting fingers).

17) Block or strike with the wrist and the top of the hand. You can use it for blocking up or striking under the chin. **18)** It is used to jab into the eyes **never to the body.**

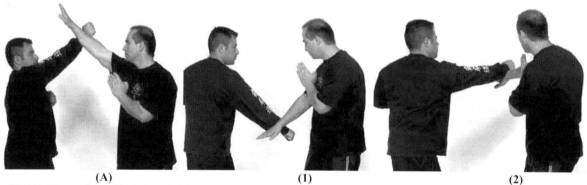

(A) (1) (2)

19) (A) Yin motion – **Fack Sow** (raising arm). Looks like **Biu Sow** but much higher. **20) (1, 2) Yin** motion - **Gwat Sow** (passing block).

19) Block using the edge of the wrist and for high attacks. **20)** Starts as **Gung Sow** motion but it carries his attack away from the target.

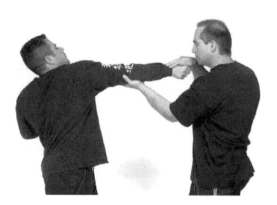 

21) Yang motion **Jeep Sow** (break block).   **22) Yang** motion – **Fook Sow** (hooking hand or bridging).

21) Push down his fist with the rear hand as you pop up his elbow joint. Both attacks must happen simultaneously and make sure that the inside of his elbow joint is up for the break to work .**22) I**t is heavily used in **Chee Sow** training. All fingers should be tight together otherwise you would be executing gum Sow. The inside palm of the hand presses down the attack, or in **Chee Sow** it just hooks on the wrist.

Palm Strikes

1) Jing Jan
2) Chung Jan
3) Chung Die Jan
4) Pow Jan
5A) Soong Lon Sow
5B) Fun Sow or Wong Jan
6) Jow Sow

1) It is used to strike to the face or to push the target back.

2) It is used to strike with an open palm to the side of the head.

1) Jing Jan (vertical palm heel strike).

2) Chung Jan (45° angle d spade palm heel strike).

3) It is heavily used to strike the kidney area or the ribs. **4)** It is used to strike down to the groin or strike up under the chin.

3) Chung Die Jan (low angle spade palm heel strike).

4) Pow Jan (low or high vertical palm heel strike).

5A,B) are both one motion, you cannot do one without the other, otherwise it will have no power behind it. Bring both arms left over right or right over left at chest level. Shoot out with a chop, horizontally. **Root** of this technique **(Siu Leem Tau)**.

5A) Soong Lon Sow (double bar arms).

5B) Fun Sow or **Wong Jan** (horizontal chop).

Jow Sow (running hand).

6) It is used heavily in trapping by striking at a curved line.

Elbow Strikes

1) **Hay Jon** (upward elbow)
2) **Gwy Jon** (over arcing elbow)
3) **Song Jon** (outward elbow)
4) **Pie Jon** (inward elbow)
5) **Sow Jon** (retracting, backwards elbow)
6) **Chum Jon** (downward elbow)

1) It is used to strike under the chin or the chest.
2) It is used to knock someone down with power by generating your whole body weight into the elbow.

1) Hay Jon (upward elbow).   **2) Gwy Jon** (over arcing elbow).

3) It is used against any side attacks.

3) Song Jon (outward elbow).

4) Pie Jon (inward elbow).

4) It is a good follow up strike to the target. It flows with all trapping hands horizontally.

5) It is used heavily to strike backwards.

6) It is used to strike downward to the back of the spine, or any downward motions.

5) Sow Jon (retracting, backwards elbow).

6) Chum Jon (downward elbow).

Jeet Kune Do Right Lead Punch

Corkscrew Punch and Shovel Hook

A Jeet Kune Punch and the Corkscrew are almost the same punch. The only difference between the two is that the Jeet Kune Do right lead punch can be executed in two ways. One way moves back and forth in a straight line, and the second takes a slight curve at impact. The corkscrew punch goes out on a straight line and it takes a sharp curve at impact. When you punch, you should hear two "whip" sounds. First you should hear the whip of the punch, and the pivoting from the hip action sound. Both sounds should be heard at the same time. To accomplish this takes a lot of practice. You must put your hip into the attack and pivot your feet simultaneously. Jeet Kune Do punch is executed in a straight line. The immovable elbow moving line plays a big part. The elbow must not stick out or kick back during execution of the punch. It should launch from position to the target and back to position. Your hip should line up with the target, feet, hand, and arm all with one motion. Everything comes from the hip; rotate at moment of impact. Your rear foot should pivot outward with the strike then turn back in to your original position (**By-Jon**). Don't lag behind after your punch, you will "open a can of worms." This means that you must try to remain on the outside of your opponent instead of his inside, because if you try to attack on the inside you can be countered much easier. Never slide your rear foot up to your front foot, because you will lose your balance. Keep a wide stance, "pyramid structure" your feet – they only pivot, they do not move. Keep your **By-Jon** stance before and after the strike. Do not move your leg just pivot your feet, everything must move simultaneously. Feet, hip, arm, everything at the same time!
It is like a door. The hinges are your feet. The punch represents a door, if you open or close the door with only one hinge it is not going to close properly. Even if it does, it is going to be crooked or it will kick out at the bottom. Try to execute a punch for instance, with a cross from an orthodox position or a jab from an unorthodox fighting position. I am sure you can deliver a lot of power, but you're sacrificing whipping power. This is because the punch might be delivered in a straight line, but only certain muscles are used such as the rear leg, the biceps, triceps, shoulders, and rear back muscles When executing a **JKD** punch, the elbow must remain in an immovable line. The punch must remain on the Center Line. Execute to the target, then come back in a curved arrow shape "1, 2, back to center" set back to ready position. Rear foot pivots on the ball of the foot out, front foot pivots on front of the foot out, hips pivot in the same direction as the foot. You are using body unity. Your body : the feet, rear and front, calves, rear and front thighs, quads, hips, chest, biceps, triceps, shoulders, and back, almost every part of your body are used. When it's fully delivered, it's a door with two big hinges and when it gets slammed shut, the whole wall vibrates on impact. Your head always stays on your Center Line. Pivot with both feet for more power. Just the back is fine but you gain more power when you use both feet. **JKD** practitioners must use the front lead punch to do most of the attacks. We do use a jab cross, but the front lead punch is more devastating. By pivoting, you add more power and reach to your punch, or any strike for that matter. The feet and hips generate the power of the upper torso when delivered by the arm and fist. When you execute your punch, clench your fist just before impact, and then relax it just after impact. An open hand is a lot easier to control than a clenched fist. Just let "it" whip, use less muscle. Just hit already! If you think, you are taking too much time. Everything works together in unity. Almost all movements can be applied to this whole pivot process. Kicks, elbows, punches, even knees are all applied. The only difference when kicking is dropping the heel for balance. Pivot, kick, then back to position.

THE SHOVEL HOOK is not a hook at all. It resembles a boxer's uppercut but is executed at a 45-degree angle. It is mainly used on the inside of the target. It is designed for body blows and head blows at short range.

Right Lead Punch (straight line)

(1) (2)

JKD right lead straight line to the target. The lower gate is very relaxed and sunk down, heel raised off the ground, shoulders very relaxed, fist not fully clenched. Execute the punch to the target by springing up for added power. Hip must line up with the target.

Right Lead Punch (curved line)

(1) (2) (3) (4)

From a **By-Jon** position, execute the punch from the Center Line or from whichever position it is at that moment. The fist is very relaxed and ready to execute the **JKD** punch. The hand is not clenched, but loose. Start clenching the fist inches before the target. Right at impact, pivot your body at a 45° angle for that added hip power.

(5)　(6)　(7)　(8)　(9)

At impact, body unity is required to create full body rotation and then return to position.

EXAMPLE: DOOR HINGE LIKE ACTION TO GENERATE FULL IMPACT. Rotate the upper and lower body simultaneously to generate power from the whole body.

The Corkscrew Punch

(1) (2) (3)

Delivering the corkscrew punch- Must be executed in a straight line but it takes a sharp curve at impact.

1) Rear corkscrew

Front and Rear arm must end up almost in a **Bong Sow** (wing arm deflection) position.
At impact rotate the hips. Both feet front and rear foot must pivot for added power.

Shovel Hook

(1) (2) (3)

Push shuffle footwork can be added when executing the shovel hook at a **45-degree** upward angle.

Figure 1   Figure 2

Front shovel hook. Rear shovel hook at a **45° Angle.**

You can also rotate the hips and pivot the rear and the front foot for that extra power when the shovel hook is executed from the front lead or rear cross.

**Many other front lead strikes are heavily used for intercepting in Jeet kune Do.
It can be a Straight Punch, Finger Jab, Backhand, open Palm, or Elbow.**

(STRAIGHT PUNCH)

BACK HAND

FINGER JAB

(OPEN PALM STRIKES)

(ELBOW)

Jeet Kune Do Hammer Principle/Straight Blast

      The Jeet Kune Do punch Straight Jab **Hammer Principle** or the **Straight Blast** Jab Cross should be executed in a circular motion to create much more power. You punch on a straight line, but return in a circular motion. On the way back reload the power for added attacks with same hand. It is like using a whip. It goes out in a straight line. It stings the target and it returns back in a circular motion without exposing the elbow. You must maintain **The Immovable Elbow Moving Line** where the elbow moves up and back in a very straight line. The Jeet Kune Do punch should be felt after the impact from its looseness and speed. When The founder of Jeet Kune Do checked the speed of students' hammer principle he never looked at the fist itself, he always watched at the elbow joint. If they had a striped shirt on then the students were in trouble because they were blocked very easily. This is because he would watch the stripes moving on the shirt, making it easy to block. You must train for speed, and practice **The Immovable Elbow Moving Line**. It does not mean that the elbow does not move, it only moves up and back in a straight line in a very deceiving way. Refer to photos below. **A. B. C.** and **D.**

The Immovable Elbow Moving Line - Hammer Principle

(A)   (B)   (C)   (D)   (E)

Launch the punch from the center outward without exposing the elbow. The elbow must stay in a straight line and return back to position in a circular motion.

LYNN WHY KUNE (continuous chain of punching)

APPLYING THE IMMOVABLE ELBOW MOVING LINE TO THE STRAIGHT BLAST PUNCHES

By-Jon 1)   Right vertical punch 2)   Drop down circle   3) Left vertical punch

4) Drop down in a circular motion   5) Right vertical punch

       You must punch in a straight line, and repeat the punches many times in a circular motion. From a **By-Jon** stance only, execute a straight right jab. After the punch lands on the target, let it drop down in a circular motion and execute a rear left punch. Apply the same exact circular motion by executing another right punch and repeat with the left punch - you must do it with speed and power. Also you must keep your elbows in on both punches, very close to your ribs to keep them protected from any side blows. The main reason that I like to do the **straight blast** only from a **By-Jon** position is that through the years I have noticed a lot of practitioners executing the straight blast in a natural position, thinking that the opponent is just going to stand still. That is not going to happen against a kicker or a grappler. I will assure you that while you're busy punching, you will be either kicked in the groin or grappled down. You must not leave the lower gate exposed, as you should be covered even when both hands are tied-up in a punching motion. Your feet should not be visible while punching and always have a backup. Have the knees and both legs always ready to use.

(1) (2) (3) (4)

Applying the straight blast against a defense line: As you punch forward with a straight vertical punch, the opponent stops it with his own upper block. Push down the defense line with the punching hand to open him up for another rear punch. He may stop this with another upper block.

(5) (6)

Push down his defense hand over the other arm trapping both hands as you finish him up with a right straight vertical punch. That's another good reason why you should be in a **By-Jon** stance, always ready.

Hip Rotation and Body Alignment

When delivering a kick, whether it is a sidekick, front kick, roundhouse, or back kick, it is very important that the front hip lines up with the target to generate full impact. Doing so, you must rotate or pivot the rear foot so your toes are in the same direction with your rear shoulder. Both the kick and the pivot must occur simultaneously, there should be no delay in motions. Do not execute the leg then pivot or vice versa, this is how full body unity is achieved.

(1)　　　　　　　　　　　(2)　　　　　　　　　　　(3)

By-Jon position. Pull the knee all the way back as far as you can for a full hip and body alignment. The hipbone should line up with the target. To release full power, rear heel should also align with the target.

Very important:
Rotate the rear foot.
Shoulder should be in same direction as toes.

Full body rotation and hip alignment will guarantee full impact.
Rotate the rear foot until the heel of the foot lines up with the target. Lock the leg and hips on impact.

Jeet Kune Do Kicking

There are only four major front kicks and one major back kick, which are executed from the front lead that I like to emphasize. There are many secondary kicks including the Sweep Kick, Heel Kick, Oblique Kick, and Inside/Outside Crescent Kicks.

(1) Jick Teck (Front kick) is launched from the ground up; you don't pull back and kick. No telegraphing. It is also a straight line to the target; it doesn't take any curves or wild turns. Use the top of the foot, not the toes.

(2) Ow Teck (Hook kick or round house) is executed the same way except you pivot the rear foot for added power.

(3) Side kick (Juck Teck) from an on guard position. Slide with the back foot, displace the front foot, then deliver the front foot in one straight line.

(4) Jeet Teck (Stop kick) is mostly used for intercepting or stopping any oncoming attacks.

(5) June Teck (Spinning back kick) step over with front foot and execute a straight back kick to the target.

(1) (2) (A) (B)

1) Jick Teck (front kick) **By-Jon** position, rear heel raised ready to trigger the front foot. Execute from the ground to target. Drop the heel for balance after executing the kick. **1) Jick Teck** (front kick)
(**No** unnecessary movement like a **(B) Cat Stance** or **(B) Chambering** before executing the kick.

(1) (2) (3)

2) Ow, Teck (hook kick) should also be executed from the ground to target. **By-Jon** position- Pivot rear heel. Hip and heel should line up with the target.

3) Juck Teck (sidekick) from a **By-Jon** position, slide the rear foot to the front foot. Sidekick with the front foot. Execute it in a straight line. Rear heel and front hip should also line up with the target.

4) Jeet Teck is mainly used to intercept or stop any oncoming attacks. Strike with the bottom of the foot.

(1) (2) (3)

5B) June Teck (spinning back kick) **By-Jon** position- Step over with your right foot all the way across your body in a small circular motion keeping your body aligned with the target. Then execute the kick back in a straight line. In case you over step in your step around, and the target is not in reach range, you need to close the gap by picking up the left foot and shuffle back. To reach your target with the same amount of power, refer to the photos **(4)** below.

(4) SLIDE THE FOOT BACK

Pick the foot up and slide back by dragging the right foot against the floor. Impact the target with the left foot.

"It's Not Just a Kick; It Is a Jeet Kune Do Kick"

       A Jeet Kune Do kick is compared to a fully loaded spring. The power that is released from the kick, not only will sweep the target off, but the impact of the kick is felt inside first, then the pain is felt outside moments after delivery. Its like a bee bite, you only feel the sting first then the swelling occurs. The speed, which is been generated by hip rotation, body alignment, and pivoting, will trigger the leg turning it into weapon.
The combination of all three will create a massive force that will knock down anything in its way.
When you kick, just kick. When you punch, just punch. Don't hold anything back, just do it. To be very honest with you, I might look like I am very flexible, but I am not. Nor is it trick photography. To reach maximum heights, you must lean back as far as you can go and rotate the hips and the rear heel. That way you are using the full length of the leg. If you keep your body in an upward position then you are forcing your leg to kick at a body level. If you lean back as far as you can when your kicking, the leg is only doing half of the work and you will achieve full height.

Kicks

1) **Jeet Teck** (stop kick)
2) **Jick Teck** (front kick)
3) **Juck Teck** (sidekick)
4) **Ow Teck** (hook kick/round house)
5) **So Teck** (sweep kick)
6) **June Teck** (spinning back kick)
7) **How Teck** (back kick)
8) **Moh Yin Teck** or **Jing Gyeuk** (oblique kick/invisible kick) 9) **Noy Huen Wong Teck** or **Gyeuk** (outside crescent kick or leg)
10) **Loy Huen Wong Teck** or **Gyeuk** (inside crescent kick or leg)
11) **Qua Teck** or **Biu Gyeuk** (inverted kick)
12) **Jung Teck** or **Gyeuk Jung** (Heel kick)

On Guard

1) Heavily used to intercept the opponent's front knee by using the bottom of the foot. 2) Execute against any part of the target, using the ball of the foot, or in an upward strike use the top of the foot.

1) **Jeet Teck** (knee kick, stop kick)   2) **Jick Teck** (straight kick, front snap kick)

3) Rotate the hips and pivot the rear foot. Strike anywhere on the target using the bottom of the foot.

4) Rotate the hips and pivot the rear foot. Strike low, mid, or high using the top of the foot or shins only.

3) Juck Teck (side kick)

4) Ow Teck (hook, kick or round house kick)

6) It looks like a back kick. Step over with left leg then spin with the right back kick.

5) So Teck (sweep kick)

5) Low sweep kick is executed at 180° circular motion, to knock the opponent off his feet by using the back of the ca lf area.

6) June Teck (spinning back kick)

- 150 -

7) **How Teck** (back kick)

7) Always look over the shoulder while executing the back kick.

8) The foot is executed at a 45° angle. This kick is heavily used from the rear against the knee.

8) **Moh Yin Teck** or **Jing Gyeuk** (invisible kick or front kick)

9) **Noy Huen Wong Teck** or **Gyeuk** (outside crescent kick or leg)

9) Start from the inside out using the outside part of the ankle.

10) Start from the outside in using the inside part of the ankle.

10) **Loy huen Wong Teck** or **Gyeuk** (inside crescent kick)

11) Qua Teck or **Biu Gyeuk** inverted kick toes pointing   **12) Jung Teck or Gyeuk Jung** (heel kick)

11) **Qua Teck** looks like an outside crescent, but it is not. You use more of the top of the front toes instead of the ankle. Use every part of your body and turn it into a weapon. You are not limited in any way in your striking.

12) **Jung Teck** is executed upward in a circular motion using the heel of the foot against the side of the opponents' face.

Tie Sut (raising knee)

It is executed upward or at an angle or straight forward using the knee and part of the front quad.
"You name it, we use what works"

Jkd Advanced Hook Kick

The advanced hook kick is mainly used to take out a front knee of an orthodox fighter. By striking the left front knee, at a downward 45-degree angle, the whole body will fall forward in one strike. This advanced hook kick must be applied at this angle and with a slight drop of weight of the rear leg to get the proper results. The kick should be executed with speed, snap, and hip rotation. Also, a slight step forward or to the side with the rear foot is needed to generate the proper power. This advanced hook kick should be delivered as if you were axing down a tree. A typical roundhouse kick is executed at a horizontal angle, which would force the leg to lift instead of collapsing from under the opponent.

(A)   (B)   (1)   (2)

(B) Is in a **By-Jon** stance facing opponent **(A)** who is in an orthodox stance. **(B)** Steps slightly to the left or slightly forward depending on how far opponent **(A)** is standing away, or how much gap **(B)** needs to close. **(B)** Executes the hook kick (round house) with the slight step and a drop of weight of the rear leg **simultaneously** at a 45° angle to the back of **(A's)** knee with full hip and body rotation.

(3)   (4)   Drop your weight slightly

The impact from the power of the kick will force him to fall forward.
Also it will result in serious injury to the opponent's knee joint.

(1)   (2)

A typical round house kick will only lift the opponent's leg upward. Also, it will not cause much injury because it doesn't have as much power as the advance hook kick.

Burning Foot Sidekick
Or
STEP SLIDE SIDEKICK

THE MOST DEVASTATING KICK IN JKD

The **Burning Foot Sidekick** should be executed left and right lead at high speed. This kick is very scientific. You must rotate the hip and the rear foot as you lock the rear knee in a straight-up position, and fully extend the front foot. In addition, the heel of the rear foot should face the opponent, and the toes should be perpendicular with the chest as you lean back. It should be practiced repeatedly to achieve full results, so when you want it to close the gap between you and your opponent, it takes out anything in its way.

By-Jon   **Step with front foot**   **Rear foot replaces front foot**

From a **By–Jon** position, step forward with the front foot. How far you step depends on how large a gap you need to close, as well as how far or how close the target is. As you step forward with the front foot, slide the rear foot behind it, and execute the front foot into the target with **Speed And Power,** holding nothing back. Do not make it mechanical, like the step slide and kick we practiced in the beginning, but make sure that all the motions become one smooth movement.

Front foot delivers to the target in a low straight line with only the rear foot pivoted. The hip and body alignment sends the target back in a straight line, or it can be delivered high, with full body rotation, picking him off his feet.

Jkd Five Corner Kicking

This drill should be done in right and left lead and with added footwork for extra power. (1) Step slide forward front kick, (2) step slide angle side kick, (3) step slide side kick, (4) step slide back corner side kick, (5) no step back kick, or no stepping at all. Just execute the kick from a **By-Jon** stance directly to the target. Always step with the front foot then slide the rear foot.

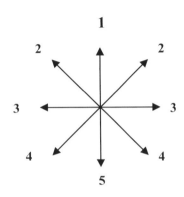

1) By-Jon front kick **(Jick Teck)**   **2) By-Jon** front corner sidekick **(Juck Teck)** at a 45° angle

(1) Maintain proper distance between you and the target. Step in a straight line with the front foot, slide with back foot, and execute the kick using the ball of the foot not the toes. Retreat back to **By-Jon** position, or you can step slide front kick using the top of the foot if you are executing the kick upwards.

(2) Step with the front foot at a 45° angle, slide with rear foot, and execute the sidekick using the bottom of the foot. Pivot the rear foot so that the toes line up with the rear shoulder. Align your hips with the target for added power. Retreat back to **By-Jon** position.

3) By-Jon side kick **(Juck Teck)** at a 90° angle   **4) By-Jon** back corner side kick **(Juck Teck)** at a 135° angle, step sidekick

(3) Step with the front foot, slide the rear foot at a 90° angle. Execute the kick putting your hip into it, pivoting and keeping body alignment. **(4)** Step with front foot, slide with the rear foot and execute the sidekick at a 135° angle. Apply the same principles to the kick as kick # **(3)**.

180-DEGREE ANGLE

1) **By-Jon** back kick **(How Teck) NO Step.** Back kick, and make sure you look back before you execute the kick for accuracy. Stay in left **By-Jon**. You must train your kicks equally; repeat the same drill on the left side, than switch to the right, etc.

All five kicks can be executed without stepping and by just exploding to the target from **By-Jon** stance. Make sure that you mix it up by creating different combinations from the drill. Example: step slide front kick, no step sidekick at any angle. Back kick step slide front left kick. Front kick no step, step slide back kick etc…

Jkd Kicking Drill

Kicking is very important with regard to long range fighting and in sparring. Reaching your opponent requires using a long weapon, and that is why kicking may become very important, but don't concentrate exclusively on kicking. Everything should have equal importance, because during close-up fighting, kicking may not always work. At times like this the hands come into play, but even hands might not work if someone grapples you to the ground. Joint locks might work better in that case. In order to be a complete **JKD** practitioner you must practice every range: long range, short range, and ground range. The drill shown below has been put together to give you a good grasp of kicking. You'll practice every kick, left and right lead, in order to build your kicking power, speed, and stamina. This drill can be practiced anywhere, whether in the dojo kwon (martial arts school) or at home. It will not only help you with speed and power, but also in timing, pivoting, turning accuracy, and coordination.

By-Jon (READY STANCE)   **(1) RIGHT FRONT KICK (JICK TECK)**   **(2) LEFT FRONT KICK (JICK TECK)**

From a fighting stance, no stepping, execute a right front kick. Plant the front foot down, execute a left front kick, plant the foot down. Remain balanced and in a straight line. Hand must remain up; don't drop your rear hand below waist level. You must maintain the guarding hand even when you are kicking.

(3) RIGHT SIDE (JUCK TECK)   **(4) LEFT SIDE KICK (JUCK TECK)**   **(5) RIGHT HOOK KICK (OW TECK)**

Rotate the hips; execute a right sidekick at waist height. Plant the foot down and sidekick with the left leg. The rear foot is pivoted all the way back so that your toes are pointing in the opposite direction. Plant the left foot down and rotate the hips and execute a right round house/hook kick; the rear heel is pivoted, and the rear hand must remain up.

(6) LEFT HOOK KICK (OW TECK)   **(7) RIGHT LOW SIDE KICK (JUCK TECK)**   **(8) RIGHT HIGH SIDE KICK (JUCK TECK)**

Plant the right foot down, execute a left hook kick, and plant it down. Remain in the same position, look to your right shoulder, execute a right low sidekick, then a right high sidekick. Plant the foot down after each kick to maintain balance.

(9) LEFT LOW SIDE KICK (JUK TECK) RIGHT FOOT   **(10) LEFT HIGH SIDEKICK JUK TECK**   **(11) STEP OVER WITH**

Look to your left shoulder; execute a low left sidekick. Plant the foot down, than execute a left high sidekick. Step over with your right foot, and look over your right shoulder to find your target.

Look over the left shoulder **(11-11A-B-C) LEFT SPINNING BACK KICK (JUNE TECK) (12) LEFT BACK HAND (GWA CHOY)**

Look over the left shoulder as you spin around with a spinning back kick at waist height. Plant the foot into a left fighting stance. With feet approx 2 feet apart, throw a backhand at head height. The spinning back kick is executed exactly as a back kick but with little spin.

RIGHT DISPLACES LEFT FOOT (13/14/15/16/17) LEFT BACK HAND (GWA CHOY) SIDE KICK (JUCK TECK)

Repeat this sequence twice in a row, for a total of three times. The footwork must be very fast. Every hit is counted as one. (Backhand slide, sidekick) (Back hand slide, sidekick.) (Back hand slide, sidekick.) Make sure that you plant the front foot after each backhand and sidekick.

(18) INVISIBLE KICK (MOW YIN TECK)   (19/20/21/22/23) BEFORE THE LEFT FOOT LANDS THE RIGHT KICK EXPLODES IN A FRONT KICK (JICK TECK)

These three kicks should be executed in mid-air and must be lateral kicks. Start with the left foot, kick forward, and jump. Execute the right front kick in mid-air, one–two, without putting the foot down. If you can't jump, just oblique kick with the left foot, put it down, execute a front kick with the right, and plant it down. Repeat three times.

STEP OVER WITH THE LEFT FOOT LOOK OVER THE RIGHT SHOULDER. (24) SPINNING BACK KICK (JUNE TECK) WITH THE RIGHT LEG.

Look for your target. Spin around with a spinning back kick with the right leg, making sure to pivot the rear foot, and lean back as far as you can to gain better height.

(29)　　　　　(30A)　　　　　(30B)　　　　　(30C)

(25) Right back hand (Gwa Choy): left foot displaces right foot (25/26/27/28/29/30). Right side kick (Juck teck). This should also be done three times in a row at a fast pace.

Backhand, slide, sidekick. Backhand, slide, sidekick. Backhand, slide, sidekick. Do it with speed, rapid backhands, and sidekicks. Make sure that you plant your foot down after each kick for balance. Note: You must backhand first in movements **12** thru **17** and movements **24** thru **30**. THEN side kick, because you are throwing a back hand to your opponent's head. If you kick him first then he will not be in range of your backhand. The sidekick will knock him back and your backhand will not hit the target. In addition, after your backhand he might not get pushed back from the hit, so that's why you need to slide, step, sidekick, not step, slide, sidekick.

ROTATE　　　　　(31A)　　　　　(31B)

(31) LEFT LEANING STANCE/ REVERSE LUNGE PUNCH

As you land on your right foot rotate the hips into a left leaning stance (karate stance) and execute a reversed vertical lung punch as you retract the left hand into a tight fist by your side.

(32) RIGHT FRONT KICK (JICK TECK)　　(33) LEFT FRONT KICK (JICK TECK)　　(34) RIGHT FRONT KICK (JICK TECK)

From a leaning stance execute a right front kick, plant it down, and repeat with a left kick. However, on the third right kick, don't plant the foot down all the way, just barely touch the floor. In other words, as you land with your front foot, you should still end up with a fighting stance. Follow photos below.

(1) (2) (3) (4) (5) (6) (7) (8)

(Slow motion only if you can't do the jump) skip photos above (1 thru 8) and go directly to the next sequence. *Do not plant* **the front foot at the start of the cyclone kick from a By-Jon on the third right front kick.**
After the third kick is executed with the front right foot, you can either plant the foot and start the cyclone kick from a **By-Jon** or continue from the third right kick, but don't let the front foot touch the ground. Just jump and execute the **Cyclone Kick**.

35) STARTING THE JUMP   **START REACHING FOR THE HEEL; KICK IN MID AIR; THE RIGHT HAND TOUCHES THE RIGHT HEEL**

As you start up in mid-air, smack the right hand against the left heel or foot.

LAND ON ONE FOOT   **START SPINNING AROUND FOR THE SECOND OUTSIDE CRESCENT KICK.**

As you land on the right foot, jump back up, maintaining your balance, and spin around.

CONTINUE CIRCLING********************IN MID AIR**

(36) BEFORE YOU LAND EXECUTE AN OUTSIDE CRESCENT KICK ON THE WAY DOWN, FINISHING WITH AN AX-KICK. LAND ON REAR LEFT FOOT FIRST, THEN DROP DOWN ONTO THE FRONT RIGHT FOOT.

Landing with proper balance, pull back to a fighting stance (**By-Jon**), spin all the way around on the front foot, and execute a spinning heel kick.

(37) Outside heel kick land into a natural wide stance

The **Cyclone kick** is very hard to achieve but with enough practice you will be able to do it very easily. **Note: the Cyclone kick was demonstrated in the movie "Enter the Dragon".**

(38) STRIKE DOWN RIGHT HEEL BLOCK (HUNG SOW) **(39) STRIKE UP RIGHT CHICKEN NECK BLOCK (J** HAND) **(DING SOW) (40) LEFT PUNCH (CHEY KUNE)** (retraction extension punch)

Place your feet about 2' apart from one another, left hand in the guarding hand position in the center. Then drop down with the right heel of the hand block, execute another block with same hand, and raise into a j-hand block. From a j-hand position retract the right hand back by your side as you punch forward with a left vertical punch in a straight line.

(41) Down left heel block **(Hung Sow)** **(42)** up left chicken neck /J-Hand BLOCK **(Ding Sow)** **(43)** right punch **(Chey Kune)** (retraction extension punch)

From a punching position drop down with the left hand into a heel block, keeping the right hand in a tight fist by your side. Execute a J-hand block upwards. From a J-hand block position retract the left hand back into a tight fist by your side, and execute a front vertical punch on a straight line.

With your fist closed, retract the right hand back as you slide both feet together. In a natural stance both hands are tight fists by your side. Open the palms up near your ribs.

Slowly inhale, exhale, pressing both palms down. Cover the right fist with the left hand, look forward, and bow. **Sow sick** (closing the stance) finish.

Kicking Drill

Directions

KICK
RIGHT FOOT FORWARD

BY-JON / RIGHT LEAD
1) R- FRONT/**FRONT KICK**
2) L-REAR **FRONT KICK**
3) R-FRONT **SIDE KICK**
4) L-REAR **SIDE KICK**
5) R-FRONT **ROUND HOUSE**
6) L-REAR **ROUND HOUSE**

7-8) RIGHT **LOW- HIGH**
9-10) LEFT **LOW- HIGH**
11) STEP OVER WITH RIGHT, **SPINNING BACK KICK WITH THE LEFT**

12-13) L-BACK HAND, **SLIDE, LEFT SIDE KICK**
14-15) L-BACK HAND, **SLIDE, LEFT SIDE KICK**
16-17) L-BACK HAND, **SLIDE, LEFT SIDE KICK**

18-19) LATERAL **L/R OBLIQUE KICK- REAR FRONT KICK**
20-21) LATERAL **L/R OBLIQUE KICK- REAR** FRONT KICK
22-23) LATERAL **L/R OBLIQUE KICK- REAR** FRONT KICK

27-28) R-BACK HAND **SLIDE, RIGHT SIDE KICK**
29-30) R-BACK HAND **SLIDE, RIGHT SIDE KICK**

31) LEFT LEANING STANCE, REVERSE RIGHT **LUNGE PUNCH**

24) STEP OVER WITH THE LEFT, **SPINNING BACK**

25-26) R-BACK HAND **SLIDE RIGHT SIDE KICK**
32) REAR RIGHT **FRONT KICK**
33) REAR LEFT **FRONT KICK**
34) REAR RIGHT **FRONT KICK**

35-36-37) **CYCLONE KICK / OUTSIDE CRESCENT AX-KICK,** SPIN SLOW **OUTSIDE HEEL KICK.**

NATURAL STANCE

38) RIGHT **PALM HEEL BLOCK DOWN** (HUNG SOW)
39-40) RIGHT **CHICKEN NECK UP** (DING SOW)

LEFT PUNCH

41) LEFT **PALM HEEL BLOCK DOWN** (HUNG SOW)

42-43) LEFT **CHICKEN NECK UP** (DING SOW)

RIGHT PUNCH, BOW, AND FINISH.

Basic Punching and Kicking Combinations

All the punching and kicking power must come from pivoting and from the hips. The hands must remain loose, not clenched, until the moment of impact on both the left and right sides. The rear hand must remain near the face, not clenched, but in a guarding hand position. The rear heel must remain up, ready for a coil spring action. Push with the ball of the foot for added power. With the heel down, you will not achieve full results. Also feel free to add footwork, advance, retreat, and get set side-to-side. Be creative: don't just stand still. Move around and circle the target. Try to hit it from every angle, because you must learn to attack from any direction. If you have a right lead, you can also train your left lead. Again, this depends on your power, the strongest side must remain forward.

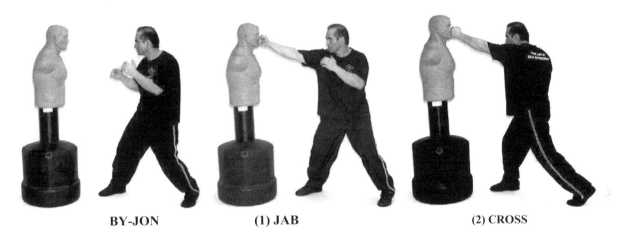

BY-JON   **(1) JAB**   **(2) CROSS**

From a fighting stance, line up with the target, feet wider than your shoulders (refer to **BY-JON** for the proper stance). Jab with a right vertical punch to the target's head in a straight line. Rotate the hips and the rear foot. Execute a rear left vertical cross. The front foot must remain at an angle. The reason for this is that you don't want to step over with the right foot, or you will open up your groin area. It's OK to do this in boxing, but in kickboxing, where there are no rules, you will get kicked in the groin. In addition, advancing a retreat gives better mobility.

(3) RIGHT HOOK   **(4) LEFT HOOK**   **(5) RIGHT UPPER CUT**

Remain in the same position. Execute a front right hook to the side of the target. Keeping the wrist bent in slightly, and the elbow also bent at a 45° angle, rotate the hips and the rear foot as you execute a rear hook in the same way as the front hook. Move back to the original position, and execute a front upper cut under the target's chin at a 45° angle. The rear hand must remain up.

(6) LEFT UPPER CUT   (7) LOW HAMMER   (8) BACK HAND

Rotate the hips and the rear foot as you execute a rear upper cut under the target's chin at a 45° angle. Return to the original position, drop down to a low hammer punch not rotating the hips, and execute a backhand to the side of the target's head.

(9) SHOULDER STOPS OPEN HAND   (10) BOB & WEAVE LEFT   (11) BOB & WEAVE RIGHT

The shoulder stop is mainly used to push the opponent back from coming in any closer, or to stop him in his tracks. Push back against the target's shoulder or collarbone with an open palm. Crouch down as you bob and weave side-to-side. Your hands must remain up and your knees bent, eyes on the target at all times. Never look down when bobbing and weaving, and never hunch your back.

| JAB | CROSS | FRONT HOOK | REAR HOOK |

BACK HAND   FRONT OR REAR UPPERCUT   FRONT OR REAR CORK SCREW   STRAIGHT ELBOW

OUTWARD ELBOW   INWARD ELBOW

Punching Combinations
BOTH SIDES RIGHT AND LEFT LEAD
Fist clenched only at moment of impact.

Jab / Cross
Jab / Hook
Jab / Uppercut
Jab / Hook / Hook
Jab / Uppercut / Uppercut
Jab / Hook / Back Hand Hook
Jab / Bob and Weave Hook / Hook
Low Hammer / Back Hand Hook
Low Hammer / Back Hand Hook / Back Hand Hook
Jab / Elbow / Back Hand Hook
Jab / Elbow / Back Hand Hook / Hook
Shoulder Stop / Cross / Hook / Backhand
Jab / Cross / Knee

IF YOU PREFER JUST TO DO BOXING COMBINATIONS, HERE ARE A FEW MORE IDEAS.
These can be done with right foot forward or left foot forward. Any foot forward is conceded (one);
rear foot is (two)

FRONT JAB IS ONE - 1
REAR CROSS IS TWO - 2
FRONT HOOK IS THREE - 3
REAR HOOK IS FOUR - 4
FRONT UPPER CUT IS FIVE - 5
REAR UPPER CUT IS SIX - 6

YOU CAN MIX THEM UP. FOR EXAMPLE:
1-2 JAB CROSS
1-3 JAB REAR HOOK
2-6 CROSS REAR UPPER CUT
1-1-4 JAB, JAB, REAR HOOK
1-2-5-3 JAB-CROSS-FRONT UPPERCUT-FRONT HOOK
5-6-3-4 FRONT UPPERCUT -REAR UPPERCUT-FRONT HOOK-REAR HOOK
THIS WAY YOU WILL HAVE AN UNLIMITED NUMBER OF COMBINATIONS

ADDED KICKING COMBINATIONS
BOTH SIDES (RIGHT AND LEFT) LEAD

FRONT KICK   **ROUND HOUSE**   **SIDE KICK**   **BACK KICK**   **INSIDE & OUTSIDE CRESCENT**

Jab / Cross / Front Kick
Hook / Hook Round House
Uppercut / Uppercut / Side Kicks
Front Kick / Round House / Round House
Front Kick / Side Kick / Back Kick
Round House / Round House / Back Kick
Round House / Hook Kick / Round House
Step / Slide / Side Kick
Step / Slide / Side Kick / Back Kick
Double Front Kicks
Oblique Kick / Round House / Round House
Inverted Kick / Side Kick / Round House
Inside Crescent / Round House
Outside Crescent / Back Kick
Rapid Round Houses on each side
Mix and Match

These combinations should be practiced every day or every other day to train your reflexes, so that they will be there when you need them. These combinations are only examples and can be mixed and matched, depending on whether you want to kick high, punch low, or vice versa. As you become better, you can change the combination any way you like to suit you, and you should feel free to improve on it.

Since JKD uses a broken rhythm, you can also use a negative (-) and positive (+) combination. A negative is any hit that will land on the target, but does not have much power. It is mostly used to fake the opponent, opening him up for a positive attack. The positive attack will land on the target to score a knock-out.

(-) R-JAB (-) L- CROSS (+) R-JAB
(+) R-JAB (-) L-CROSS (+) R- HOOK

(-) R-JAB (+) L-CROSS
(-) JAB (+) L-HOOK (+) R-HOOK

(-) R-JAB (+) R-JAB (+) L-CROSS   (+) R-JAB (+) L-CROSS (-) R UPPER CUT(+)
R-UPPER CUT (-) L-UPPER CUT   (+) R-HOOK (+) LEFT HOOK (-) R-UPPER CUT

YOU CAN ALSO ADD KICKS TO THE BROKEN RHYTHM COMBINATIONS.

(-) R-JAB (+) L-CROSS (-) R- FRONT KICK
(-) R-JAB (-) L- CROSS (+) R-JAB (-) L-FRONT KICK
(+) R-JAB (-) L-CROSS (+) R- HOOK (+) ROUND HOUSE
(-) JAB (+) L-HOOK (+) R-HOOK (+) R-SIDE KICK
(-) R-JAB (+) R-JAB (+) L-CROSS (+) L-ROUND HOUSE
(+) R-JAB (+) L-CROSS (-) R UPPER CUT (-) L-SPINNING BACK KICK
(+) R-UPPERCUT (-) L-UPPERCUT (+) R-SIDE KICK
(+) R-HOOK (+) LEFT HOOK (-) R-UPPERCUT (+) L- OUTSIDE CRESCENT KICK

USE ANY KICK COMBINATION.

(-) LOW KICK (+) HIGH KICK   (+) HIGH KICK (+) HIGH KICK (-) LOW KICK) (+)
LOW KICK
(+) LOW KICK (+) HIGH KICK   (+) MID KICK (-) HIGH KICK (-) LOW KICK
(-) HIGH KICK (+) LOW KICK   (-) LOW KICK (-) MID KICK (+) MID KICK
(+) MID KICK (+) HIGH KICK   (+) HIGH KICK (+) LOW KICK) (+) MID KICK

(-) LOW KICK (+) MID KICK (-) LOW KICK (+) MID KICK (-) HIGH KICK
(+) HIGH KICK (+) MID KICK (+) HIGH KICK
(-) LOW KICK (-) MID KICK) (+) HIGH KICK (+) LOW KICK
(+) LOW/LOW KICK (+) HIGH/LOW LOW
(-) MID/HIGH KICK (+) HIGH/HIGH KICK
(+) MID/LOW KICK (-) HIGH/MID/LOW KICK
(+) HIGH/MID KICK (+) HIGH/LOW HIGH
(-) HIGH/LOW KICK (-) MID/LOW/HIGH KICK
(+) HIGH/LOW/HIGH (-) LOW/LOW/MID
(+) LOW/HIGH/HIGH KICK (-) LOW/HIGH/LOW KICK (+) LOW/LOW/MID/MID/HIGH/HIGH KICKS

Reaching Your Destination!

Sensitivity Drills

Chee Don Sow
Chee Sow

Energy Drills

Gock Ing Sing (Five Star Blocking)
JKD Ten (10) Blocks With a Partner
Teet Sa Jan (Iron Palm Training)
Pock Sow /Gwa Choy Drill
Kune Sue Kune /Pock Sow Kune Sue Kune Drill
Tun Lop Sow Drill
Fon Sow (Trapping Hands) Drill
Lop Sow (Grabbing or Pulling) Gwa Choy (Back Hand) Drills
Pock Sow Gwa Choy/Bong Lop Gwa Choy Drills
Pock Tun /Da pock Drill
Pock Da (Slap Hit) Drill

The Gates

Hand Traps
Trapping Reversals - Stupid Traps
FIA (Foot Immobilization Attack)

The Wooden Dummy Form

Small Joints Lock Manipulations

FLUIDITY

The Application Stage!
The two stages are part of one stage.

Developing and Sharpening Your Tools!

Sensitivity Drills

CHEE DON SOW (Single Sticky Hand)

Your goal is to be able to strike back from any point. You can strike from a low, medium, or high point. You will also be able to block from a very short distance, responding to an attack by building good sensitivity and reaction. Normally, in real situations, you're not just standing. The drill will help you develop awareness and reaction for a counter attack. When you are practicing this drill, treat it like a **"Small play"**.

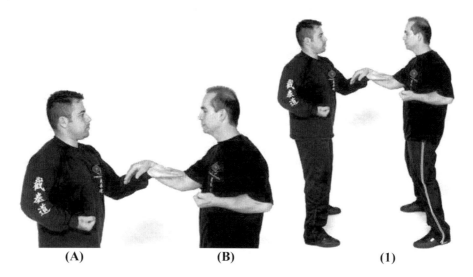

(A) (B) (1)

Both partners are in a **natural stance.** Keep your elbow in, other hand by your side but not touching your ribs. Rest the **Fook** (bridging) hand on your partner's wrist, which should barely be felt. Do not press down or apply any pressure, just let it dangle against your partner's wrist.

(2)

Both practitioners should be very relaxed, with hands and arms always maintaining contact throughout the drill. In a natural stance position **(B)** is in **Fook Sow** (bridging hand), and **(A)** is in **Tun Sow** (showing hand) position. **(A)** Strikes **(B's)** abdomen with **Jing Jan** (vertical open hand strike), then **(B)** pulls in and **Jut Sow** (jerking hand).

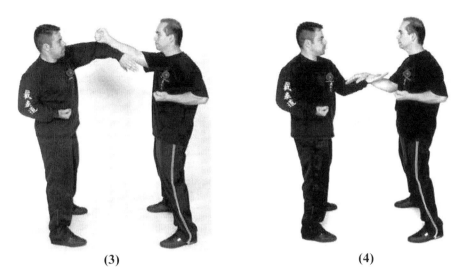

(3) (4)

From a **Jut** position **(B) Tie Kune** (raise vertical punch), with hands in contact, and **(A)** counters with **Bong Sow** (wing arm deflection). Then both partners go back to original position.

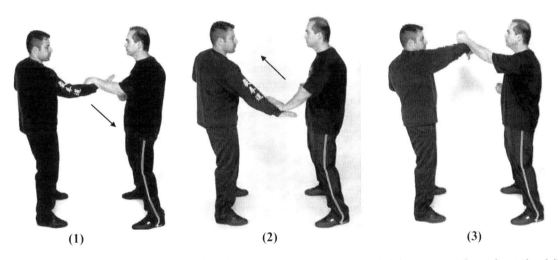

(1) (2) (3)

Both practitioners should be very relaxed, with hands and arms maintaining contact throughout the drill. In a natural stance position, **(B)** is in **Fook Sow** (bridging hand), and **(A)** is in **Tun Sow** (showing hand). **(A)** Strikes with **Jing Jan** (vertical open hand strike). **(B)** Pulls in and down **Jut Sow** (jerking hand). From a **Jut** position **(B) Tie Kune** (raise vertical punch), hands in contact, **(A)** counters with **Bong Sow** (wing arm deflection). Then both partners go back to original position.

(4)

Partners **(A)** and **(B)** back to original position with fists by the side, but not touching the ribs.

Right Side `

(1)   (2)   (3)   (4)

(1) **(A)** is in high **Fook Sow** position and **(B)** is in low **Tun Sow** position. (2) **(A)** is in **Jut Sow** position and **(B)** is in **Jing Jan** position. (3) **(A)** is in **Tie Kune** position and **(B)** is in **Bong Sow** position.

Switch to the left side

(5)   (6)   (7)   (8)

(5) **(A)** is in high **Fook Sow** position **(B)** is in low **Tun Sow** position. (6) **(A)** is in **Jut Sow** position **(B)** is in **Jing Jan**. (7) **(A)** is in **Tie Kune** position **(B)** is in **Bong Sow** position. (8) **(A)** and **(B)** return to original **Fook** and **Tun Sow** position.

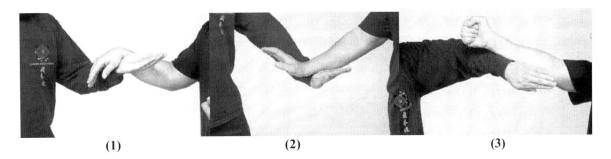

(1) Fook Sow/Tun Sow (bridging hand /showing hand) **(2) Jing Jan/Jut Sow** (vertical spade palm/jerking hand) **(3) Tie Kune/Bong Sow** (raise punch/wing arm deflection)

Note: open hand on the **Bong Sow**, finger must point at your partner's throat to guarantee perfect **Bong**. If the fingers are not at the same level as the throat, his punch will hit you. To test proper **Bong**, have one partner in **Bong** and one in **Tie Kune** position. One must slide the punch forward to see if it hits the face. If it does, then you have wrong **Bong**. If you slide it through and the **Bong** goes up on an angle passing his head, then you have the proper **Bong Sow.**

APPLICATION BEHIND THE DRILL

Applying the **Yut Fook Yee** principles to a straight jab cross attack: By deflecting both attacks without retracting the hand, either practitioner will be able to block with one hand without retracting for reloaded power. **Yut Fook Yee** principle (one hand Carries two attacks or blocks two strikes with the same hand) is either blocked with **Bong Sow** to **Tun Sow**, from **Bong Sow** to **Choon Choy** (straight punch), or **Kune Sue Kune** (fist Perris fist).

Deflect a straight jab attack with **Bong Sow** and block the cross with **Tun Sow** (showing hand) without retracting the hand all the way back.

Block the jab cross from **Fook Sow** to **Tun Sow**, strike the face with **Tie Kune** (raised punch).

Chee Sow (Double Sticky Hands)

ALSO KNOWN AS **LOOK SOW** ROLLING HANDS.

You will learn sensitivity and timing so you can respond as soon you are touched. You can feel your opponent's energy. This is a sparring drill, but its main purpose is sensitivity. As you get better at it, you can add your own attacks and counters to the drill to make it more challenging. Both partners should be in a very calm state of mind and relaxed. You should let the flow of your energy rotate from one side to the other in a very relaxed manner. The lower part of your body should be sunk down, while your hands are resting on your partner's hands. Your whole posture is relaxed but ready. In a real life situation, you and your opponent might not be as close, or in a set position. However, the attack might come from a grab or a bear hug. If you build very good sensitivity, your reaction to any attack will be good. The good sensitivity is what this drill will help you develop.

At a natural position, partner **(B)** is in high **Bong Sow** (wing arm block) and partner **(A)** is in high **Fook Sow** (bridging hand), resting on partner **(B's)** Bong arm. Partner **(B's)** other arm is in low **Fook** (bridging hand), and partner **(A)** is in low **Tun Sow** (showing hand) as both partners roll. Then partner **(A)** is in high **Bong Sow** (wing arm block), and partner **(B)** is in high **Fook Sow** (bridging hand). Partner **(A's)** other hand is in **Low Fook** (bridging hand), and partner **(B)** is in low **Tun Sow** (showing hand), and the cycle continues. Repeat the circling motions as many times as you need until you feel very confident to add your own techniques to make it a sparring drill.

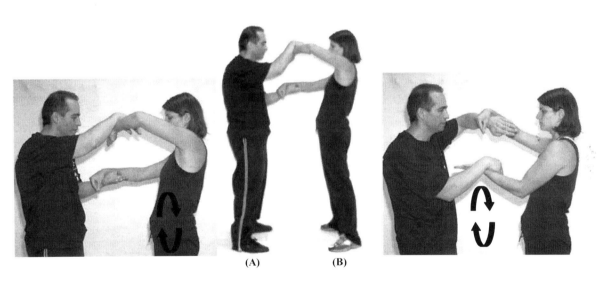

A) High **Fook Sow** low **Tun Sow**, (B) high **Bong Sow** low **Fook Sow** rotate so (B) high **Fook** low **Tun**, (A) low **Fook** high **Bong Sow.**

Either hand position, a classical Wing Chun sticky hands, or a JKD sticky hand are both correct.

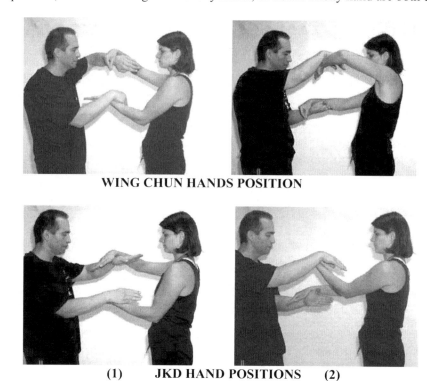

WING CHUN HANDS POSITION

(1)   **JKD HAND POSITIONS**   (2)

(A) And **(B)** rotate back and forth in circular motions many times until one partner sees an opening for attack, or weakness. You can also add different energy drills, kicks, or even foot work by moving forward and backward into each other while maintaining full contact with your partner's hand throughout the entire **Chee Sow** cycle, until you are ready to attack.

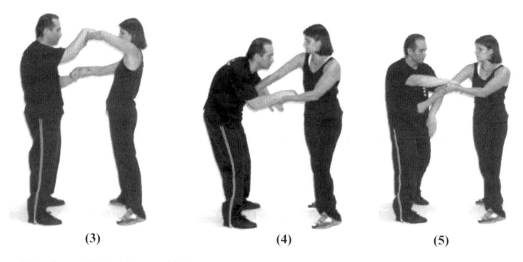

(3)   (4)   (5)

In high bong, **(B)** strikes at **(A's)** abdomen with **Chop Kune** or **Ping Choy** (horizontal punch) and **(A)** might respond with low **Bong Sow**.

By adding strikes from **Chee Sow** (sticky hands), **(A)** or **(B)** can strike from any position. The other partner should respond to the attack by blocking or striking back. You must be very aware of your partner's hands at all times in order to build your sensitivity and reaction in a front touching position. Your goal is to be able to respond to a person's touch, regardless of whether it comes from the front, side, back, or any angle.

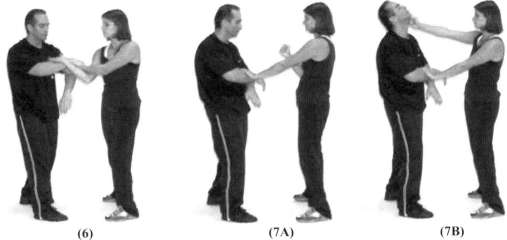

(6)   (7A)   (7B)

(B) Low **Fook** switches hand up to **Tun Sow** (showing hand), followed by **Gum Sow** (pressing hand), then **Choon Choy** or **Tie Kune** (straight punch/raising punch) to **(A)**'s face.

(1)   (2)

(B) Low **Fook** hand becomes **Gum Sow,** and high **Bong** hand becomes **Lop Sow** (grab and pull), followed by a strike to the knee with **Jing Gyeuk** (front kick).

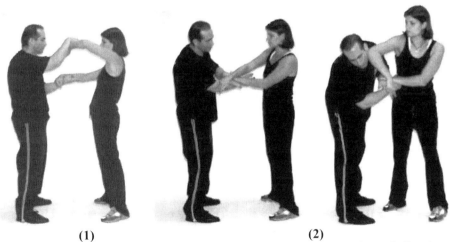

(1)   (2)

(B) High **Bong Sow** becomes **Lop Sow,** and low **Fook** becomes a **Pie Jon** (horizontal elbow) strike to the face.

(1)　　　　　　　(2)　　　　　　　(3)

(4)

(B) High **Bong** low **Fook,** and partner **(A)** high **Fook** low **Tun Sow (B) Quack Sow** (spreading hands) turn outward simultaneously to strike with **Soong Chung Die Jan** to the body (double spade palm), followed with a head butt to the face.

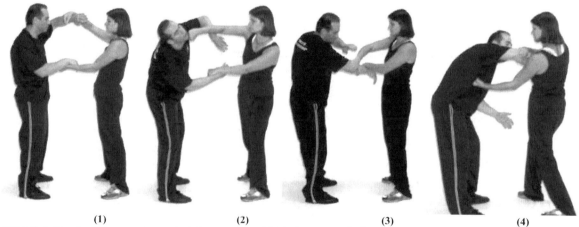

(1)　　　　　　　(2)　　　　　　　(3)　　　　　　　(4)

(B) High **Fook, (B)** executes a straight punch to **(A's)** face or switches to **Huen Sow** (circling hand), and locks **(A's)** elbow. **(B)** follows with a left **Cho Kune** (shovel hook) to the ribs.

Energy Drills

The drills below should help you develop blocking and striking, leading with either side, left or right. Many people think JKD is strictly right lead, but this is not true. The way I teach it is to train both sides equally, but when we are in a **real** fight or **sparring** match we strictly use the right lead to reach the opponent with more speed, less effort, and much more power. This is achieved by using non-telegraphic movements, as you will see in the drills that follow.

THESE DRILLS SHOULD HELP YOU DEVELOP SPEED COORDINATION POWER, SNAP, SENSITIVITY, AND REACTION.
Both Partners Should Either Be In A Natural Stance Or The By-Jon Position.

GOCK ING SING: FIVE STAR BLOCKING

WING CHUN DRILL

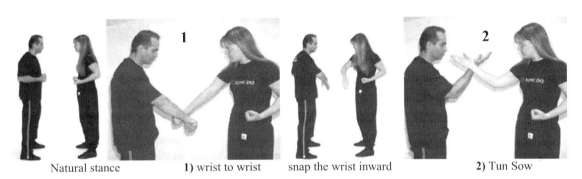

Natural stance   1) wrist to wrist   snap the wrist inward   2) Tun Sow

3) Gung Sow   circle around to generate power   4) Jom Sow

- 185 -

Snap the wrist inward   5) Woo Sow

This drill should be done on wooden dummy **(Mook Joang),** with a partner at a natural stance, or in **By-Jon**: left and right side. This will build the practitioners forearms and toughen them for later blocks or for a workout on the wooden dummy **(Mook Joang).**

Start with the right hand fist fully clenched, turned inward.
1) Low **Gung Sow** (low sweep block) fist closed smash your wrist against your partner's wrist.
2) High **Tun Sow** block (showing hand).
3) Low **Gung Sow** (low sweep block) open hand.
4) Circle the hand in front of your forehead with **Jom Sow** (chop block).
5) Index finger and thumb pinched together pointing at your chest **Huen** (circling hand) to **Woo** block (guarding hand).
Repeat many times.

JKD TEN (10) BLOCKS WITH A PARTNER

By-Jon or Natural Stance This drill should be done left and right repeatedly to build fast reaction during blocking. Every block should have a snap behind it so it can build striking power with your block.
A block must **become a strike.** JKD ten blocks will help you build very strong hands and forearms by blocking using every part of the hand or arm. Also it will help develop speed and power in your blocking.

1) KUNE SUE KUNE (Fist Perris Fist)

Both partners thrust straight vertical punches at each other's centerline. Both must **INTERCEPT** each other at the center using the forearm. Retract the other hand, place it on your centerline. Count to total of **ten** between blocks, left and right. Then switch to the next block. You can also add pivoting like **Cho Ma** (pivoting stance) pivoting on the heel of foot, or you can add step slide or step retreat. You can add side to side footwork to make it more challenging with added power. Once you feel comfortable with the block, then you can add kicks. The same exact add on should be applied to all of the next blocks.

2) WOO SOW (Guarding Hand)

Both partners block with **Woo Sow** in the center which is between both partners. Use the edge of wrist. Other hand must retract to the center with **Woo Sow**. Count to ten then switch to the next block.

3) BIU SOW, BIU JEE OR BIU JON SOW (Finger Jab or Shooting Fingers)

Thrust forward with **Biu Sow** meeting each other at the center and using the outside edge of the wrist retract the other hand back to center.

4) JOM SOW (Chopping Block)

Both partners chop at a 45-degree angle. Rear hand remains in **Woo Sow** (guarding hand), and both intercept each other using the inside of wrist.

5) BONG/TUN/ LOP SOW (Wing Arm Deflection Showing Hand, Grabbing)
All Three Motions Are Part of One Motion

Both partners block each other with outside edge of the forearm using **Bong.** Then both partners flip up to **Tun Sow** using the outside edge of the hand. The rear hand remains in **Woo sow,** and both partners grab and pull each other with **Lop Sow** at shoulder level.

REPEAT THE SAME THING ON THE LEFT SIDE

Both partners block each other with outside edge of the forearm using **Bong.** Then both partners flip up to **Tun Sow** using the outside edge of the hand. The rear hand remains in **Woo Sow,** and both partners grab and pull each other with **Lop Sow** at shoulder level.

6) *LOY JUT SOW* (Inside Jerking Hand)

In a circular inward motion both partners block each other with the inside edge of the wrist palm down.
Use **Loy Jut Sow,** right and left.

7) NOY JUT SOW *(Outside Jerking Hand)*

In a circular outward motion both partners block each other with the inside edge of the wrist palm up.
Use **Noy Jut Sow,** right and left.

8) GUNG SOW *(Low Sweep Block)*

Both partners block each other at a hip height with **Gung Sow** using the outside edge of the wrist. Rear hand remains in **Woo Sow** (guarding hand).

9) POCK SOW (Slapping Hand)

(B) (A)

Partner **(A)** strikes at partner **(B)** with right **Choon Kune** (vertical punch). Partner **(B)** blocks with left **Pock Sow** (slapping hand), partner **(A)** counters with left **Choon Kune**, and partner **(B)** blocks with right **Pock Sow**. Then partner **(B)** strikes at partner **(A)** with left **Choon Kune** (vertical punch), and partner **(A)** blocks with right **Pock Sow** (slapping hand). Partner **(B)** counters with right **Choon Kune**, and partner **(A)** blocks with left **Pock.**

10) GUM SOW/ JING JAN/ JING GYEUK OR MOY YIN GYEUK
(Pressing Hand Vertical Punch, Front/ Invisible Kick)

(A) Strikes at (B's) midsection with **Chop Kune** (horizontal punch), (B) blocks and counters with left **Gum Sow** right **Jing Jan** to the face and left **Jing Gyeuk** to the knee. All three blocks and two strikes are done simultaneously. (A) Repeats the same strike with left hand, and (B) blocks and counter the same way with the right side block.

(B) Strikes at (A's) midsection with **Chop Kune** (horizontal punch). (A) blocks and counters with left **Gum Sow** right **Jing Jan** to the face and left **Jing Gyeuk** to the knee. All three blocks and two strikes are done simultaneously. (B) repeats the same strike with left hand, and (A) blocks and counter the same way with the right side block.

Teet Sa Jan (Iron Palm Training)

Iron palm training is very important. It helps toughen up your hands and gets you ready for further developing. Bag must be filled with sand or rice to give you maximum results. There are **ten** strikes in iron palm. Herbal liniment **(Leen Gon Jow/ Dit Da Jow)** must be applied before training to prevent blood clots and bruising, and should be done lefty and righty. After practicing iron palm for a long period you should be able to generate power without telegraphing the hit or pulling the hand all the way up and then release the power. You should be able to generate power from only **1"** distance.

ONE: PALM DOWN

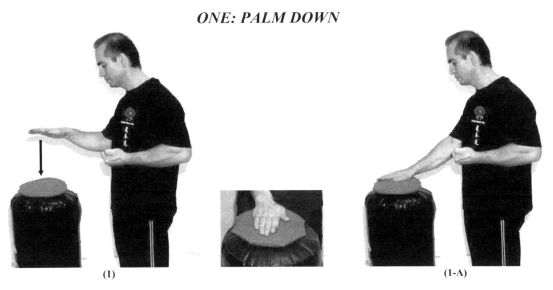

Raise the hand chest height, palm down, knuckles facing the ceiling, and let it fall down smashing against the bag not using too much muscle power. Only use whip power with the other hand fully clenched, by your side, but not touching the ribs.

TWO: TURN BACK OF THE HAND

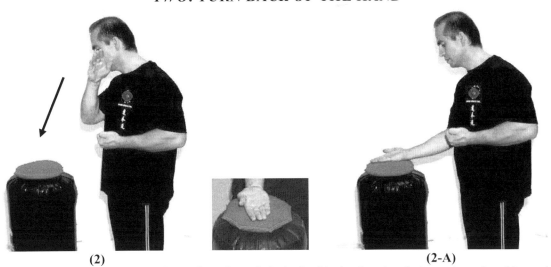

Bring the hand by left side of your face. Flip and smash the back of the hand against the bag palm up knuckles against the bag.

THREE: EDGE OF THE HAND

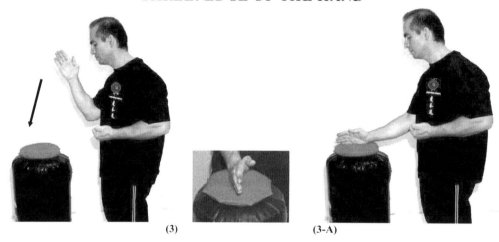

Raise the hand at shoulder height. Chop down with edge of the hand.

FOUR: HEEL OF THE HAND

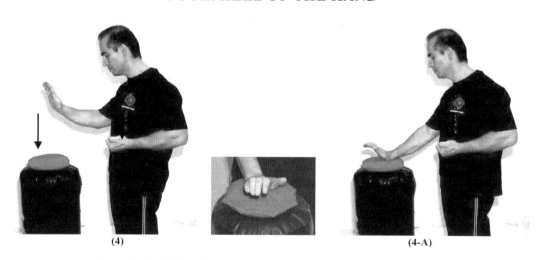

Raise the hand chest height. Drop down using the back heel of the hand.

FIVE: FRONT KNUCKLES

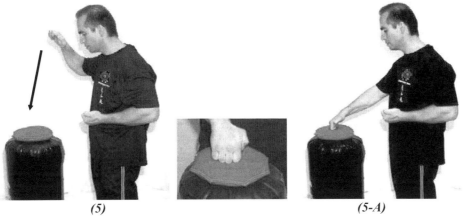

(5) (5-A)
Bring the hand head height and drop down with the front knuckles thumb tucked in.

SIX: PHOENIX PUNCH

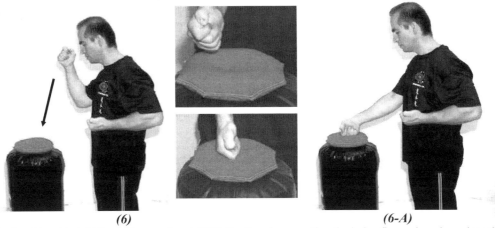

(6) (6-A)
Bring the hand head height three fingers closed. With the thumb supporting the index finger drop down into the bag.

SEVEN: INWARD PUNCH

(7) (7-A)
Bring the hand chest height fist fully closed, turn the fist inward fingers facing out knuckles in, and strike down into the bag.

EIGHT: HAMMER PUNCH

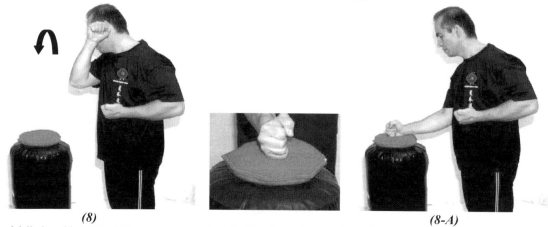

(8)   (8-A)

Hand full closed bring it all the way up near the left side of your face, and in a hammering circular motion drop down into the bag using the bottom of the fist when its fully closed.

NINE: FINGERS

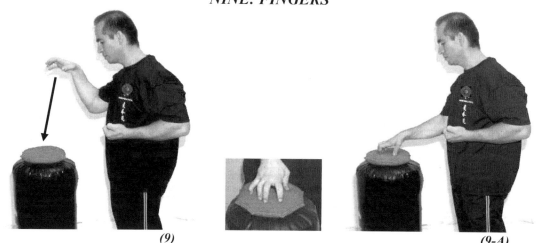

(9)   (9-A)

RAISE THE HAND HEAD HEIGHT, AND OPEN THE HAND FINGER BENT LIKE SPIDER LEGS. DROP DOWN INTO THE BAG.

TEN: ELBOW

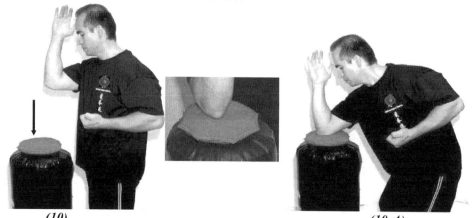

(10)   (10-A)

Raise the elbow shoulder height hand open in woo sow position, and drop down into the bag.

POCK SOW /GWA CHOY (Slapping Hand Block /Back Hand)
Both partners in **By-Jon.**

Partner **(A)** back hand **(Gwa Choy)** partner **(B) pock sow** (slapping hand).
Then partner **(B) Gwa Choy,** partner **(A) Pock Sow. T**his is repeated many times, something like playing patty cake but much more intense. Counter blocking and striking should be done in a circular motion, with **Pock Sow /Gwa Choy** counted as one**.** Switch and repeat on the left side. Do this a total of ten times, then switch. The sequence is **1,2,3,4,5,6,7,8,9,10;** switch to the left side.

(A)   *(B)*

(1) **(B)** *GWA* CHOY **(A)** POCK SOW   *(2)* **(A)** *GWA CHOY*   *(3)* **(B)** BLOCKS WITH POCK SOW

(4) **(B)** COUNTERS WITH GWA CHOY   *(5)* **(A)** BLOCKS WITH POCK SOW

KUNE SUE KUNE /POCK SOW KUNE SUE KUNE (Fist Intercept or Perris Fist and Slapping Hand)

Both partners in the **By-Jon** or natural position, both fists intercepting each other. This helps to build very good forearms and teaches you to punch right through the centerline, starting with the right, then the left. Each punch is counted as one, up to a count of ten. Once you feel confident, add pock sow (slapping hand). This is a more advanced drill, which teaches you how to block at a very short distance, and will build your blocking speed.

(A) RIGHT PUNCHES
(B) RIGHT INTERCEPTS

(A) LEFT PUNCHES
(B) LEFT INTERCEPTS

(B) RIGHT PUNCHES
(A) LEFT **POCK SOW**

(1) (A) LEFT BLOCK RIGHT PUNCH
(B) RIGHT PUNCH

(2) (A) FRONT BLOCK
(B) REAR PUNCH

(3) (A) LEFT PUNCH
(B) LEFT PUNCH

(4) (A) LEFT BLOCK
(B) RIGHT PUNCH

(5) (A) RIGHT PUNCH
(B) RIGHT PUNCH

(6) (A) LEFT PUNCH
(B) LEFT PUNCH

Cont.... **(A)** Left **Pock Sow**; right **Choon Kune** **(B)** left **Choon Kune**, as **(B)** executes a rear **Choon Kune**.
(A) Blocks it with the same hand that he punched with without retracting the hand.
As you continue to immobilize his punching hand using a right **Pock Sow**, intercept it with a left **Choon Kune**. The cycle continues, so that both partners get the chance to do the same drill. Both partners' wrists must touch after each punch.

TUN LOP SOW DRILL

TUN SOW (SHOWING HAND) LOP SOW (GRABBING OR PULL HAND) DRILL

Both practitioners are in **Woo Sow** (guarding hand) or **Tun Sow** (showing hand) position.
Partner **(B) Lop Sow** (grabs and pulls) partner **(A's) Tun Sow** hand as partner **(B)** punches with **Chey (Kune)** (retracting straight punch). Partner **(A)** blocks with **Tun Sow** (showing hand block), then partner **(B)** grabs and pulls partner **(A)'s Tun Sow** (showing hand). Partner **(A)** then punches with her own **Chey kune** (retracting straight punch), as partner **(B)** blocks with his own **Tun Sow** (showing hand). The cycle continues. You can also add pivoting, such as **Cho Ma** (side to side) as you practice the drill, to add more snap to your block or hit.

A CLOSER LOOK AT THE DRILL

(A) WOO SOW   **(B) WOO SOW**   **(B) LOPS CHEY KUNE AS (A) TUN SOW**   **(B) LOPS (A)'S TUN SOW**

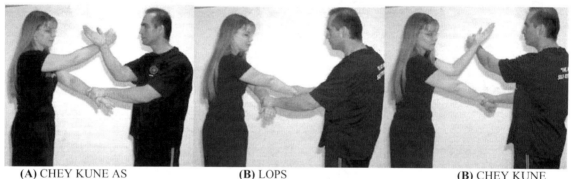

(A) CHEY KUNE AS   **(B) LOPS**   **(B) CHEY KUNE**
(B) LOP/ TUN SOW   **(A) REMAINS CHEY KUNE**   **(A) TUN SOW**

The cycle continues, with added footwork or kicks to make it more challenging.

NATURAL POSITION; PIVOT ON THE HEEL OF YOUR FOOT, SIDE TO SIDE.

CHO–MA (pivoting stance) right to left for added power.

THIS DRILL CAN BE CALLED MANY NAMES
FON SOW (TRAPPING HANDS) DRILL
LOP, BONG SOW CHEY KUNE DRILL, OR LOP SOW CYCLE.

Lop (grab or pull)- **Bong** (wing arm deflection)- **Chey Kune** (retracting straight punch)
This drill will help to toughen up your forearms for future training with the **Mook-Jon** (wooden dummy). It also helps develop natural trapping from a block position.

Both practitioners begin in the pivoted **(Cho Ma)** position. Forearms must be **touching. (A)** Is in left **Bong Sow** (wing arm deflection), **(B)** in right **Choon Kune** (vertical straight punch) position.
Note -The cycle (**one Lop, one Chey Kune** for each partner) count 1-2-3-4-5 –6-7-8-9-10, then switch to the other side.

(A) BONG SOW (LEFT)
(B) CHEY KUNE (RIGHT)

(A) LOP SOW   CHEY KUNE

AS (B) BONG SOW

(B) LEFT LOP SOW SWITCH

(A) BONG SOW

(A) RIGHT LOP SOW LEFT CHEY KUNE
(B) RIGHT BONG

As **(B)** reaches to grab **(A'S)** left hand with her right, **(A)** grabs it and pivots left to do the switch to the right side.

PIVOT LEFT **CHO-MA (A)** LOP CHEY KUNE **(B)** BONG SOW   **(B)** RIGHT LOP   LEFT CHEY KUNE
(A) RIGHT BONG SOW

LOP SOW (GRABBING OR PULLING) GWA CHOY (BACK HAND)

Both practitioners should be in the **Woo Sow** (guarding hand) position.
(A) Outside **Lop** (grabs or pulls) left **Gwa Choy** (backhand). **(B)** Responds with a left **Tun Sow** (showing hand). **(A)** outside **lop** (grabs) right **Gwa Choy** (backhand). **(B)** Responds with a right **Tun Sow** (showing hand).
(A) Lops (grabs) **(B)**'s

Outside left hand followed with right **Gwa Choy**. **(B)** Responds with a right **Tun Sow** (guarding hand). **(A) Lops** (grabs) **(B)**'s right **Tun Sow** (showing hand) with a left hand followed with right **Gwa Choy** (backhand). **(B)** Responds with a left **Pock Sow**. Switch, and the cycle continues on the left side.

(1) (A and B) in Woo Sow position. (2) (A) Lops (B)'s right outside arm followed with left **Gwa Choy**.
(3) (B) Responds with left **Tun Sow**.   (4A) (A) Lops on the outside.

(4B) (A) **lops** on the outside followed with right **Gwa Choy**. (5) (B) Responds with right **Tun Sow**. (6A,B) (A) **Lops** on the inside.

(7) (A) Strikes with right **Choon Choy**, (B) responds with left **Pock**. (8A,B) (A) **Lops** on the outside followed with right **Gwa Choy**. (9) (B) Responds with right **Tun**.

REPEAT THE DRILL

(A) Inside **lop**   right **Gwa Choy**   (B) Responds with **Tun**   (A) Outside **Lop**

(A) Right **Gwa Choy** (A) Right **Tun**

Switch to the left side

Note – there will be no change of partner position. You remain in the same place as you started, only pivot on the heel of your feet with a **Cho Ma** (pivoting stance).

(1) (A) **Lops** on the outside followed with left **Gwa Choy**. (2) (B) Responds with left **Tun Sow.**

Do not switch sides with your partner. Showing left side drill position only.

From an outside right **lop**, left **Gwa Choy** position **(3)** **(A)** reaches on the inside of **(B)**'s arm and grabs and pulls, followed with a left **Gwa Choy**. **(4)** **(B)** Responds with right **Tun**. **(5)** **(A)** **Lops** on the outside, followed with left **Gwa Choy**.

(A) Responds with right Tun Sow.

Switch back to the original right side position. Repeat the drill.

Lop Gwa Choy inside outside.

POCK SOW GWA CHOY/BONG LOP GWA CHOY
ADVANCE

This is where you put all the skills together and combine all the drills. You should practice until you feel totally confident, then change and modify the drills to suit. It might seem very hard at first, but will become much easier as you practice it and understand the drill better. What you are trying to accomplish is blocking, responding, and trapping. Whether it's in a straight line, inside line, outside line, or curved line: they should all become one.

BOTH PARTNERS IN EITHER BY-JON OR NATURAL POSITION

BY-JON   NATURAL

(A) - Rear **Pock Sow**, followed with a front **Gwa Choy**. **(B)** Stops it with her own rear **Pock Sow** block as she responds with a front **Gwa Choy.**

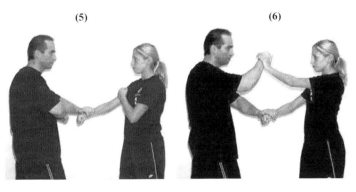

(A)- Rear **Pock Sow**, front **Gwa Choy.**   **(B)** Rear **Pock.**   Repeat cycle, counting 1-2-3-4-5, then switch and make the exercises more difficult.

As (**B**) tries to attack with her back hand (**A**) switches the rear **Pock** hand to a **Bong** arm blocking it. Then (**A**) **Lops** on the outside.

(**A**) **Lops** and executes a front **Gwa Choy**, but (**B**) stops it with her own rear **Woo.**

(**A**) Turns the striking hand to a front **Bong Sow** blocking arm, then he **Lops** on the outside of (**B**)'s arm, but (**B**) stops it with a front **Woo.** (**A**) **Lops** the attack on the inside.

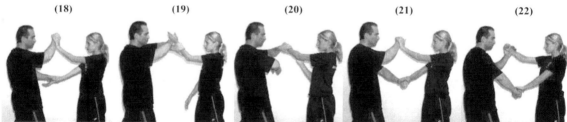

(**A**) **Lops** and executes a front **Gwa Choy**, (**B**) stops it with rear **Pock**. (**A**) Continues by **Lopping** on the outside followed with a front **Gwa Choy**, but (**B**) stops it with rear **Pock** and the cycle continues.

CONTINUE THE CYCLE: (**A**) REAR **POCK SOW** FRONT **GWA CHOY** (**B**) REAR **POCK SOW** FRONT **GWA CHOY.**

Pock Tun / Da Pock

The job of one of the partners is only to pivot and strike at the other partner while the other partner carries out the drill, then they should switch so both partners receive equal training time.
Pock (slap block)- **Tun Sow** (showing hand block)- **Da** (hit)
This drill requires footwork and pivoting.

Both partners should begin in the natural stance. **(B)** Pivots **(Cho-Ma) Chey Kune** (retracting straight punch/side pivot), then **(A)** side pivots **(Cho –Ma)** rear **Pock Sow** (slapping hand). **(B)** Then pivots rear **Chey Kune** (retracting straight punch) and **(A)** responds with a step slide **Tun /Da** simultaneous attack. For a more **complex drill**, both step slide /block/hit, all at the same time. **(A)** Then switches back to rear **Pock** (slap block), **(B)** pivots front **Chey Kune** (retracting straight punch). You can make it very rhythmic at first but remember that JKD uses a **broken rhythm.** Try to keep your partner guessing by using moves like **Pock /Tun/Da Pock, Pock/Pock Tun Da, Pock Tun Da Bong** (wing arm deflection block) or even **Bong Tun/Da Pock** etc. Be creative: add your own blocks and attacks, like backhand, kicks, knees, or take downs.

RIGHT SIDE

(1) **(A)** Steps and blocks with rear **Pock,** **(B)** front **Chey Kune.** (2) **(A)** Step slide to the outside **Tun /Da,** **(B)** rear **Chey Kune.** (3) **(A)** Steps back and pivots rear pock, **(B)** rear **Chey Kune.**

LEFT SIDE

Repeat the same movement as above on the left side.

<u>You can also switch it up, such as using **Pock /Pock Tun/Da** left</u>

<u>**Pock, Pock Tun/Da** right.</u>

(1) (A) Steps and blocks with front **Pock Sow**, **(B)** rear **Chey Kune**. **(2) (A)** Pivots rear **Pock Sow**, **(B)** front **Chey Kune**. **(3) (A)** Steps back and pivots **Tun Da**, **(B)** rear **Chey Kune**.

FRONT OR REAR **BONG SOW TUN/DA**

(1) (A) Steps forward and blocks with rear **Bong Sow**, **(B)** front **Chey Kune**. **(2) (A)** Step slide **Tun /Da**, **(B)** rear **Chey Kune**. **(3) (A)** Steps back rear **Bong**, **(B)** front **Chey Kune**.

(4) (A) Steps forward and blocks with front **bon sow**, **(B)** rear **Chey kune**. **(5) (A)** Step slide **Tun /Da**, **(B)** front **Chey kune**. **(6) (A)** Pivots rear **Bong**, **(B)** rear **Chey Kune** etc.

POCK DA (SLAP HIT)

This drill should help you with trapping and will get you ready for the next level of training: the **Gates.**

Both partners start in the **By-Jon** (fighting stance) and in the **Woo Sow** (guarding hand) position. **(B)** Slaps down **(A)'s** guard hand as he punches forward with a straight vertical punch, but partner **(A)** stops it with a rear **Pock sow** (slapping hand).

Partner **(B) Lop Sow** (grabs) the outside of **(A)'s** blocking hand and strikes with a front **Gwa Choy** (back hand), but **(A)** again stops it with a **Woo Sow** (guarding hand). They then both fade back to the original position.

Partner **(B) Lop Sow** (grabs) the outside of **(A)'s** blocking hand and strikes with a front **Gwa Choy** (back hand), but **(A)** again stops it with a **Woo Sow** (guarding hand). They then both fade back to the original position.

Partner **(A) Lop Sow** (grabs) the outside of **(B)'s** blocking hand and strikes with a front **Gwa Choy** (back hand), but **(B)** again stops it with a **Woo Sow** (guarding hand) or **Tun Sow** (showing hand). They then both fade back to the original position.

Right to right **Woo Sow**.   **(B) Pock Sow** to the outside of **(A)'s** arm as he punches forward with a right **Choon Choy/Kune**. **(A)** Blocks with a left **Pock Sow**.

B) Lop Sow with the left hand the outside of **(A)'s** left arm as he strikes with a right **Gwa Choy**. **(A)** Stops it with a right **Woo Sow**, then both fade back.

(A) Left **Pock Sow** to the outside of **(B)**'s right hand as he strikes forward with a right **Choon Choy**, but **(B)** stops it with left **Pock Sow**. **(A)** **Lop Sow** the outside of **(B)**'s arm as he strikes forward with a right **Gwa Choy.** Again **(B)** stops it with a right **Woo Sow** or **Tun Sow**. Both fade back to the original position.

The "Gates" (Moon) Trapping Hands (Fon Sow)
Must Be Done With Front Lead Only, Right Or Left.

GATES (MOON). I refer to gates as doors or openings of opportunity for intercepting. As the opponent strikes, we intercept at either the opening or retracting of the attack. You have an opportunity to break down the gate if an opponent stops you from intercepting by blocking or placing a gate in front of your attack. You do so with your own block or strike. For example, if he strikes with a straight jab or cross, you can either intercept before his attack reaches you or stop it with your own block. If he stops your counter strike with his own block, then your punch never retreats back to position to reload, instead it continues by immobilizing his blocking hand and hitting the target. In JKD, we intercept whatever is in front of us by breaking down that gate. Breaking down the gate can either be done by a single direct attack **(SDA)**, a Hand Immobilization Attack **(HIA)**, Trapping Hand **(FON SOW)**, **(ABC)** Attack By Combination, **(PIA)** Progressively Indirect, **(ABD)** Attack By Drawing, and taking away the attacker's entire weapon by closing in on the attacker. The five ways of attack are a massive force that will take down anything standing in its way, no matter how plugged or protected the blocker is. You should be able to take down any barrier that goes in front of you. Remember, for every attack there is a counter **(BAK GUY BAK GEE)**. I will demonstrate 27 **GATES** in this book. **Why 27 gates**? The specific number chosen is relative to Bruce Lee's birthday, and is purely in recognition of this date. These gates are not to be taken lightly. They are the backbone of JKD training. If you master these gates, you will have an unlimited amount of blocking and striking, therefore it is not necessary for you to only use these twenty-seven techniques. You have unlimited techniques. By unlimited I mean you can switch them around, generate from them, add kicks, and take downs, whatever works at the time. This way you are not limited to these techniques alone, but when it really comes down to it, you only need to do one in real life situations. That is why you must become these techniques, so when you need them they are there because in real situations you not going to say, "If he comes this way, I will block him this way. Then I will trap this way." Well, let me assure you that it will not work. No matter how the attack has been brought on you, you should respond to it very naturally. We start from **Woo** or touching hand position. That is **Not** how a fight starts in most situations. What it's teaching you is that both practitioners can be in a block position. For instance, if he punched then I blocked, I punch then he blocks instead, that's why we start in block position. Therefore, both partners get a lot of repetition and you are already one step ahead. In addition, 95% of people strike with the right hand, so these gates are not designed to fight against another JKD student; their purpose is to block an orthodox fighter. Because when they strike with a telegraphic punch or cross hook or what ever they use, they end up right foot forward. So why not take advantage of their attack by counter attacking with JKD, and trapping their hands to use the front lead to the fullest? Footwork, pivoting, and hip rotation are used heavily to achieve full results. **THE GATES** should be practiced right lead unless you're lefty. Then you will realize why we depend on the front lead so heavily because if you strike from the rear you are not going to be able to strike with power. You will end up trapping yourself because you will be going against the Yin and Yang structure and you are going to shorten yourself. When you put your right hand forward, you're already halfway there with much more power and speed, which is very unlikely to be blocked even with a first strike.

LEAK: leak attack is normally executed by the opponent against a very well plugged defense lines. Normally the leak attack is executed between the lower and the upper defense lines; no matter how well your gates are closed, a good JKD practitioner will always find a way to land an attack.

Speed; snap hip and footwork are heavily required. Your rear heel must remain up because you are lunging forward before each strike. After practicing these gates, your JKD punch will be **"felt before it is seen"**.

Note: every **Pock Sow** (slapping hand) will become **Gum Sow** (pressing hand) but with speed they both become one so don't get confused which one you should do. It always starts with **Pock Sow** and finishes with **Gum Sow**.

GATE ONE (1) *(YUT MOON) POCK SOW* CHOON CHOY OR POCK DA (SLAP/ HIT)

Pock Sow (slapping block) **Choon Choy** (straight punch) or **Gwa Choy** (back hand)

To me this gate is the most effective gate in trapping hands **(SDA)** single direct attack. **"Simplicity."**
This will teach you how to block a straight jab or cross.
All gates should be done on **Wooden Dummy** (Mook Joang) or with a partner at **By-Jon** stance.
Gate: By- Jon right hand open with your wrist touching your partner's wrist in **Tun Sow**(showing hand) or **Woo Sow**(guarding hand).
Push his hand down with your left hand, punch with your right. *Note that the left hand should pin partner's elbow or forearm, until the punch is fully delivered and returned back to position. This drill should be done with speed to build that elastic **"IT"** punches.
"I don't hit, "IT" hits all by itself. Don't think, feel. The punch should be felt before it is seen"

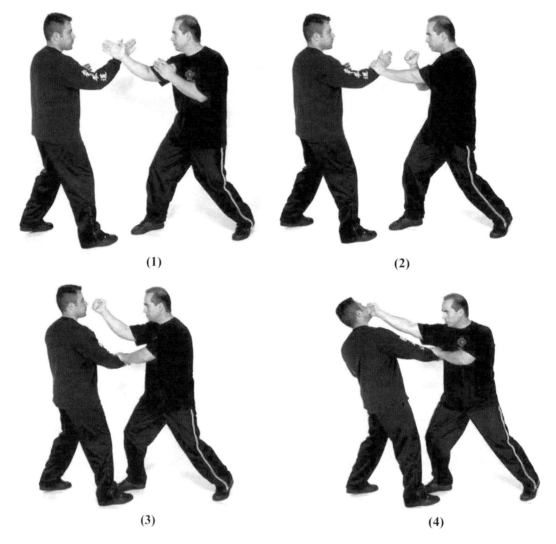

(1) (2)

(3) (4)

Both partner's hands are touching in **Woo Sow** (guarding hand) or **Tun Sow** (showing hand) **Pock Sow/Gum Sow** (pressing hand) with rear hand right **Choon Choy** (JKD vertical punch) or **Gwa Choy** (back hand) as you push forward with the ball of your rear foot to add power. All moves as one. Trap, push shuffle, and punch, all three motions should be done as one motion with speed. You should practice this trap until you can barely see the punch being delivered to your partner's head. With the proper footwork and speed, your opponent should only see a blur before he gets hit. It is almost impossible for any one to be able to block it.

GATE TWO (2) *(YEE MOON)* POCK CHOON CHOY LOP GWA CHOY

Pock Sow (slapping hand), **Choon Choy** (straight punch), **Lop** (grab) (pull back), **Gwa Choy** (back hand)
All gates should be done on a Wooden Dummy **(Mook Joang)** or with a partner at **By-Jon** stance:

Gate: start in **By-Jon** position with your right hand open and your wrist touching your partner's wrist. In **Tun Sow** (showing hand), press down with your left hand and punch with your right. Note: your left hand should pin your partner's elbow or forearm until the punch is fully delivered, and then, return to position. The opponent blocks your punch with a **Pock Sow** (slapping hand). You then **Lop Sow** (grab) his wrist, and pull back on the outside, and deliver a devastating **Gwa Choy** (back hand) to the head.

(1) (2) (3)

Both partner's hands are touching in **Woo Sow** or **Tun Sow** (showing hand), pressing down with rear **Pock Sow/Gum Sow** as you strike with a straight vertical punch (**Choon Choy**) to the face. **Same as gate one.**

(4) (5) (6)

As he blocks your attack to the outside with rear **Pock Sow** (slapping hand), grab the outside of his wrist and pull **Lop Sow** with rear hand as you rotate the hips and deliver a front **Gwa Choy** (Back hand) to the face.

GATE THREE (3) (SUM MOON) POCK SOW CHOON CHOY COW CHOON CHOY

Pock Sow (slapping hand) **Choon Choy** (straight punch), **Cow Sow** (hooking or catch back), **Choon Choy**(straight punch)

All gates should be done on a Wooden Dunmny **(Mook Joang)** or with a partner at **By-Jon** stance:

<u>Gate</u>: both partners stand in a **By-Jon** position with your right hand open and your wrist touching your partner's wrist. In **Tun Sow** (showing hand) position, push down with your left hand against his elbow or wrist. Punch with your right. Note that your left hand should pin partner's elbow or forearm until the punch is fully delivered; then return back to position. The opponent then blocks your punch with a **Pock Sow** (slapping hand), and you **Cow Sow** (hooking hand) on the inside and pull back to deliver a devasting **Choon Choy** (JKD vertical punch**).**

(1)　　　　　　　　　　　(2)　　　　　　　　　　　(3)

Both partners will start in **By-Jon** hands touching. Then in **Tun Sow** (showing hand) position, press down with rear **Pock/Gum Sow strike** with front straight punch **(Choon Choy).** He blocks your outside with rear slapping hand **(Pock Sow).**

(4)　　　　　　　　　　　(5)　　　　　　　　　　　(6)

Grab the inside and jerk back with **Cow Sow** step slide **Choon Choy** (straight punch) to the facc. Always bring back the hand. Never leave out for any one to grab it.

GATE FOUR (4) *(SEE MOON)* CHOP CHOY GWA CHOY LOP SOW JOW SOW

Chop Choy (low hammer) **Gwa Choy** (back hand) **Lop Sow** (grab or pull) **Jow Sow** (running hand)
All gates should be done on a Wooden Dummy (Mook Joang) or with a partner at **By-Jon** stance.

Gate: start in **By-Jon** with your right hand open and wrist touching your partner's wrist. Then in **Tun Sow** (showing hand) position, drop down to **Chop Choy** (low hammer), **(PIA)** push down with your left hand and punch with your right. Note that your left hand should pin your partners elbow or forearm until the punch is fully delivered, then return to position and your opponent will block your punch with a **Pock Sow** (slapping hand); then **Lop Sow** (grab) the wrist on the outside and pull back as you deliver a powerful **Jow sow** (running hand) to the face.

(1)   (2)   (3)

Both partners will start in **By-Jon** position. Next, with hands in **Tun Sow** (showing hand) position, drop down to a **Chop Choy** (low hammer), not connecting, only **FAKE** to cause him to drop his hand thinking to block the attack. Then **Gum Sow** (pressing hand) with rear hand against his elbow as you front **Gwa Choy** or **Choon Choy**

(Back hand or straight punch) to the face.

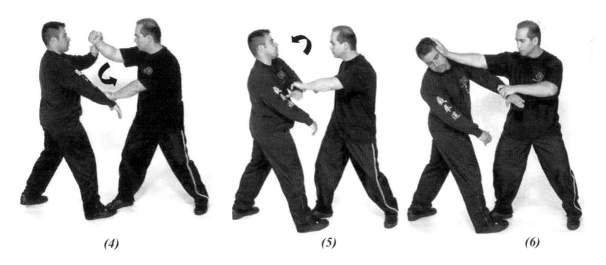

(4)   (5)   (6)

He blocks with **Pock Sow** (slapping hand), you counter with **Jow Sow** (open hand resembles a slap / running hand) to the side of the face, make sure that you rotate the hips for added power.

ANOTHER FINISHING OPTION FOR GATE FOUR

Strike to the side of the head

GATE FIVE (5) *(UMM MOON)* - **Tun Sow** (showing hand) position **Lop Sow** (pull or grab) **Choon Choy** (straight punch) / **Lop Sow/Choon Choy**

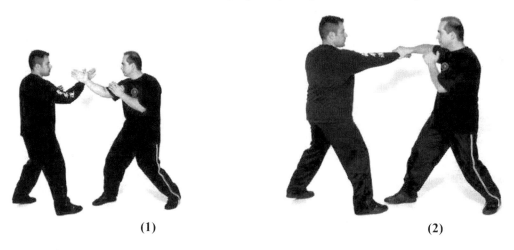

(1) (2)

Start in **By-Jon** position with hands touching. In **Tun Sow**, front **Lop Sow** to the outside as you strike with rear **Choon Choy** to the face.

(3) (4) (5)

He blocks with rear **Pock Sow**. Circle the hand to the outside and counter with rear **Lop Sow**, followed with front **Choon Choy** to the face.

GATE SIX (6) *(LOOK MOON)* Tun Sow - (showing hand) position Lon Sow (bar arm) Chop Kune (horizontal punch) leak. Lop Sow (grab) Choon Choy (straight punch)

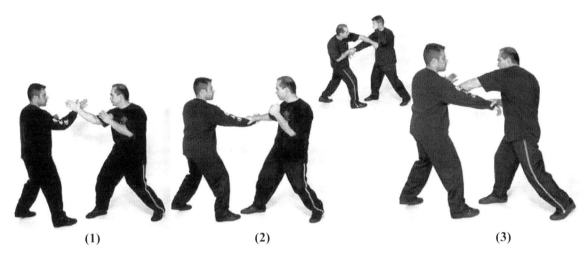

(1)　　　　　　　　　　(2)　　　　　　　　　　(3)

Both start in **By-Jon** position with hands touching. In **Tun Sow**, grab pull front **Lon Sow** to the outside as you open the line of attack and strike his abdomen with rear **Chop Kune** or **leak**.

(4)　　　　　　　　　　(5)

As he keeps his guard up, grab and pull his hand with rear **Lop Sow**; then rotate the hips and strike with front **Choon Choy** to the face.

GATE SEVEN (7) *(TIT MOON)* Tun Sow - showing hand position. Pock Sow (slapping hand), Choon Choy (straight punch), Jow Sow (running hand or circling)

(1)　　　　　　　　(2)　　　　　　　　(3)

Both partners start in a **By-Jon** position with hands touching. In **Tun Sow**, press with rear **Pock/Gum Sow** against the forearm, and push shuffle front **Choon Choy** to the face.

(4)　　　　　　　　　　　　　(5)

He blocks with rear **Pock Sow** to your outside, and you counter with front **Jow Sow** to the side of the face, open hand.

GATE EIGHT (8) *(BOT MOON)*-Tun Sow (showing hand) position. Pock Sow (slapping hand), Choon Choy (straight punch), and Pie Jon (horizontal elbow) Lop Sow (grab), Fun Sow (chop), or Gwa Choy (backhand)

(1) (2) (3)

Both start in **By-Jon** position with hands touching. In **Tun Sow** position, press with rear **Pock/ Gum Sow** against his forearm, followed with front **Choon Choy** to the face.

(4) (5) (6)

He blocks with rear **Pock Sow** to the outside of your hand, and you counter with front **Pie Jon,** followed with **Gwa Choy** to the side of the head or **Fun Sow** (chop) to the throat.

GATE NINE (9) *(GIU MOON)* Tun Sow - (showing hand) position, Lop Sow (grab or pull) fake high; Gwa Choy (backhand) **"don't connect"**, only cause him to put his blocking hand up. Rear Chop Kune (horizontal punch); Lop Sow (grab or pull) Choon Choy (straight punch).

(1)   (2)   (3)

Start in **By-Jon** position with both hands touching. **Lop Sow** his hand on the outside as you strike with rear **Choon Choy** to the face, he blocks the attack with his own **Pock Sow** on the inside.

(4)   (5)   (6)

As you still control his hand at waist level, drop a rear **Chop Kune** the abdomen, grab and pull his other hand on the outside, **Lop Sow** to open him up for more attack, then strike him with front **Gwa Choy** to the face.

GATE TEN (10) (SUP MOON) Pock Sow (slapping hand), Choon Choy (straight punch), inside Lop (grab), Jing Jan (vertical palm heel strike) or Fun Sow (chop), Cow Sow (jerking hand back), Choon Choy (straight punch)

(1) (2) (3)

Start in **By-Jon** position with both hands touching, then in **Tun Sow** you rear **Pock/Gum Sow** and front **Choon Choy**. He blocks with rear **Pock Sow** to the outside.

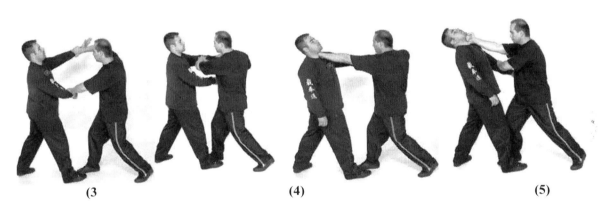

(3) (4) (5)

You will counter with front **Lop Sow**, pulling on his inside strike with rear **Jing-Jan** to the face, and simultaneously re-trap with **Cow Sow** pinning his biceps. Strike with **Choon Choy** to the throat.

GATE ELEVEN (11) *(SUP YUT MOON)* - **Tun Sow** (showing hand), **Pock** (slapping hand), right **Chop Kune** (horizontal punch), outside **Lop Sow** (grab or pull), **Gwa Choy** (back hand)

(1)   (2)   (3)   (INSIDE VIEW)

(4A)   (4B)

Start in **By-Jon** position with both hands touching, then in **Tun Sow** position, press down with rear **Gum Sow** to clear his arm out of the way, and drop down with front **Chop Kune** (leak horizontal punch). Grab his rear hand on the outside with rear **Lop Sow,** and strike with front **Gwa Choy** to the face.

GATE TWELVE & THIRTEEN (12, 13) *SUP YEE MOON / SUP SUM MOON)* Tun Sow (showing hand), inside **Huen sow** (circle**), Pock** (slap), **Woo Sow** (guarding hand), **Lop Sow** (grab or pull) **Gwa Choy** (back hand), **Huen sow** (circling hand), **Chung Die Jan** (low spade palm strike), **Gwa Choy** (back hand).

(1) (2) (3)

Both partners start in **By-Jon** position with both hands touching. In **Tun Sow**, front **Huen Sow/ Pock Sow** to the inside of his wrist.

(4) (5) (6)

As you push the inside, place the rear hand against the inside of his wrist with **Woo Sow**. **Woo** switches to **Lop Sow** to the inside as you strike with front **Gwa Choy** to the side of the face. ***Continue - do not just stop, 12 and 13 should become one.

From **Gwa Choy,** position circles the front hand on the outside of his elbow and hooks it. Strike with rear **Chung Die Jan** to the ribs, front hand strikes with **Gwa Choy** to the side of the face.

CLOSER LOOK AT GATES 12/13

GATE FOURTEEN (14) *(SUP SEE MOON)* - **Pock** Sow (slapping hand), **Choon Choy** (straight punch), reverse **Woo Sow** (guarding hand), head butt.

(1)   (2)   (3)

Start in **By-Jon** position with hands touching. In **Tun Sow**, press down with rear **Pock/Gum Sow** against his elbow as you strike with a front **Choon Choy**. He blocks with rear **Pock Sow** to the outside.

(4)   (5)   INSIDE VIEW OF PHOTO (5)

Place rear **Woo** hand behind his left tricep and pull, striking him with a head butt at the same time.

GATE FIFTEEN (15) (SUP UMM MOON) **Lop Sow** (grab or pull), **Chow kune** (uppercut), **Lop Sow** (grab or pull), **Gwa Choy** (backhand).

(1)   (2)   (3)   INSIDE VIEW OF PHOTO (3)

(4)   (5)   INSIDE VIEW OF PHOTOS (4, 5)

Both partners are in a **By-Jon** position with both hands touching. Then in **Tun Sow**, grab and pull his **Tun** hand to the outside as you rotate the hip, and strike up with **chow kune** uppercut to the chin. Switch to the inside and **Lop Sow** with rear hand, and **Gwa Choy** with front hand to the side of the face.

GATE SIXTEEN (16) *(SUP LOOK MOON)* - **Tun Sow** (showing hand), **Lop Sow** (grab), **Jom Sow** (chop), **Huen Sow**, (circle), **Choon Choy** (straight punch).

(1)   (2A)   (2B)

(3)   INSIDE VIEW   (4)   INSIDE VIEW OF PHOTO (4)

Start in **By-Jon** position with hands touching. In **Tun Sow**, grab and pull **Lop Sow** on the outside, and chop his elbow with **Jom sow** using the forearm for wider surface. Circle **Huen Sow** on his inside to open him up for the **Choon Choy,** or **Shovel Hook** to the abdomen.

GATE SEVENTEEN (17) *(SUP T IT MOON)* - **Tun Sow** (showing hand), **Pock Sow** (slapping hand), **Choon Choy** (straight punch), **Chum–Q** (bridge block), **Huen** (circle), **Jing Jan** (vertical palm heel strike), **Chop Kune** (leak horizontal punch).

(1) (2) (3)

Partners start in a **By-Jon** position with both hands touching. In **Tun Sow**, press down with rear hand **Pock/Gum Sow** against his forearm, and strike with **Choon Choy**. He blocks with rear **Pock Sow** to the outside.

(4) (5) (6)

Striking hand converts to a **Chum-Q.** Right forearm strikes the outside of the elbow joint, as the rear forearm strikes the inside of the wrist, they should both be done simultaneously. Then circle **Huen Sow** on the inside of his elbow.

(7) (8) (9) (10)

Strike with rear **Jing-Jan** to the face, maintaining rear **Woo** hand up, and finish with a **Chop Kune** to the abdomen.

GATE EIGHTEEN- (18) *(SUP BOT MOON)* - Tun Sow (showing hand), Pock Sow (slapping hand), Lop Sow (grab or pull), Gwa Choy (backhand), under Lon sow (pull low), over Gwa Choy.

(1)　　　　　　　　　(2)　　　　　　　　　(3)

Start in **By-Jon** with both hands touching. In **Tun Sow**, press down with rear hand **Pock/ Gum Sow** against the forearm. Strike with front **Choon Choy**. He blocks with rear **Pock Sow** to the outside.

(4)　　　　　　　　　(5)　　　　　　　　　(6)

Rear hand converts to **Lop Sow** to the outside. Strike with **Gwa Choy** from under his armpit, and pull down his arm. Waist height **Lon Sow,** and strike **with Gwa Choy** to the side of the face.

GATE NINETEEN (19) *(SUP GIU MOON)* - Rear **Gum Sow** (pressing hand), **Jow Sow** (running hand), **Loy Jut** (inside jerking hand), **Gum Sow** (pressing hand), **Gwa Choy** (back hand).

Both partners start in **By-Jon** position with hands touching. In **Tun Sow**, press down with rear **Pock/Gum Sow** against his elbow, and strike with front **Jow sow.**

If he blocks with rear **Tun Sow**. Pull his hand in with front **Loy Jut Sow** and trap both hands, then switch the hand and pin down both of his hands with rear **Gum Sow**, trap **Gwa Choy** to the side of the head.

GATE TWENTY (20) *(YEE SUP MOON)* Tun Sow (showing hand), rear Pock Sow (slapping hand), **Choon Choy** (straight punch), **and Chum Jon** (downward elbow), **Chow Kune** (uppercut/shovel hook).

(1) (2) (3)

Start in **By-Jon** stance with both hands touching. In **Tun Sow**, press down with rear hand **Pock/Gum Sow** against the forearm, and strike with front **Choon Choy**. He then blocks with rear **Pock Sow** to the outside.

(4) (5) (6)

Circle your elbow over his, then with a blocking hand, trap it down with **Chum Jon** to force his hands down. Strike up with **Chow kune** or **Shovel Hook** under the chin.

GATE TWENTY ONE (21) *(YEE SUP YUT MOON)* - Rear **Pock,** (slapping hand) **Choon Choy** (straight punch), **Gwy Jon** (over the top elbow), **Gum Sow** (pressing hand), **Song Jon** (outward elbow).

(1) (2) (3)

Start in **By-Jon** stance with both hands touching. In **Tun Sow**, press down with rear hand **Pock/Gum Sow** against his elbow, and strike with front **Choon Choy**. He then blocks with rear **Pock Sow** to the outside.

(4) (5)

As he blocks, circle his **Pock Sow** over, using the front elbow. Trap both hands by pressing down with the elbow, and switch to rear hand **Gum Sow** with his hand against the elbow, then strike with front **Song Jon** to the throat.

GATE TWENTY-TWO (22) *(YEE SUP YEE MOON)* rear **Pock** (slapping hand), **Choon Choy** (straight punch), and press against his **Pock Sow** then trap the hand against his head, **Lop Sow** (grab) **Tie Sut** (raising knee).

(1) (2) (3)

Start in **By-Jon** stance with both hands touching. In **Tun Sow**, press down with rear hand **Pock/ Gum Sow** against his elbow, and strike with front **Choon Choy.** He then blocks with rear **Pock Sow** to the outside.

(4A) (4B) (5)

Press your hand against his block, pinning it to his neck. As you **Lop** his front hand, pull down his head, and **Tie Sut** with front knee to the face.

GATE TWENTY THREE (23) *(YEE SUP SUM MOON)*

rear **Pock Sow** (slapping hand) **Choon Choy** (straight punch), trap thumb and elbow, with **Gum Sow** (pressing hand) left **Choon Choy** (straight punch), right **Gwa Choy** (back hand). Pin the back of the head, **Tie Sut** (raising knee) to the face.

(1) (2) (3)

Start in **By-Jon** stance with both hands touching. In **Tun Sow**, press down with rear hand, **Pock/ Gum Sow** against his forearm. Strike with front **Choon Choy**. He then blocks with a **Pock Sow** to the outside.

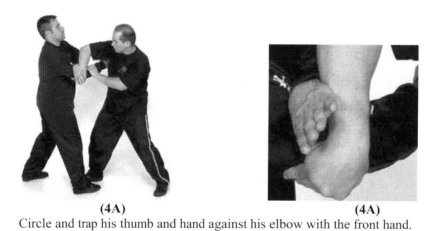

(4A) (4A)

Circle and trap his thumb and hand against his elbow with the front hand.

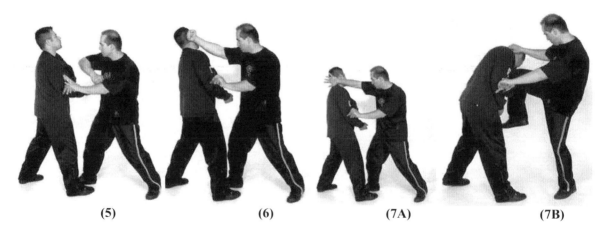

(5) (6) (7A) (7B)

Re-trap and pin down both hands with rear **Gum Sow,** and strike with front **Gwa Choy** to the side of the head. Grab the side of the face and pull down as you introduce his face to your knee.

GATE TWENTY-FOUR (24) *(YEE SUP SEE MOON)* front **Lop Sow**, rear **Biu Sow** (finger jab) to the eyes. Place reverse **Woo Sow** (guarding hand), and lock the elbow take down.

(1)　　　　　(2)　　　　　(3)　　　　　(4A)

In a **Tun Sow** position, front **Lop Sow** to the outside as you strike with rear **Biu Sow** to the eyes. Place rear open hand against the inside of his elbow joint.

(4B)　　　　　(4C)　　　　　(4D)

Push his hand out as you pull in against the elbow joint, place the right hand against his wrist and clamp it as you force his shoulder and elbow joint out of place. This will cause the shoulder and elbow to separate out of the joint.

(5A)　　　　　(5B)

The pressure from the lock will force him to land flat on his back. Continue with your **Z** lock on the ground until he taps out; it will not take more than 2 seconds for him to do so, if it is executed correctly.

GATE TWENTY-FIVE (25) *(YEE SUP UMM MOON)* -

In a **Tun Sow** (showing hand) position rear **Pock/Gum Sow** (pressing hand), front **Choon Choy** (straight punch). He blocks with rear **Pock Sow** (slapping hand). You counter with rear **Biu Jee** (finger jab) to the eyes. Rear **Lop/ Gum Sow** (grab/press), front **Choon Choy** (straight punch).

(1)　　　　　　　　　(2)　　　　　　　　　(3)

Start in **By-Jon** stance with both hands touching. In **Tun Sow**, press down with rear hand **Pock/ Gum Sow** against his elbow, and strike with front **Choon Choy.** He then blocks with rear **Pock Sow** to the outside.

(4)　　　　　　　　　(5)　　　　　　　　　(6)

Counter with rear **Biu Jee** to the eyes, then re-trap rear **Lop Sow /Gum Sow,** and strike with front **Choon Choy** to the face.

GATE TWENTY-SIX (26) *(YEE SUP LOOK MOON)* front **Biu Sow/Jee**
(finger jab) to the eyes, switch to **Lop Sow** (grab or pull) rear **Choon Choy** (straight vertical punch) re-trap **Lop Sow** (grab or pull) **Choon Choy** (straight vertical punch).

(1)　　　　　　　　(2)　　　　　　　　(3)

(3)　　　　　　　　(4)

Start in **By-Jon** stance with both hands touching. Front **Biu Sow** to the eyes as you **Lop Sow** his front lead, and strike with rear **Choon Choy.** Re-trap **Lop Sow** his rear hand on the outside, and strike with front **Choon Choy** to the side of the head.

GATE TWENTY-SEVEN (27) *(YEE SUP TIT MOON)* -THIS DRILL SHOULD BE DONE ON A WOODEN DUMMY (Mook Joang), OR WITH A PARTNER AT BY-JON STANCE:

Drill: both partners stand in **By-Jon** position with your right hand open, and your wrist touching your partner's wrist. In **Tun Sow** (showing hand) position, push down with your left hand against his elbow or wrist. Punch with your right. Note that your left hand should pin your partner's elbow or forearm until the punch is fully delivered. Then return to position.

Front **Lop Sow** (grab or pull) and rear **Gwa Choy** (back hand), he blocks with **Woo Sow** (guarding hand). Front hand converts to **Ping Choy** (Horizontal punch). Then **Lop** (grab) the inside of his blocking hand to open him up for the second strike, **Fun Sow** (chop) to the throat. **Gum Sow / Choon Choy** (pin down/vertical punch) to the chin. Re-trap again with **Lop Sow / Fun Sow** (grab/chop) to the throat again.

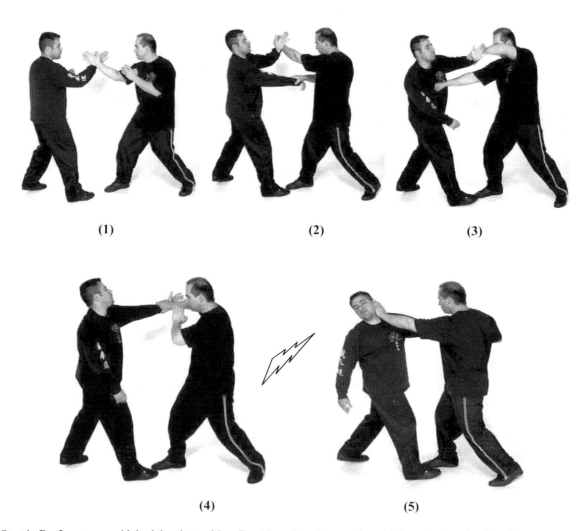

(1)   (2)   (3)

(4)   (5)

Start in **By-Jon** stance with both hands touching. Front **Lop Sow** the outside of his front lead, and strike with rear **Choon Choy**. He blocks with rear **Woo Sow**. Execute front **Choon Choy** to his abdomen, and re-trap the inside of his **Woo Sow** hand with front hand.

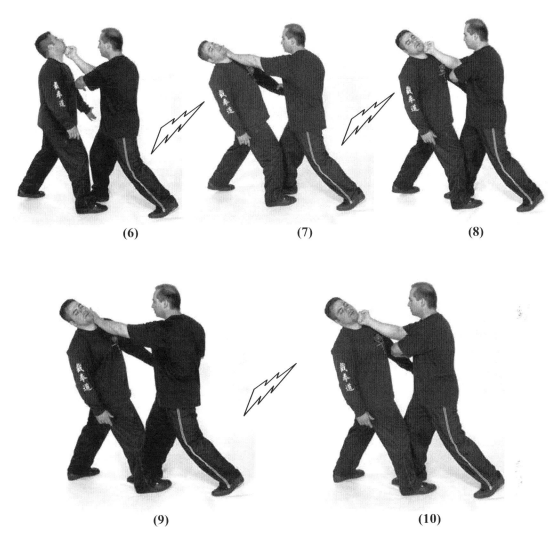

Lop Sow/ Fun Sow to the throat, and re-trap. **Choon Choy** to the chin, re-trap **Fun Sow** again, re-trap **Choon Choy** to the throat in case the first hit did not hurt. Photos - 5-6-7-8-9-10 should be executed with lightning speed

All six hits should take under 2 seconds, this is the type of thing you have to train your self into. Your hits should be felt before they are seen.

Trapping Reversal
Or Stupid Trap

Why do I call it "**Stupid Trap**"? Because the opponent is grabbing very hard, but will not realize that the trap will not work if he lets go. It will be too late because he will have been hit. Reversal trapping is done when the opponent's trapping is sloppy or too slow, and you are able to use his own trapping against him. For every trap, there is almost always a trap reversal or counter attack. You can apply many of the reversal traps against any of the gates. I am only going to demonstrate few of the most commonly used reversal traps, and the most effective in actual situations. In addition, the trapping reversals can be used against any of the gates for countering. Stupid traps will only work against a **tight grip.**

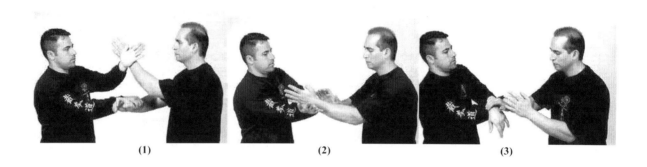

(1)　　　　　　　　(2)　　　　　　　　(3)

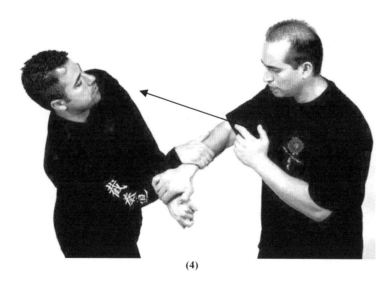

(4)

You can trap and follow it with a punch or a finger jab to the face.

From A Grab And Strike Position: Fold over his striking hand with your blocking hand, as you clamp the left hand on his right forearm, lock both arms long enough that you can execute a strike to his face.* **Note: make sure that you drop the right hand down, as you raise the left hand simultaneously, if you do not, he will have enough time to release his grab, and your trap will not work.**

From A Pin, Strike Position: as you stop his first attack, he circles around for with an open hand strike to your face, simply stop it with your own open hand block. Fold his right hand over his left arm, as you clamp your left hand over both of his arms controlling long enough, that you can execute a strike to the face or you can shovel hook to his ribs.

REVERSAL TRAP (ONE)

(A) (B)

Both partners in a fighting touching hand position, partner **(A)** drops his front hand, faking partner **(B)** causing him to fall for the fake. Then partner **(B)** pins partner **(A's)** hand with rear hand followed with a front punch to the face. Partner **(A)** blocks the attack with the rear hand to the outside of **(B's)** striking hand.

Partner **(B)** grabs and pulls **(A's)** defending block to the outside as he back hands to **(B's)** face, but **(B)** blocks the attack to the outside with an open hand block. With a quick response partner **(A)** pulls down the right hand as he clamps the left over the right hand of partner **(B)** simultaneously locking both hands into a trap, with quick speed **(A)** strikes **(B's)** face with a vertical straight punch.

INSIDE VIEW OF REVERSAL TRAP (ONE)

(1) (2) (3)

(4) (5)

(6) (7) (8)

REVERSAL TRAP (2)

(1) He grabs and pulls your left hand to strike to the face; you block his attack with the front hand. He continues his attack by circling his right hand around to land a strike to the side of the head.

(2) You stop his attack with the front hand

3) block and fold his hand down by trapping both hands

From A Grab Strike: as you stop his attack, he will continue his attack with an open hand strike to the face, you stop him with your own open hand block. At moment of contact, with the opponent's hand, fold his blocking hand down as you clamp the left hand on both of his arms, which will give an opportunity to respond with a quick strike to his face.

(4) Clamp and control both of his arms   **(5)** as you pull back both of his of his arms execute a strike to his face.

Inside view of above movements (4 and 5)

Note: always be creative, do not just be limited to the above reversal traps. You have to be able to apply your reversal traps against any attack.

F.I.A (FOOT IMMOBILIZATION ATTACK)

F.I.A is used when you close the gap between your opponent and yourself as you step slide or push shuffle. Your front foot will act as a bearing wall in front of your opponent's leg to the outside, inside, or the top. This will prevent him from kicking you. By placing your front lead in front of his front lead, you will totally eliminate his weapon. Or, you could plant your front foot on top of his front foot, pinning it down during your attack, and leaving your opponent with no place to go. All movements must be done in one motion, it cannot be done in steps or it will not be effective. You must execute the block, push shuffle, and strike simultaneously, giving him no time to retreat. By doing so, you can also snap his ankle out of the joint by applying pressure against his shins, and rotating the front foot at a 45° angle. By kneeling and pushing forward, you will trap his leg between your shin and the foot, and will leave him no room to retreat.

(1) (2A) (2B)

Facing the opponent in **By-Jon** stance, block his attacks with the front hand as you push shuffle as he strikes. Place the rear hand on the outside of his attacking arm, and slide your front foot to the outside of his front foot and park it. You have many options because you are in full control. You can strike to the face, or you can simply sweep him down.

(3) OR (3) OR (3)

Second option: pivot the foot at a 45° angle and press down against the back of the calf area to knock him down, or slide to the inside of his leg and kneel down forward against his front knee to snap the ankle and knee.

(1)

(2)

1) Block and pin the foot down by stepping on his front toes nailing him down to the floor. You can kick him in the groin or strike him.

2) If he attacks with the right lead, slide to his outside by blocking and trapping his leg as you kneel forward against his knee, knocking him back.

Step-1- either slide to the inside or plant the foot down

Step-2-slide to the inside   **Step-3-kneel and push forward**

THE PERFECT TRAINING PARTNER

MOOK YAN JOANG FOT YUT LING BOT "108 WOODEN DUMMY MOTIONS"
MOOK JOANG (Wooden Dummy)

Why is it so important that a JKD practitioner should learn this form?
Benefits of the Wooden Dummy: It teaches the practitioner to strike, block, pivot, step, sweep, and hand-trap, as well as how to handle simultaneous attacks. It also toughens the hands, wrists, forearms, shins, knees, and bones. It also acts to mold your form, as it teaches you to place your hands precisely on the target. Because the Dummy is stationary, it forces the practitioner to move around it by pivoting, stepping side to the side, stepping and sliding, and stepping and facing. It's a great partner because it's there whenever you need to practice, and it doesn't bruise or complain. Bruce Lee practiced the Wooden Dummy form and like I said previously, to be like Bruce Lee you have to follow in his footsteps.

The Wooden Dummy that I train on is a replica of the original Dummy that Bruce Lee trained on. The difference between the traditional Wooden Dummy and the JKD Wooden Dummy is that the traditional Dummy has a rounded trunk, and is approximately 9 inches in diameter and about 4½ to 5 feet in height. It consists of three wooden poles that represent the arms. The part that is sticking out of the trunk is a rounded, smooth shape. The part that is in the trunk is square-shaped, and it fits into a small square in the trunk somewhat bigger than the square on the "arms". This will allow the "arms" to move slightly in the hole in four different directions. It can go left, right, up or down very slightly, and one Wooden, leg-shaped piece is somewhat moveable.

The Jeet Kune Do Dummy has almost the same exact measurements, except it has shaping within the trunk that represents the head, neck and body. Also, the leg-shaped areas are made of steel instead of Wood and are much longer from the knee section down, and it mounts higher than the traditional leg. Additionally, it has two leg-shaped parts that pass through the bottom sides of the trunk. They, too, are Made of steel, stationary and approximately 2½ inches in diameter. Bruce and James Lee, who was one of Bruce Lee's Oakland school students and one of the only three students that were certified by Bruce Lee, designed the extra features on the Dummy. When using this Dummy, it feels like you are practicing on a person, and you can strike more than one leg. The Wooden Dummy that I train on converts into two: one is JKD and the other is Wing Chun. This way, when I need to sharpen my form, I like to use the traditional wing Chun leg, but I also like the shape of the neck and the side legs. This allows me get the best of both worlds. When practicing the form, the side legs cannot be used — because they are not part of the form — but when I practice freestyle JKD Wooden Dummy techniques, I use the side legs for low kicking and sweeping. I find them very useful.

The Wooden Dummy is the third form in Wing Chun. It's taught after the second form chum –q (searching for the bridge). The Wooden Dummy techniques are divided into two Major sections or 18 SETS (Number of sets may vary among practitioners). Repetition is very important, as one must Master the first 60 motions before he can proceed on to the next 48 motions. Grandmaster yip Man, who is Bruce Lee's only known wing Chun instructor, felt that the original 140 movements were quite overwhelming, so he rearranged them into 108 movements. The number 108 is also preferred by the Chinese people, having significance in Chinese lunar mathematics, superstitions and religion. After years of experience, he felt that 108 movements were overly repeated and did not address the most important parts of the Dummy, so he change them to 116 total movements, left and right. However, by using the way that I have learned the Dummy, I will demonstrate the original 108 motions as practiced on the right side and the left side. Repeating these motions will enable the practitioner to become fluid in pivoting, stepping, sweeping, and the blocking of different angles. The more the practitioner performs these movements the faster he will become; the movements will become second nature, and they will be executed without even thinking.

The first 60 motions in the section are based on applications and techniques from Siu Leem Tau (little idea) and Chum -Q (searching for the bridge) form. These techniques are used to teach you hand-and-legs flow in JKD. Principles of simultaneous blocking and attacking, and theory concerning the alternating of hands in the centerline, are incorporated into the motions. Each technique should be completed, and the power released on contact with the Dummy, before the next motion has begun. This will develop the correct power for the motion. Moving around the Dummy with the correct stance, and completing the motion by the time the next stance stops, will develop body unity. By using natural power, not strength, when striking the Dummy and by releasing power at the correct time, you develop stronger hands, forearms, and legs by bone-packing. All of these skills, developed on Mook John, will build a better Jeet Kune Do foundation.

The second half of the Dummy form is based on applications of emergency techniques from the Biu Jee form (shooting fingers), which is the fourth form in Wing Chun Gung Fu. You are shown Biu-Jee only if you can first demonstrate the 60 motions fluidly. The Wooden Dummy will help develop more JKD hand-and-leg combinations. In addition, Biu Jee emergency techniques are designed to recover or regain the line when you have lost it during a close fighting situation. In the second half of the Dummy form, there are many kinds of hand-and-leg combination techniques to regain lost position. There are also ginger fist and phoenix punches, which are considered more advanced because, to be effective, they require more body unity and coordination. The very last set with the Dummy combines a series of leg attacks and blocks, coordinating with hand control to develop leg flow. Practicing the Mook Joang will improve your overall ability in JKD, and develop many valuable skills in fighting. You will also find it very useful in tight fighting, as it helps deliver much more power from a very short distance (like the 1" PINCH). What it will also help you with is developing your simultaneous blocking/striking, with added footwork. Through the years, I have found it to be one of the most practical forms that I have ever practiced. This is not to knock the other forms down, as I think they are very important; but as for me, I have gained from always having a partner, 24 –7, and whenever I needed to practice, it was always there. Furthermore, it did improve my speed, coordination, and complex motions like block punch, and block punch kick, etc. That is why I am demonstrating this form: hopefully you will find it very useful, and will help improve your training.

TRADITIONAL WING CHUN DUMMY

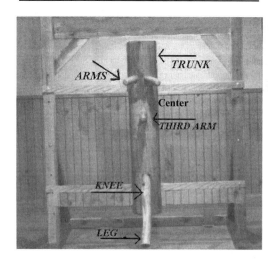

JKD WOODEN DUMMY

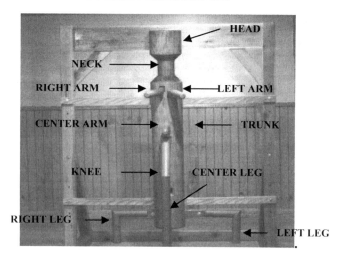

EXPLANATION OF THE DUMMY

The techniques are executed as if the Dummy is a real opponent, facing you for an attack.

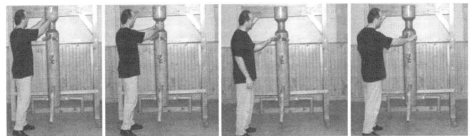

SHAPED LIKE HEAD   SHAPED LIKE NECK   RIGHT ARM   LEFT ARM

CENTER ARM   THE TRUNK OR THE BODY   THE KNEE   THE LEG

THESE FEATURES ARE AVAILABLE ONLY ON THE JKD DUMMY, NOT THE TRADITIONAL DUMMY

RIGHT SIDE LEG   LEFT SIDE LEG   THE KNEE   CENTER LEG

THE JKD LEG IS USED FOR MANY DIFFERENT APPLICATIONS

FOOT WORK

FOOT WORK IS REQUIRED TO PRACTICE THE (MOOK JOANG)

1) **JING MA** (CENTER NATURAL STANCE)
2) **CHO MA** (STANCE PIVOT OR SIDE PIVOT)
3) **TOH MA** (STEP SLIDE ADVANCE)
4) **TOY MA** (RETREATING STANCE)
5) **SEEP MA** (MOTION-INTERCEPTING, OR THREE-POINT STANCE)
6) **SOONG MA** (ADVANCE STEP THROUGH)
7) **LOY SEEN WHY** (INSIDE STEP AND FACE)

CHO MA (PIVOT STANCE)

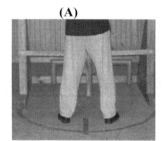
(A) NATURAL STANCE (JING MA)

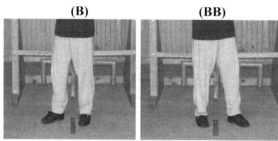
(B, BB) PIVOT ON THE HEEL OF THE FOOT, SIDE TO SIDE, SIMULTANEOUSLY

SEEP MA (MOTION INTERCEPTING OR THREE POINT STANCE)

RIGHT SIDE

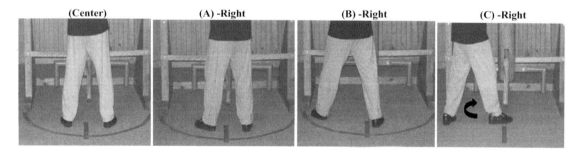
(Center)   (A) -Right   (B) -Right   (C) -Right

LEFT SIDE

(Center) (A) -Left) (B) -Left) (C) -Left

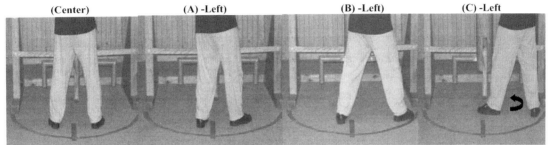

From a starting point **Jing Ma)**, pivot out **(Cho Ma)**, and step with the front foot as the rear foot circles around and slides behind the leg of the Dummy. The rear foot becomes the front foot by sliding behind the leg. Repeat the same footwork on the opposite side. You must remain inside the imaginary red circle to maintain the proper distance between you and the Dummy.

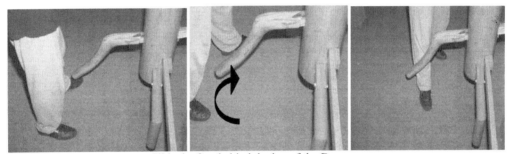

Slide the foot behind the leg of the Dummy.

TOH MA/ SOONG MA/ TOH MA

Toh Ma (step-slide advance), **Toy Ma** (retreating stance), and **Soong Ma** (advance step through) all have the same motion and positioning of the feet.

PROPER HANDS POSITIONING

TUN SOW — LOP SOW — CHUNG GANG — NOY KWAN SOW

Showing hand — Grab or pull — Throat squeeze — outside rolling hands

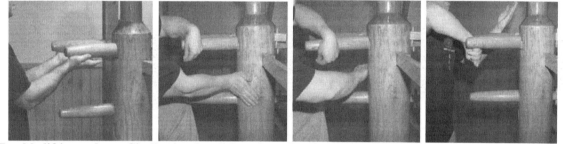

NOY KWAN SOW — LOY JUT SOW — BIU JON SOW — SOONG LOY JUT SOW

Outside rolling hands - Inside jerking hand - Thrusting hand - Double inside jerking hand

SOONG POW JAN - HUEN / CHUNG DIE JAN - HUEN / FUN SOW - HUEN / JOM SOW OR LOY KWAN

Double lifting palms - Circling/angle spade palm - Circling/ chopping hand - Inside rolling hand

HUEN / JOM SOW OR LOY KWAN - WOO/BONG SOW - DIE BONG — HUEN SOW

Inside rolling hand - Wing arm deflection - Low wing arm deflection - Circling hand, two fingers pinched, three closed

| LOP /CHUNG JAN | LOY JUT SOW/CHUNG JAN | LOY JUT/JING JAN | TUN SOW/CHUNG DIE JAN |

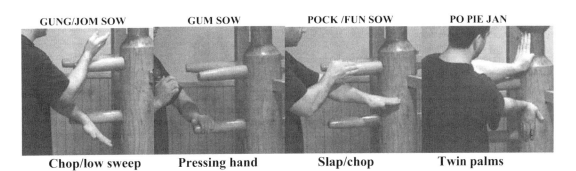

Grab/angle spade palm - Inside jerking hand/angle spade palm Vertical palm - Showing hand /angle spade   palm

| GUNG/JOM SOW | GUM SOW | POCK /FUN SOW | PO PIE JAN |

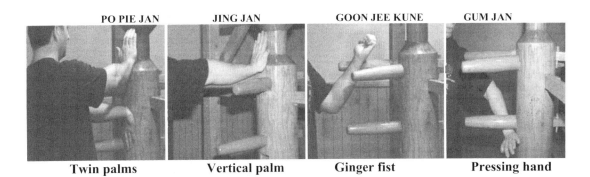

Chop/low sweep   Pressing hand   Slap/chop   Twin palms

| PO PIE JAN | JING JAN | GOON JEE KUNE | GUM JAN |

Twin palms   Vertical palm   Ginger fist   Pressing hand

| HUEN/FUN SOW | JEEP SOW | LOY JUT/CHOON CHOY | TUN DA |

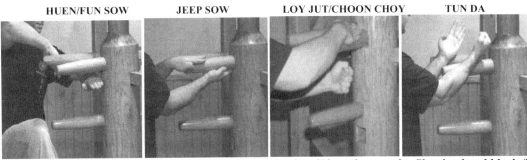

Circle /chopping hand - Catching hand - Inside jerking hand/thrusting punch - Showing hand block /hit

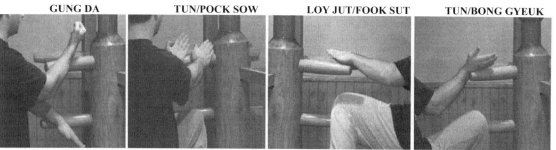

GUNG DA — TUN/POCK SOW — LOY JUT/FOOK SUT — TUN/BONG GYEUK

Low sweep block /hit - Showing/slapping hand- Inside jerking hand/bridging knee - Showing hand/wing leg

CHOP CHOY/CHO KUNE — POCK/ FOON NON-KUNE — POCK/ CHO KUNE

Low hammer — Phoenix punch — Slapping hand/low hammer

POCK/CHO KUNE — LOY JUT/CHOON CHOY — L OY JUT/CHOP KUNE

Slapping hand/low hammer - Inside jerking hand/vertical punch - Inside jerking hand/ horizontal punch

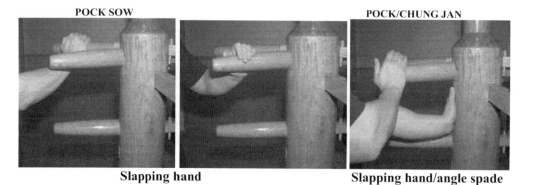

POCK SOW — POCK/CHUNG JAN

Slapping hand — Slapping hand/angle spade

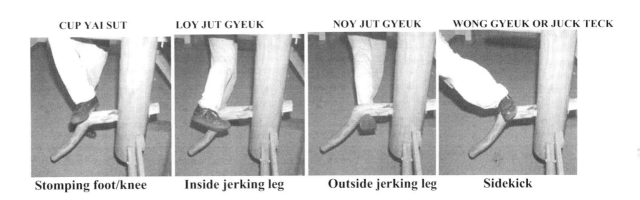

| TUN/POCK SOW/TIE SUT | GUNG /JOM SOW | QUACK SOW/SOONG HUEN SOW |

Showing/slapping hand/raising knee - Low sweep /chop - Spreading hand/double circling hands

| CUP YAI SUT | LOY JUT GYEUK | NOY JUT GYEUK | WONG GYEUK OR JUCK TECK |
| Stomping foot/knee | Inside jerking leg | Outside jerking leg | Sidekick |

JING GYEUK

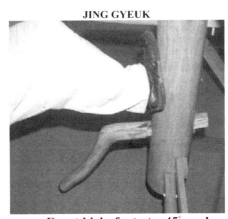

Front kick: foot at a 45° angle

WOODEN DUMMY APPLICATIONS

  These Dummy applications will give you a general idea of how the techniques are applied in real-life situations. The techniques are not executed exactly as they are portrayed on the Wooden Dummy. This is so because a real person moves and the Wooden Dummy does not. However, the principle of the techniques are executed the same way in real-life situations, depending on the attack and how it is brought on: either just from standing still, or from a raging charge. No Matter what the attack is, after practicing with the Wooden Dummy you should be able to apply the techniques to their fullest. Also you should be able to block and counter, from any position, without even thinking. This is good, because in real-life situations, you're are not going to say "Maybe movement #5 or movement #10 will work well against this attack" — because if you think, you have lost already. I am only demonstrating some of the applications, just to give you a jump-start. I believe that every practitioner should be able to come up with his or her applications from the same technique. For example, from the photo below, there are many applications I could generate from this technique. It can be a throat squeeze (which it is), but I could strike to the throat with a tiger's mouth — or it could be a grab just to control his neck for a take-down. Each person should have his or her own ideas of what the technique can or can't do. Don't be limited. Also, my defense will be somewhat <u>classical</u>, and not from a By-Jon fighting stance. The reason is that a JKD practitioner should be able to block from any position, whether it's a fighting stance, or a natural stance. Also, you do not walk on the street in a By-Jon stance, but you can switch from a natural stance to a fighting stance and execute the same techniques that are done on the Dummy. From a pivoted position, you can apply them to a real person from a By-Jon position.

LOP or TUN SOW/ CHUNG GANG

  Apply this defense against a hook, cross or jab by pivoting at a 45° angle and counter-attack with a block strike to the throat. Also, you can step forward as you still control the neck and arm, slide your right foot behind his right foot and take him down.

BONG SOW   **TUN CHUNG DIE JAN**

If he attacks with a jab cross or vice versa, you simply carry both attacks with the same-hand **Yut Fook Yee** principle. (One hand carries two attacks.) Deflect the first attack, then block on the outside of his second attack as you strike him to the rib with an open palm.

Example (1)   **Example (2)**   **Example (3)**

GUNG /JOM SOW is never executed simultaneously in a real-life situation, as far as JKD is concerned, because you don't want to tie up both hands in a blocking position. Always use either a high or low block, then strike. If the attack is executed with a cross, you defend it by chopping the outside of his arm at a 45° cutting angle, then counter attack. If he attacks with a straight punch to the abdomen, then you still block on the outside and counter-strike. If you block on the inside of his attack, then you're opening a can of worms: he can come with his own counter-attack.

DIE BONG SOW

The low arm deflection block is used against a low attack; by deflecting his attack, you can follow up with a counter-strike. Also, I like to use it in a tight place or when pinned against the wall — when you don't have much room, all you need is a pivot of the hips, and then the block is executed effectively.

TUN/CHUNG DIE JAN

Outside block and counter with an open palm to the ribs, against a cross or a jab. In the same position against the same attacks, you can simply deflect his attacks by chopping his elbow. There is no need for an extra strike unless necessary because by training on the Wooden Dummy for a long time your blocks become strikes.

HUEN /CHOON KUNE   **SOONG JUT SOW.**

This defense is used as an add-on to the outside block, like the **Jom Sow.** You can simply circle the rear hand on the inside of his wrist as you strike to the face with a straight punch or an open hand. You must execute both block-strikes simultaneously; otherwise, you're going to open yourself up for an attack. The next attack can be a lapel grab or front choke — just simply jerk him inward to loosen him up as you give a knee to the groin or a head-butt to the face.

SOONG POW SOW   **POCK SOW**

If your opponent's grasp is particularly tight, pop both of his elbows up lifting him off his feet. He will let go. The **Pock Sow** block is effective against a straight cross or jab. You can parry using **Pock Sow** followed up with a strike

POCK SOW   **WOO / FUN SOW**

Another use of a **Pock Sow** block is to clamp on the wrist as a full committed block. You can also follow up with a chop to the throat from a **Pock Sow** blocking position.

JUT DA /CHOW KUNE /or TIE KUNE **LOY JUT SOW**

After blocking an upper cut jab or cross, you have a choice of either striking low to the abdomen or high to the head.
By redirecting your opponent's line of attack, you open him up for a counter attack under the chin with either a shovel hook attack or a raised punch.

LOY JUT SOW **BIU JON SOW**

In deflecting your opponent's double hook attacks on the inside, your rear hand must remain in the guarding hand position for an effective defense. Rotating your hip and pivoting your feet will strengthen your center of gravity adding power to your stance.

HUEN/ CHUNG DIE JAN

Your opponent attacks with a jab, block from the inside with a **Biu Jon,** then circle his wrist out with **Huen Sow** as you strike him on the outside with an open palm to the ribs.

HUEN SOW OR GWAT SOW/ PO PIE JAN

From an outside block, position yourself to circle on the inside of your opponent's attack. As you step slide, simultaneously strike low to the groin area and high to the face both with open palms.

JUT SOW JING JAN

Deflect your assailant's attack using the heel of your hand as you strike with your open palm to the face.

TUN SOW/JING GYEUK /CHUNG JAN

You can either block high and kick low; or block and strike high with an open palm to the face as you kick low to the knee.

POCK SOW /CHUNG JAN OR CHOON CHOY

A simultaneous block strike counter attack can be used against any jab or cross. Step forward and meet the attack with a block and a counter strike to the ribs. This Maneuver can also be executed with a left tun Sow to the outside as you strike to the ribs.

POCK SOW /NOY JUT GYEUK **CUP YAI SUT OR JING GYEUK/ POCK SOW/ FOON NON-KUNE**

As your opponent jabs, block the attack, hook your front foot behind his knee, and then pull him off balance. Alternative maneuvers would be to block strike and stomp his knee simultaneously, or just block strike and front kick him to the groin.

BONG SOW

For added power and to throw your opposition off target, deflect a jab or cross as you pivot both feet and rotate the hips.

WOO SOW **JING JAN**

As you block an attack on the inside, maintain your rear hand on guard for extra defense. Step slide and strike your adversary in the face with the same hand.

JING JAN

You can strike your attacker with an open palm to the face from any position.

TIE SUT

It can be used to strike or block. In addition, it can be used against any circular kick (front round house or rear round house), by raising the knee to waist level.

JUCK TECK **TUN DA**

Counter a roundhouse kick with a sidekick to your opponent's base leg thereby knocking him off balance. You can also block his jab or cross with either a simultaneous or complex attack block hit with the left or right hand.

TUN DA

GUNG DA

Another complex attack can be executed against a strike to the abdomen by simultaneously blocking low and striking high to the face.

LOY FOOK SUT   **JUCK TECK OR WONG GYEUK**

Raise your knee to waist level to block your attacker and force him back off balance. You can stop an attack of kicks to the knee by intercepting your opponent before he executes any kick attacks at all.

JUCK TECK OR WONG GYEUK

Side kick to the knee area when he raises his leg to execute a kick.
The counter kick will stop your assailant's attack and knock him backwards.

Hoy Sick Sequence (OPENING THE STANCE)

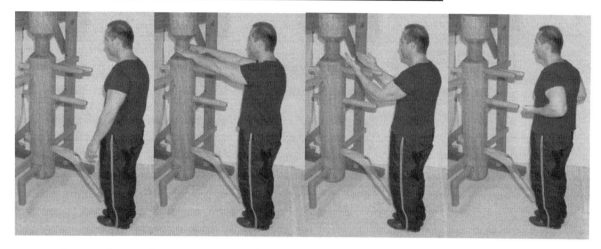

In a natural stance, feet together, arms very relaxed by your side, the **Hoy Sick** sequence (opening stance) begins. With both hands open, touch the edge of your finger against the neck of the Dummy at shoulder height. Chop **Soong Jom Sow** (double chopping hands) to the outside arms of the Dummy. Retract the fists (**Sow Kune**), back straight, elbows approximately one fist distance away from the ribs, fists about one finger distance away from the hips.

Front view only.   Bend the knees forward   **Hoy Ma** (open the horse)

Open the horse, **Front view only.**   **Yee Jee Kim Yin Ma** (character 2 pigeon toe horse stance).   **Front view only'**

Open both feet in a wide "**V**" formation, heel to heel, but without actually touching. With a slight bend of the knees pivot both feet pointing inward.

1) Left side set

Movement (1) a

Movement (1) b

Movement (2) a

1) A – both hands in **Woo Sow**- (guarding hand) position. Place left hand right on the centerline. **1) B** - left **Tun Sow** (showing hand) or **Biu Jon Sow** (shooting hand) **2) A** - **Cho Ma** (pivot stance) left **Lop Sow** (grab or pull)

In a **Yee Jee Kim Yin Ma,** right and left hand in **Woo Sow** position block the inside right arm of the Dummy with a left **Biu Jon Sow**, rear hand in **Woo Sow**. Grab the inside right arm of the Dummy and pull **Lop Sow** with the left hand as you pivot out **(Cho Ma)**. "Note" both feet pivot simultaneously on the heel of the foot when you **Cho -Ma.**

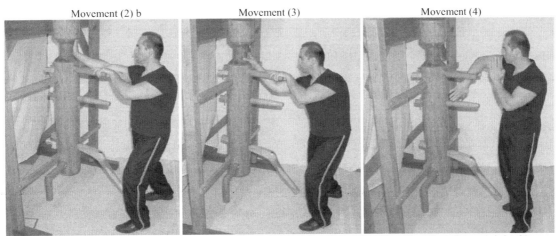
Movement (2) b   Movement (3)   Movement (4)

2) B-Cho Ma (pivot stance) **Lop/Chung Die Jan** (grab/spade palm strike) **3)** - **Cho Ma** left **Lop**/ right **Chung Gang** (squeeze the throat)
4) -**Cho Ma** (pivot stance) right **Bong Sow** (wing arm deflection)

In pivoted position left **Cho Ma**, left **Lop Sow** to the inside right arm of the Dummy, with the right hand **Chung Die Jan** to the head or the neck. While still controlling the arm with **Lop Sow**, right squeeze the neck and sink the elbow down slightly. Right block to the inside arm of the Dummy with **Bong Sow** as you still maintain the left **Woo** and **Cho Ma** pivoted position.

Movement (5) a

Movement (5) b

5) A, B- Seep Ma (motion intercepting) **Tun Sow** (showing hand) **Chung Die Jan** (low spade palm)

Circle and slide around the leg of the Dummy. Then step around the leg of the Dummy and slide through all three moves. Motion intercepting is also called **Seep Ma** (three point stance), right **Tun Sow**, to the outside right arm .of the Dummy, then left **Chung Die Jan** to the body.

Movement (6)

Movement (7)

6) - Toy Ma (retreating stance) **Gung/Jom Sow** (chopping hand, low sweep block) **7) – Toh Ma** (step slide) **Noy Kwan Sow** (out side rolling hand)

Toy Ma left **Jom Sow** to the outside right arm of the Dummy, right low **Gung Sow** to the center arm, **Jom /Gung Sow** simultaneously. Then **Toh Ma/ Noy Kwan Sow** right hand strikes the inside left arm of the Dummy as the left hand strikes the center arm. Both **Die Bong** and **Tun Sow** are called **Noy Kwan Sow.**

8) A -**Seep Ma** (three point stance)   8) B- **Tun Sow** (showing hand) **Chung Die Jan** (low spade palm)
9) -**Toy Ma** (retreating stance) **Gung / Jom Sow** (chop, low sweep block)

Seep Ma around the leg of the Dummy. Place left **Tun Sow** against the outside left arm of the Dummy, and **Toh Ma** low **Chung Die Jan.** Strike with the right hand to the body as you **Toy Ma/ Gung Sow** with your left arm to the center arm of the Dummy. Right **Jom Sow** to the outside left arm of the Dummy. You must execute the footwork and the strikes simultaneously.

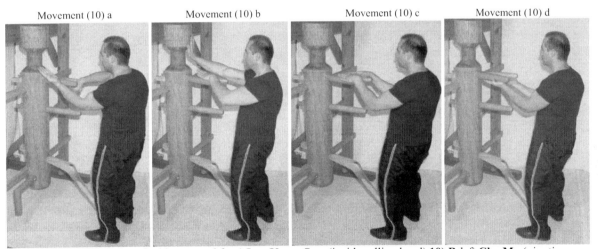

10) A - **Loy Seen Why** (inside step and face) **Loy Kwan Sow** (inside rolling hand) 10) B-left **Cho Ma** (pivoting stance) left **Jut Sow** (jerking hand), right **Jing Jan** (vertical palm) 10) C **Jing Ma** (center stance) **Soong Loy Jut Sow** (double inside jerking hands) 10) D - Feet together **Soong Pow Jan** (double lifting palms)

Loy Seen Ma. Huen Sow (circling hand) to the inside left arm of the Dummy, left **Jom Sow** to the outside right arm of the Dummy. Done simultaneously, they are called **Kwan Sow** (rolling hand). Left **Jut Sow** to the top right arm of the Dummy, right **Jing Jan** to the face. Pivot back to position at a natural stance **Soong Loy Jut Sow**, **Soong Pow Jan** to both arms.

2) Right side set

The same exact techniques that were done on the left side will now be done on the right side. The only difference is that the last motion has a slight change.
Do not confuse the position of the Dummy. Some shots were taken from the left side to give a better view.

Movement (11) a   Movement (11) b   Movement (12) a

11) A - right and left **Woo Sow** (guarding hand) **11) B** - right **Tun Sow** (showing hand) or **Biu Jon Sow** (shooting hand) **12) A** - right **Cho M**a (pivoting stance) right **Lop Sow** (grab or pull).

Face the Dummy with the left and right hands in **Woo Sow** or **Biu Jon Sow,** block the inside left arm of the Dummy with a right **Biu Jon Sow**, and maintain your rear hand in **Woo Sow**. Grab and pull **Lop Sow** the inside left arm with the right hand as you pivot out **(Cho Ma)**.

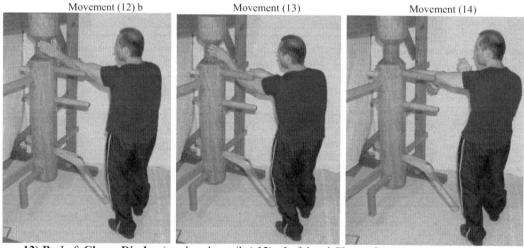

Movement (12) b   Movement (13)   Movement (14)

12) B - Left **Chung Die Jan** (spade palm strike) **13)** - Left hand **Chung Gang** (squeezes the throat)
14) - Left **Bong Sow** (wing arm deflection)

In pivoted position right **Lop Sow** the inside left arm of the Dummy to the left. **Chung Die Jan** striking to the head or the neck. Left squeeze, as you sink the elbow down slightly. Right **Cho Ma**, left arm blocks **Bong Sow** to the inside left arm of the Dummy as you maintain right **Woo** in a pivoted position.

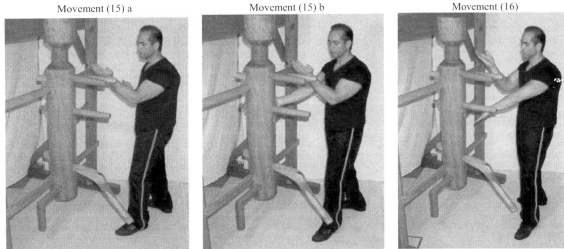

15) A – Seep Ma (three point stance) **15) B - Tun Sow** (showing hand) **Chung Die Jan** (low spade palm) **16)** - **Toy Ma** (retreating stance) **Gung Jom Sow** (chop, low sweep block) **19)** -**Toy Ma** (retreating stance) **Gung /Jom Sow** (chop low sweep)

Seep Ma step and face around the leg of the Dummy. Place left **Tun Sow** against the outside left arm of the Dummy. As you step slide execute a low **Chung Die Jan** strike with the right hand to the body. Step out **Toy Ma, Gung Sow** with the left hand to the center arm. Right **Jom Sow** to the outside left arm of the Dummy. You must do both strikes simultaneously.

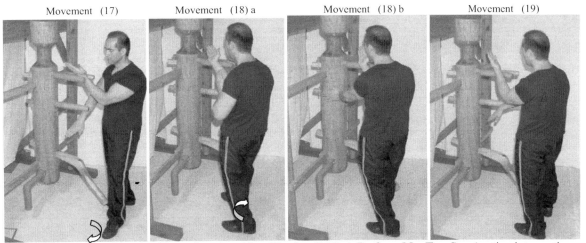

17) -**Toh Ma** (step slide) **Noy Kwan Sow** (outside rolling hand) **18) A-B** - **Seep Ma, Tun Sow** (motion intercepting, showing hand) **Chung Die Jan** (low spade palm)
19)-**Toy Ma** (retreating stance) **Gung /Jom Sow** (chop low sweep)

Toh Ma left **Tun Sow** to the inside right arm of the Dummy, right **Die** (low) **Bong Sow** to the center arm (done together, this sequence is called **Noy Kwan Sow**). **Seep Ma** step around the leg of the Dummy, block **Tun Sow** with the right hand to the outside right arm of the Dummy, **Chung Die Jan** with the left hand to the body. Step slide left **Jom Sow** to the outside right arm of the Dummy. Right **Gung Sow** to the middle arm.

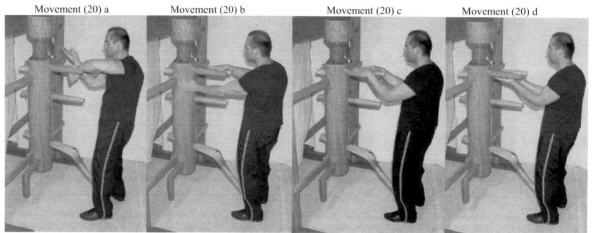

20) A - Loy Seen Why (inside step and face) **Loy Kwan Sow** (inside rolling hand) **20) B - Cho Ma** (pivot stance) **Jut Sow** (jerking hand) **Chung Die Jan** (low spade palm) **20) C- Jing Ma** (center stance), **Soong Loy Jut Sow** (double inside jerking hands). "Note- the **Low Chung Die Jan** is the only difference between the left set and the right set."
20) D- Jing Ma (center stance) **Soong Pow Jan** (double lifting palms)

Pivot left **Cho Ma,** left **Huen Sow** (circling hand) to the inside right arm of the Dummy. Right **Jom Sow** to the outside left arm of the Dummy. When they are done simultaneously, this sequence is called <u>**Kwan Sow**</u> (rolling hands). Right **Jut Sow** to the top left arm. Left **Chung Die Jan**, to the body of the Dummy. Pivot back into position. In a natural stance, **Jing Ma /Soong Loy Jut Sow** to both arms.

3) Starting right side set

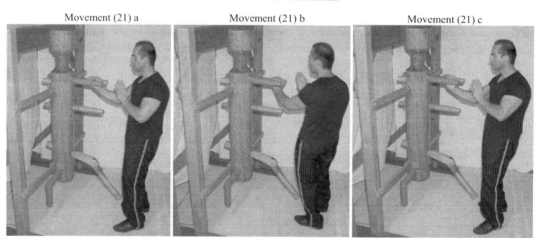

21) A - left pivot (**Cho Ma**) right **Pock Sow** (slapping hand) **21) B** - right pivot (**Cho Ma**) left **Pock Sow** (slapping hand) **21) C** - left pivot (**Cho Ma**) right **Pock Sow** (slapping hand)

Start with the right hand and left hand in **Woo Sow** (guarding hand) position. Left **Cho Ma** as you **Pock Sow** the inside right arm of the Dummy. Pivot left **Cho Ma** as you **Pock Sow** the inside left arm of the Dummy. Rear hand in **Woo Sow** (guarding hand) pivot, **Cho Ma Pock Sow** the inside right arm of the Dummy, rear hand in **Woo Sow** (guarding hand). "Note both the hands and feet must move simultaneously for body unity."

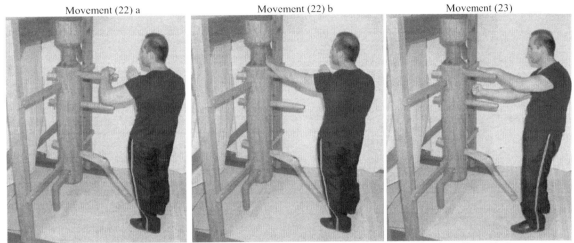

Movement (22) a   Movement (22) b   Movement (23)

22) A - pivot right (**Cho Ma**) left **Cow Sow** (catching hand) **22) B** - left **Fun Sow 23)** -pivot **Jing Ma** (center stance left) **Jut Sow** (jerking hand) right **Choon Kune** (straight vertical punch) or **Tie Kune** (raising punch)

Right pivot **Cho Ma**, as you pull in **Cow** with left hand to the top right arm of the Dummy. Right hand in **Woo Sow**, left **Fun Sow** to the neck, right hand in **Woo Sow** (guarding hand). Pivot back to the center. **Jing Ma** left **Jut Sow** to the top right arm. Right **Choon Kune** to the center, without making contact with the Dummy.

Movement (24) a   Movement (24) b   Movement (25) a

24) A - pivot left (**Cho Ma**) right **Cow Sow** (catching hand) **24) B** - right **Fun Sow 25) A** - pivot **Jing Ma** (center stance) right **Jut Sow** (jerking hand) left **choon kune** (straight vertical punch) or **tie kune** (raising punch)

Left pivot **Cho Ma** as you pull in **Cow** with right hand to the top left arm of the Dummy. Right **Fun Sow** to the neck. Left hand in **Woo Sow** (guarding hand) position, pivot back to the center with **Jing Ma**. Right **Jut Sow** to the top left arm, left **Choon Kune** to the center, without making contact with the Dummy.

25) B - Soong Loy Jut Sow (double inside jerking hands) **25) C - Soong Pow Jan** (double lifting palms)

Right on center. Pull in **Soong Loy Jut Sow**, push up. **Soong Sow Jan** to both arms.

4) Right side set

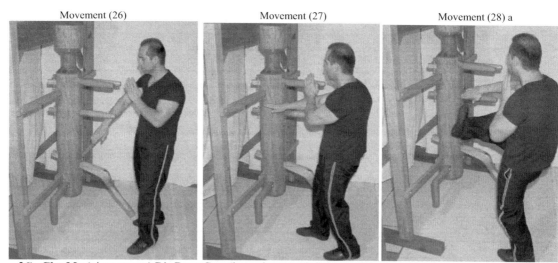

26) -Cho Ma (pivot stance) **Die Bong Sow** (low wing arm deflection) **27) - Toh Ma** (step slide) **Pock/ Fun Sow** (slapping hand/ chop) **28) A - Jick Teck** or **Jing Gyeuk** (front kick)

Pivot left, **Cho Ma** right, and **Die Bong** to the center arm. Left hand in **Woo Sow** (guarding hand), **Toh Ma** around the leg of the Dummy. Left **Pock Sow** to the outside right arm of the Dummy, right **Fun Sow** to the body. "Note: with the step around, **Pock Sow** and **Fun Sow** must be done simultaneously." Step back with your left hand in **Woo Sow,** right arm in **Bong Sow**. Right **Jick Teck** to the body of the Dummy. "Note: When kicking you must use the bottom of the foot and should connect at a 45° angle against the trunk."

28) B - step forward **28) C** - **Die Bong Sow** (low wing arm deflection) **29)** - **Toh Ma** (step slide) **Pock/ Fun Sow** (slapping hand/ chop) **30) A-Jick Teck** or **Jing Gyeuk** (front kick)

As you step in front of the Dummy left **Die Bong** to the center arm, right hand in **Woo Sow** (guarding hand), step around the leg of the Dummy and right **Pock Sow** to the outside left arm of the Dummy. Left **Fun Sow** to the body. "Note: the step around, **Pock Sow** and **Fun Sow** must be done simultaneously." Pull back, left **Jick Teck** to the body of the Dummy, foot at a 45° angle. Maintain front **Bong** and rear **Woo Sow**.

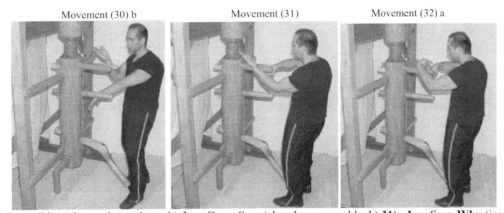

30) B - **Soong Ma** (advanced step through) **Jom Gung Sow** (chop low sweep block) **31)** - **Loy Seen Why** (inside step and face) **Loy Quack Sow** (inside rolling hands) **32)A** - start double **Huen Sow** (circling hands)

Pivot left **Soong Ma**; strike with right **Jom Sow** to the outside left arm of the Dummy. Left **Gung Sow** to the center arm. Pivot **Loy Seen Why** to the center, and right hand **Huen Sow** to the inside left arm of the Dummy. Left **Jom Sow** to the outside right arm of the Dummy. Circle in both hands to start the **Qwak Sow** motion.

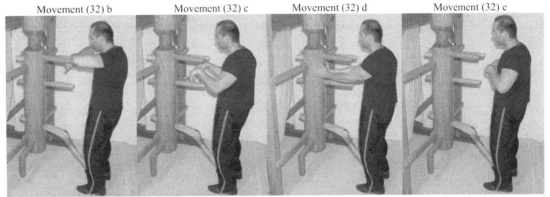

32) B- Jing Ma (center stance) **Quack Sow** (spreading hands) **32) C,D-Soong Chung Die Jan** (double low spade palms) **32) E** -pull the hands back

Right on center, two fingers pinched three closed, double **Huen Sow** (**Quack Sow**) to the inside arms of the Dummy. Strike, **Soong Chung Die Jan** to the body of the Dummy. Pull back toward your chest to generate power.

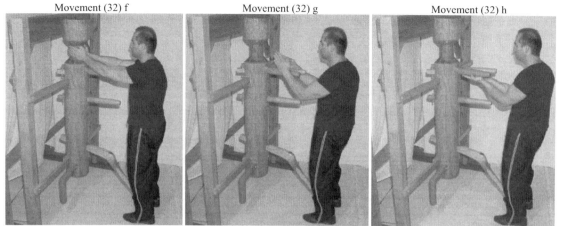

32) F- Soong Chung Jan (double angle spade palm strikes) **32) G - Soong Jut Sow** (double jerking hands)
32) H - Soong Pow Jan (double lifting palms)

Strike with **Soong Chung Jan** to the neck of the Dummy. Pull back **Soong Jut Sow** to the left and right arm. Using the edge of the wrist, elbows in, push up, **Soong Pow Jan** to the bottom of the arms.

5) Left side set

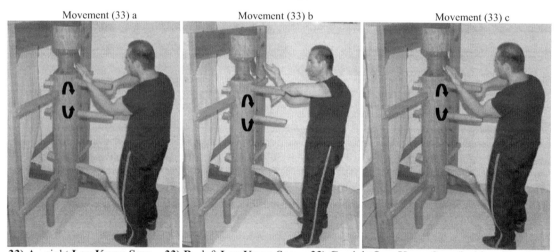

33) A - right Loy Kwan Sow   **33) B - left Loy Kwan Sow**   **33) C - right Loy Kwan Sow** (inside rolling hand)

Pivot right (**Cho Ma**) **Loy Kwan Sow**, pivot left (**Cho Ma**) **Loy Kwan Sow** pivot right (**Cho Ma Loy Kwan Sow**)
1) Right **Cho MA** right hand, two fingers pinched three closed, circle **Huen Sow** to the inside left arm of the Dummy. Left hand **Jom Sow** to the outside right arm of the Dummy. **2)** Left **Cho Ma**, left hand two fingers pinched three closed, circle **Huen Sow** to the inside right arm of the Dummy. Right hand **Jom Sow** to the outside left arm of the Dummy. **3)** Right **Cho Ma**, right hand, two fingers pinched three closed, circle **Huen Sow** to the inside left arm of the Dummy. Left hand **Jom Sow** to the outside right arm of the Dummy. Make sure you don't loose any contact with the arms as you circle with your hands in a clockwise circular motion.

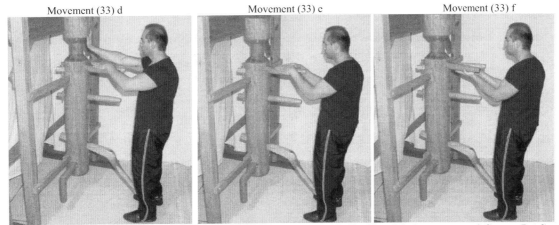

33) D - Cho Ma -Jut Sow (jerking hand) **Jing Jan** (vertical palm) **33) E - Jing Ma** (center stance) **Soong Jut Sow** (double jerking hands)   **33) F -Soong Pow Jan** (Double lifting palms)

Facing the Dummy, your left hand pulls in the top right arm of the Dummy with **Jut Sow,** as the right hand strikes the face with **Jing Jan**. Back to the center, pull in **Soong Jut Sow** to the top of the arms, and push up **Soong Pow Sow/ Jan** to the bottom of the arms.

6) Right side set

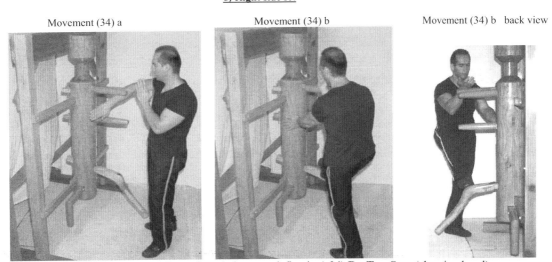

34) A- left pivot **(Cho Ma) Bong Sow** (wing arm deflection) **34) B - Tun Sow** (showing hand)
Chung Die Jan (low spade palm) **Cup Yai Sut** (knee stomping kick)

Pivot left, **Cho Ma** right **Bong Sow** to the inside right arm of the Dummy. Left hand in **Woo Sow** (guarding hand), step around the leg of the Dummy. Maintain contact with the right arm. Block **Tun Sow** with the right hand to the outside right arm of the Dummy. Left **Chung Die Jan** to the body. Right **Cup Yai Sut** to the knee of the Dummy. All three motions, **Tun, Chung Die Jan,** and **Cup Yai Sut** are done simultaneously.

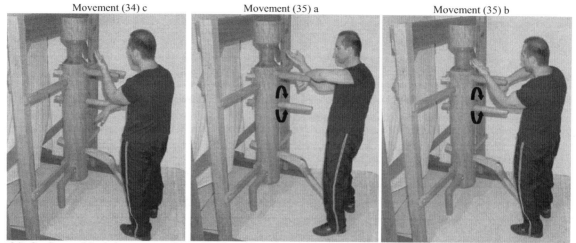

34) C - **Soong Ma** (advance step through) **Gung/Jom Sow** (chop, low sweep) pivot 35) A - **Loy Seen Why** (inside step and face) the Dummy **Loy Kwan Sow** (inside rolling hand) 35) B - pivot right **Cho Ma, Loy Kwan Sow.**

Right **Soong Ma**, left arm strikes the outside right arm of the Dummy with **Jom Sow** as right arm strikes the center arm. With **Gung Sow**, pivot to the center **Loy Seen Why**. Facing the Dummy, left hand, two fingers pinched three closed, **Huen Sow** to the inside right arm, and the right hand **Jom Sow** the outside left arm of the Dummy. **Huen** and **Jom Sow** are done simultaneously. Pivot right **Cho Ma**, right hand **Huen Sow**, two fingers pinched three closed, to the inside left arm, as left hand **Jom Sow** to the outside right arm of the Dummy in clock wise circular motion. This sequence should be executed without losing contact with the Dummy.

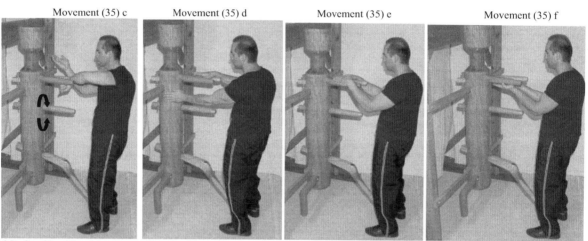

35) C - **Cho Ma -Loy Kwan Sow** (inside rolling hand) 35) D - **Cho Ma -Jut Sow** (jerking hand) **Chung Die Jan** (low spade palm) 35) E - **Jing Ma** (center stance) **Soong Jut Sow** (double jerking hands) 35) F - **Jing Ma** - (center stance) **Soong Pow Jan** (double lifting palms)

Pivot left **Cho Ma** facing the Dummy, left hand two fingers pinched three-closed, **Huen Sow** to the inside right arm of the Dummy as the right hand **Jom Sow** the outside left arm. **Huen** and **Jom Sow** are done simultaneously. Pivot right **Cho Ma**, right hand pulls in **Jut Sow** to the top left arm of the Dummy. Left hand **Chung Die Jan** to the body. **Jut Sow** and **Chung Die Jan** are done simultaneously. Face the Dummy, **Jing Ma**, feet together, pull in **Soong Jut Sow** to both arms of the Dummy. Feet together, push up **Soong Pow Jan** to both arms.

7) Left side set

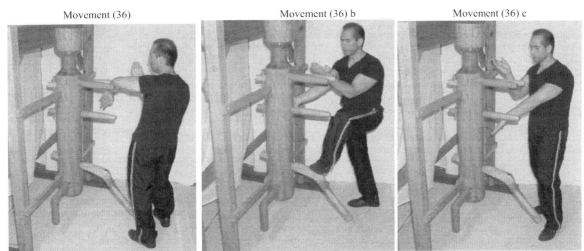

36) - **Cho Ma** (pivot stance) **Bong Sow** (wing arm deflection) 36) B - **Tun Sow** (showing hand) **Chung Die Jan** (low spade palm) **Cup Yai Sut** (stomping knee kick) 36) C - **Soong Ma** (advance step through) **Gung Jom Sow** (chop, low sweep)

Pivot right, **Cho Ma** left **Bong Sow** to the inside left arm of the Dummy. Right hand in **Woo Sow** (guarding hand), step around the leg of the Dummy, Maintain contact with the left arm, as you block **Tun Sow** with the left hand to outside left arm of the Dummy. Right **Chung Die Jan** to the body, left **Cup Yai Sut** to the knee of the Dummy. All three motions, **Tun, Chung Die Jan/Cup Yai Sut** are done simultaneously. Left **Soong Ma**, right hand strikes the outside left arm of the Dummy with **Jom Sow**, as the left hand strikes the center arm with **Gung Sow**.

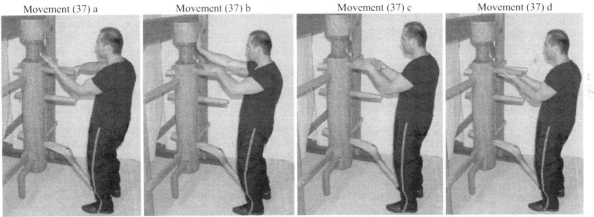

37) A - **Loy Seen Why Loy Kwan Sow** (inside step and face/inside rolling hand) 37) B - **Cho Ma Jut Sow** (jerking hand) **Jing Jan** (vertical palm) 37) C - **Jing Ma** (center stance) **Soong Loy Jut Sow** (double inside jerking hands) 37) D - **Jing Ma** (center stance) **Soong Pow Jan** (double lifting palms)

Right **Loy Seen Why**, right hand two fingers pinched three closed, **Huen Sow** to the inside left arm of the Dummy. The left hand strikes with **Jom Sow** to the outside right arm of the Dummy. Done together the sequence is called **Kwan Sow**. Pivot left, **Cho Ma** left, **Jut Sow** to the top right arm. Right **Jing Jan** to the face of the Dummy. Pivot to center **Jing Ma**, **Soong Loy Jut Sow** to both arms of the Dummy, elbows in. **Jing Ma Soong Pow Jan** to both arms of the Dummy.

8) Right side set

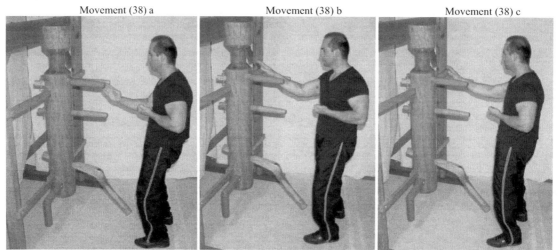

38) A - **Jing Ma** center stance **Fook Sow** (bridging hand) 38) B - **Jing Ma** (center stance) **Loy Jut Sow** (inside jerking hand) 38) C - **Jing Ma** (center stance) **Biu Sow** (thrusting hand)

Both feet on center **Jing Ma**, left hand is in a tight fist by your side, but not in contact with the ribs. Right hand is in center of both arms of the Dummy in **Fook Sow** position. Strike with right hand to the inside right arm of the Dummy with **Loy Jut Sow**. Maintain your stance; do not pivot. Strike the inside left arm of the Dummy with **Biu Sow**. Again, do not pivot.

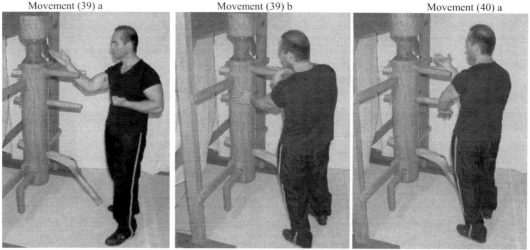

39) A - **Cho Ma** (pivot stance) **Jom Sow** (chopping hand) 39) B - **Loy Seen Why** (step and face) **Huen Sow** (circling hand) **Chung Die Jan** (low spade palm) 40) A - **Toh Ma** (step slide) **Noy Kwan Sow** (outside rolling hand)

Pivot left **Cho Ma** /**Jom Sow** to the inside right arm of the Dummy. **Loy Seen Why**, **Huen Sow**, the outside right arm of the Dummy. Left **Chung Die Jan** to the body, then **Toh Ma Noy Kwan Sow**. The right hand strikes the inside left arm of the Dummy as the left hand strikes the center arm. Then **Die Bong** and **Tun Sow** (done together this sequence is called **Noy Kwan Sow**).

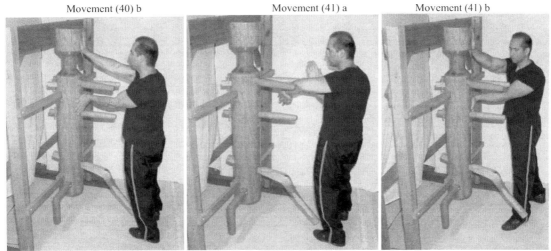

40) B - Jing Ma (center stance) **Po Pie Jan** (twin palm strike) **41) A - Cho Ma** (pivot stance) **Bong Sow** (wing arm deflection) **Woo Sow** (guarding hand)

41) B - Seep Ma (three point stance), **Po Pie Jan,** high **Jing Jan** (vertical palm), low **Pow Jan** (lifting palm). Done together this sequence is called **Po Pie Jan.**

Face the center **Jing Ma**; right hand strikes the face of the Dummy with **Jing Jan** as the left hand simultaneously strikes the body of the Dummy with **Pow Jan**. Pivot right **Cho Ma**, left **Bong Sow** to the inside left arm of the Dummy, and step around the leg with **Seep Ma.** Right hand strikes the face of the Dummy with **Jing Jan** while the left hand simultaneously strikes the body of the Dummy with **Pow Jan**.

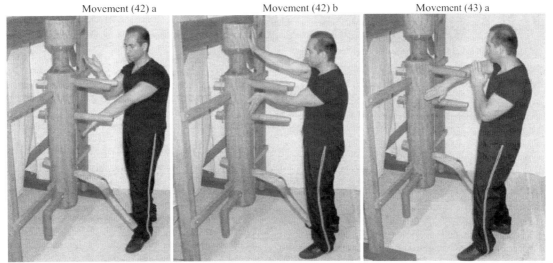

42) A - Toy Ma (retreating stance) **Gun/Jom Sow** (chop/low sweep) **42) B - Jing Ma** (center stance) **Po Pie Jan** (twin palms) **43) A -Cho Ma** (pivot stance) **Bong Sow** (wing arm deflection) **Woo Sow** (guarding hand)

Pivot left **Toy Ma**, right hand strikes the outside left arm of the Dummy. The left hand strikes the center arm of the Dummy. Both moves must be done simultaneously. Face the center **Jing Ma**, right hand strikes the face of the Dummy with **Jing Jan** as the left hand strikes the body with **Pow Jan.** Simultaneously pivot left **Cho Ma.** Right **Bong Sow** to the inside right arm of the Dummy as you Maintain rear **Woo Sow**.

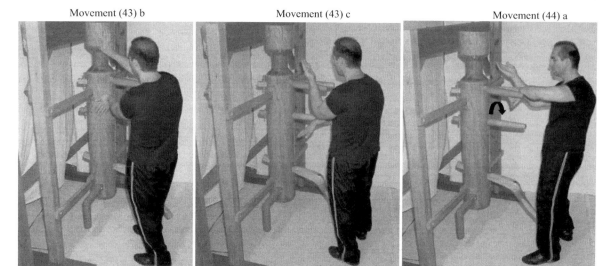

43) B - Seep Ma (three point stance) **Po Pie Jan** (twin palms) **43) C - Cho Ma** (pivot stance) **Gung Jom Sow** (chop low sweep) **44) A - Noy Seen Why** (outside step and face) **Loy Kwan Sow** (inside rolling hand)

Step around the leg of the Dummy with **Seep Ma**. Right hand strikes the face of the Dummy with **Jing Jan** as the left hand simultaneously strikes the body of the Dummy with **Pow Jan**. Pivot right **Cho Ma**, **Gung /Jom Sow** left arm strikes the outside right arm of the Dummy as the right hand strikes the center arm simultaneously. Pivot to the center and face the Dummy **Noy Seen Why/ Loy Kwan Sow**, left hand two fingers pinched three closed, **Huen Sow** (circling hand) with left hand to the inside right arm of the Dummy as the right hand strikes the outside left arm of the Dummy with **Jom Sow**. When the **Huen** and the **Jom Sow** are executed together they are called **Kwan Sow**.

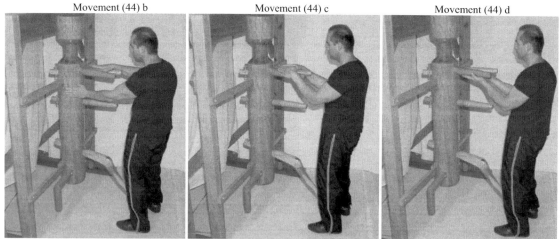

44) B - Jut Sow (jerking hand) **Chun Die Jan** (low spade palm) **44) C - Jing Ma** (center stance) **Soong Loy Jut Sow** (double inside jerking hands) **44) D - Jing Ma** (center stance) **Soong Pow Jan** (double lifting palms)

Pivot right **Cho Ma**, right hand **Jut Sow** to the top left arm of the Dummy as the left hand strikes the body with **Chung Die Jan**. Pivot to the center and face the Dummy. Pull in **Soong Jut Sow** to both arms of the Dummy, remain on center and push up, **Soong Pow Jan,** to both arms.

9) Left side set

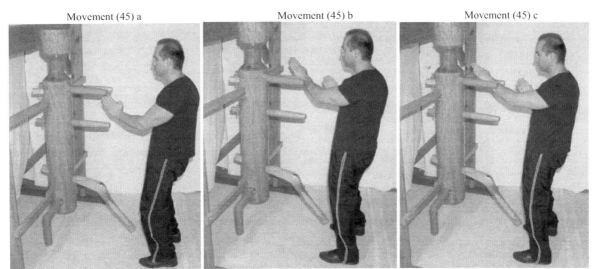

45) A - Jing Ma (center stance) **Fook Sow** (bridging hand) **45 B - Jing Ma** (center stance) **Loy Jut Sow** (inside jerking hand) **45) C - Jing Ma** (center stance) **Biu Sow** (thrusting hand)

With both feet on center **Jing Ma**, right hand is in a tight fist by your side. It is not however, in contact with the ribs. Left hand is in the center of both arms of the Dummy in **Fook Sow** position. Strike with left hand to the inside left arm of the Dummy with **Loy Jut Sow.** Do not pivot. Strike the inside right arm of the Dummy with **Biu Sow,** without a pivot.

46) A - Cho Ma (pivot stance) **Jom Sow** (chopping hand) **46) B - Loy Seen Why** (step and face) **Huen Sow** (circling hand) **Chung Die Jan** (low spade palm)
47) A - Toh Ma (step slide) **Noy Kwan Sow** (outside rolling hand)

Pivot right **Cho Ma**, left **Jom Sow** to the inside left arm of the Dummy. **Loy Seen Why**, **Huen Sow**, the outside left arm of the Dummy. Right **Chung Die Jan** to the body. **Toh Ma Noy Kwan Sow** left hand strikes the inside right arm of the Dummy, as the right hand strikes the center arm. Both **Die Bong / Tun Sow** are called **Noy Kwan Sow**.

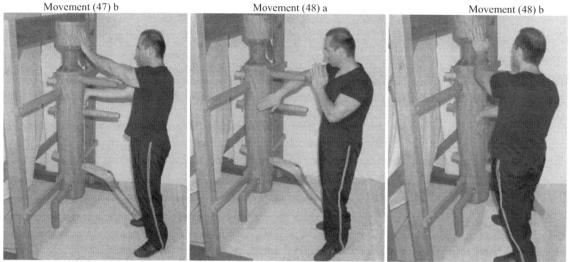

47) B - **Jing Ma** (center stance) **Po Pie Jan** (twin palm strike) 48) A - **Cho Ma** (pivot stance) **Bong Sow** (wing arm deflection) **Woo Sow** (guarding hand) 48) B - **Seep Ma** (three point stance) **Po Pie Jan** high **Jing Jan** (vertical palm) and low **Pow Jan** (lifting palm) together are called **Po Pie Jan.**

Face the center **Jing Ma**; left hand strikes the face of the Dummy with **Jing Jan** as the right hand simultaneously strikes the body of the Dummy with **Pow Jan**. Pivot left **Cho Ma**, right **Bong Sow** to the inside right arm of the Dummy. Step around the leg of the Dummy with **Seep Ma**. With your left hand strike the face of the Dummy with **Jing Jan** at the same time as the right hand strikes the body of the Dummy with **Pow Jan.**

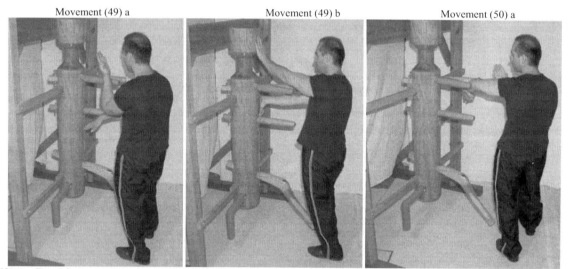

49) A - **Toy Ma** (retreating stance) **Gun/Jom Sow** (chop/low sweep) 49) B - **Jing Ma** (center stance) **Po Pie Jan** (twin palms) 50) A - **Cho Ma** (pivot stance) **Bong Sow** (wing arm deflection) **Woo Sow** (guarding hand)

Pivot right **Toy Ma**. Left hand strikes the outside right arm of the Dummy, as the right hand strikes the center arm of the Dummy. Both moves must be done simultaneously. Face the center **Jing Ma**. Left hand strikes the face with **Jing Jan** as the right hand strikes the body of the Dummy with **Pow Jan**. Simultaneously pivot right **Cho Ma**, left **Bong Sow** to the inside left arm of the Dummy as you maintain rear **Woo Sow**.

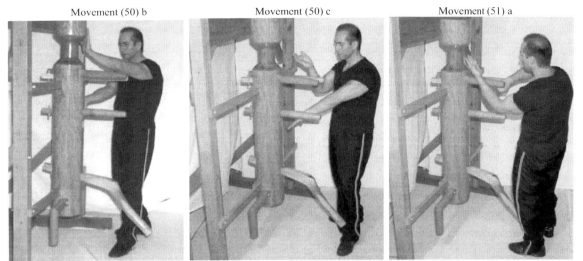

50) B - Seep Ma (three point stance) **Po Pie Jan** (twin palms) **50) C - Cho Ma** (pivot stance) **Gung Jom Sow** (chop low sweep) **51) A - Loy Seen Why** (inside step and face) **Loy Kwan Sow** (inside rolling hand)

Step around the leg of the Dummy with **Seep Ma.** Left hand strikes the face of the Dummy with **Jing Jan** as the right hand strikes the body of the Dummy with **Pow Jan.** Simultaneously pivot left **Cho Ma. Gung /Jom Sow** right arm strikes the outside left arm as the left hand strikes the center arm of the Dummy. Simultaneously pivot to the center and face the Dummy **Loy Seen Why Loy, Kwan Sow** right hand, two fingers pinched three closed. **Huen Sow** (circling hand) with right hand to the inside left arm of the Dummy as the left hand strikes the outside right arm of the Dummy with **Jom Sow.** When the **Huen** and the **Jom Sow** are executed together, they are called **Kwan Sow**.

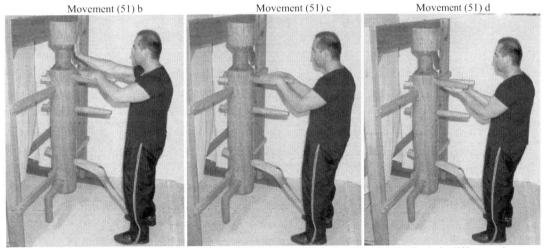

51) B- Jut Sow (jerking hand) **Jing Jan** (vertical palm) "Note: **Jut Da Jing Jan** is the only difference between movement **44) B** and **51) B**."
51) C- Jing Ma (center stance) **Soong Loy Jut Sow** (double inside jerking hands) **51) D - Jing Ma** (center stance) **Soong Pow Jan** (double lifting palms)

Pivot left **Cho Ma,** left hand **Jut Sow** to the top right arm of the Dummy as the right hand strikes the head with **Jing Jan.** Pivot to center and face the Dummy. Pull in **Soong Jut Sow** to both arms of the Dummy. Remain on center; push up **Soong Pow Jan** to both arms.

10) Left side set

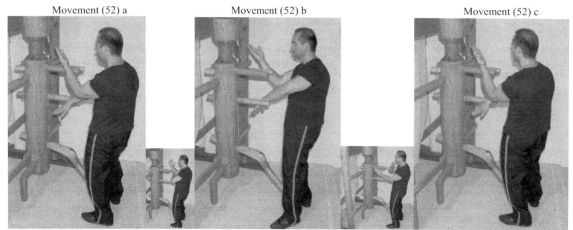

52) A - Cho Ma (stance pivot) **Gung/Jom Sow** (low sweep chop) **52) B - Cho Ma** (stance pivot) **Gung/Jom Sow** (low sweep chop) **52) C - Cho Ma** (stance pivot) **Gung/Jom Sow** (low sweep chop)

Pivot right **Cho Ma,** left hand strikes the outside right arm of the Dummy as the right hand strikes the center arm. All three motions: **Cho Ma/ Gung /Jom Sow** are executed simultaneously.

Pivot left **Cho Ma,** right hand strikes the outside left arm of the Dummy as the left hand strikes the center arm. All three motions: **Cho Ma /Gung /Jom Sow** are executed simultaneously.

Pivot right **Cho Ma,** left hand strikes the outside right arm of the Dummy as the right hand strikes the center arm. All three motions: **Cho Ma /Gung /Jom Sow** are executed simultaneously.
Practice to attain body unity in all three movements.

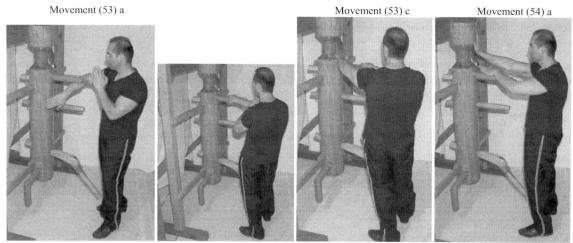

53) A-Cho Ma (pivot stance) **Bong Sow** (wing arm deflection) **53) C- Loy Seen Why** (inside step and face) **Lop Fun Sow** (pull or grab/ chop) **54) A - Noy Seen Why** (outside step and face) **Jut Sow** (jerking hand) **Jing Jan** (vertical palm strike)

Pivot left **Cho Ma,** strike the inside right arm of the Dummy with right **Bong Sow** maintaining rear hand in **Woo Sow** (guarding hand). Without breaking contact with the arm of the Dummy, step around the leg of the Dummy with **Noy Seen Why.** Grab, **Lop Sow** with the right hand to the outside right arm of the Dummy, and left **Fun Sow** to the throat of the Dummy.

Movement (54) b   Movement (54) c

54) B - Jing Ma (center stance) **Soong Loy Jut Sow** (double inside jerking hands) **54) C - Jing Ma** (center stance) **Soong Pow Jan** (double lifting palms)

Pivot left and face the center of the Dummy, left **Jut Sow** to the top right arm of the Dummy, as the right arm strikes the face or the neck, simultaneously with **Jing Jan**.
Remain in the same position. Facing the Dummy, pull in **Soong Jut Sow** to both arms of the Dummy as you push up, **Soong Pow Jan** to both arms.

11) Right side set

Movement (55) a   Movement (55) b   Movement (55) c

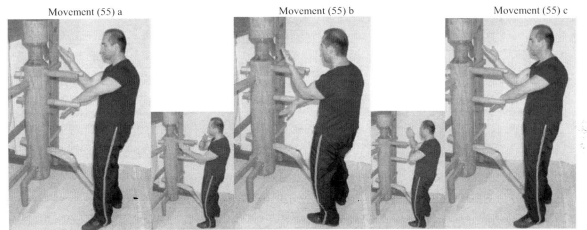

55) A - Cho Ma (stance pivot) **Gung/Jom Sow** (low sweep chop) **55) B - Cho Ma** (stance pivot) **Gung/Jom Sow** (low sweep chop) **55) C- Cho Ma** (stance pivot) **Gung/Jom Sow** (low sweep chop)

Pivot left **Cho Ma**, right hand strikes the outside left arm of the Dummy as the left hand strikes the center arm. All three motions: the **Cho Ma /Gung /Jom Sow** are executed simultaneously.

Pivot right **Cho Ma**, left hand strikes the outside right arm of the Dummy as the right hand strikes the center arm. All three motions: the **Cho Ma /Gung /Jom Sow** are executed simultaneously.

Pivot left **Cho Ma**, right hand strikes the outside left arm of the Dummy as the left hand strikes the center arm. All three motions: the **Cho Ma /Gung /Jom Sow** are executed simultaneously.
Practice to attain body unity in all three movements

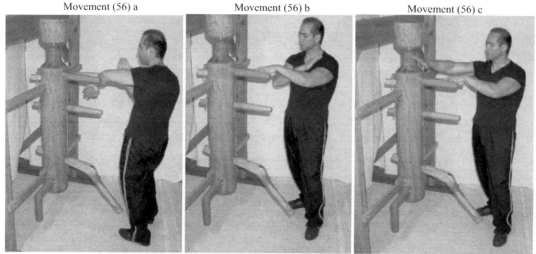

Movement (56) a   Movement (56) b   Movement (56) c

56) A - Cho Ma (pivot stance) **Bong Sow** (wing arm deflection) **56) B-C - Noy Seen Why** (outside step and face) **Lop Fun Sow** (pull or grab/ chop)

Pivot right **Cho Ma,** strike the inside left arm of the Dummy with left **Bong Sow** maintaining rear hand in **Woo Sow** (guarding hand). Step around the leg of the Dummy with **Noy Seen Why,** grab **Lop Sow** with the left hand to the outside left arm. Strike right **Fun Sow** to the throat.

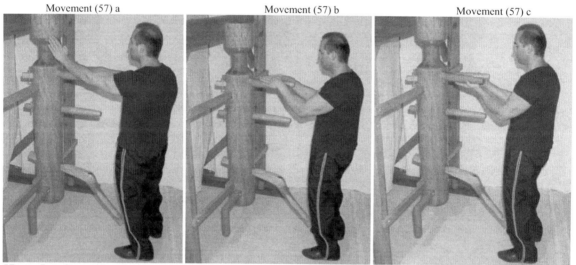

Movement (57) a   Movement (57) b   Movement (57) c

57) A - Loy Seen Why (inside step and face) **Jut Sow** (jerking hand) **Jing Jan** (vertical palm strike) **57) B - Jing Ma** (center stance) **Soong Loy Jut Sow** (double inside jerking hands) **57) C- Jing Ma** (center stance) **Soong Pow Jan** (double lifting palms)

Pivot right and face the center of the Dummy. Right **Jut Sow** to the top left arm as the left arm simultaneously strikes the face or the neck with **Jing Jan**. Still facing the Dummy, pull in **Soong Jut Sow** to both arms of the Dummy. Remaining on center, now push up **Soong Pow Jan** to both arms.

- 292 -

12) Right side set

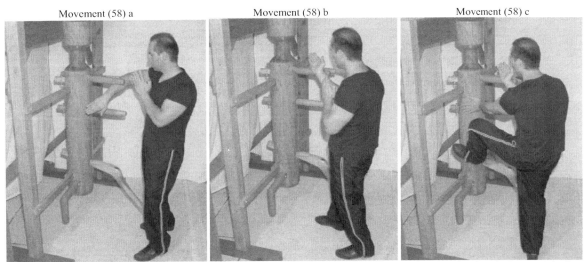

58) A – Cho Ma (pivot stance) **Bong Sow** (wing arm deflection) **58) B - C- Tun Sow** (showing hand) **Chung Die Jan** (low spade palm) **Mo Yin Teck** (invisible kick) or **Yai How Gyeuk** (rear stomp kick)

Pivot left **Cho Ma,** block with **Bong Sow** to the inside right arm of the Dummy. Without breaking contact with the arm, flip up to a **Tun Sow** strike to the body of the Dummy with a left **Chung Die Gyeuk,** done simultaneously.

58) D – Soong Ma (advanced step through) **Gung/Jom Sow** (low sweep chop)

Pivot right and strike with both hands. Left hand strikes the outside right arm of the Dummy as the right hand strikes the center arm.

59) A - Toh Ma (step slide) **Bong Sow** (wing arm deflection) **Woo Sow** (guarding hand) **59) B - C-Tun Sow** (showing hand) **Chung Die Jan** (low spade palm) **Mo Yin Teck** (invisible kick) or **Yai How Gyeuk** (rear stomp kick)

Pivot right **Cho Ma**, block with **Bong Sow** to the inside left arm of the Dummy. Without breaking contact with the arm, flip up to a **Tun Sow** strike to the body of the Dummy with a right **Chung Die Jan** as you execute a rear kick to the lower trunk. All three motions: the **Tun/Chung Die Jan /How Yai Gyeuk** are done simultaneously.

59) D - Soong Ma (advanced step through) **Gung/Jom Sow** (low sweep chop) **60) A– Loy Seen Why** (inside step and face) **Loy Kwan Sow** (inside circling hand) **60) B - Cho Ma** (pivot stance) **Jut Sow Jing Jan**

Pivot left, **Gung/Jom Sow** right hand strikes the outside left arm of the Dummy as the left hand simultaneously strikes the center arm. Pivot right **Cho Ma**, right hand with two fingers pinched and three fingers closed, **Huen Sow** to the inside left arm, as the left hand strikes with **Jom Sow** to the outside right arm of the Dummy, (both together are called **Kwan Sow**). Pivot to center and face the Dummy **Loy Seen Why**, left **Jut Sow** to the top right arm of the Dummy. Right **Jing Jan** to the face of the Dummy.

Movement (60) c   Movement (60) d

60) C - Jing Ma (center stance) **Soong Loy Jut Sow** (double inside jerking hands) **60) D - Jing Ma** (center stance) **Soong Pow Jan** (double lifting palms)

Facing the Dummy, pull in **Soong Jut Sow** to both arms of the Dummy. Remain on center and push up **Soong Pow Jan** to both arms of the Dummy.

(A) **Sow Kune**   (B) **Sow Sick**

Sow kune (retracting fist)   **Sow Sick** (closing the stance)

With both fists tight by your side, without touching your ribs -- elbows are one fist distance from your sides. Open your hands slowly then drop them down **Soong Gum Jan** (double pressing hands). **Sow Kune/Sow Sick** (A-B) are only optional for teaching purposes. You do not stop at the end of the 60 motions. The movements continue.

****

End of first 60 motions

13) Right side set

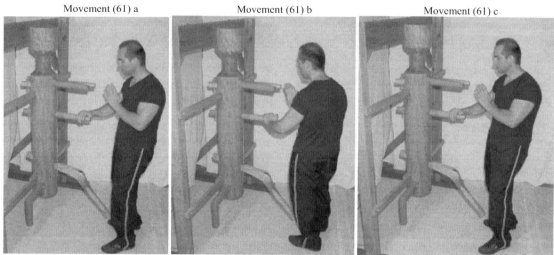

61) A - Cho Ma (pivot stance) **Gum Sow** (pressing hand) **61) B - Cho Ma** (pivot stance) gum Sow
61) C - Cho Ma (pivot stance) **Gum Sow** (pressing hand)

Pivot left **Cho Ma,** right **Gum Sow** the top center arm of the Dummy. Pivot right **Cho Ma,** left hand **Gum Sow** to the top of the center arm. Pivot again, left **Cho Ma,** right **Gum Sow** the top center arm, the rear hand must remain in **Woo Sow** position (guarding hand) on all three movements. In order to maintain body unity, your feet and hands must move simultaneously.

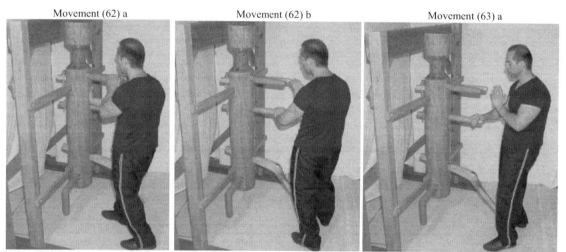

62) A - Seep Ma (three point stance) **Pock Sow, Chung Die Jan** (slapping hand, low angle spade palm) **62) B - Toy Ma** (retreating stance) **Gum Sow** (pressing hand) **63) A - Cho Ma** (pivot stance) **Gum Sow** (pressing hand)

Step around the leg of the Dummy with **Seep Ma.** Left hand **Pock Sow** to the outside right arm of the Dummy as the right hand strikes the body with **Chung Jan.**
Retreat **Toy Ma** as you block the center arm of the Dummy with left **Gum Sow.** Pivot left **Cho Ma**; block the center arm of the Dummy with right **Gum Sow.** Rear hand must remain in **Woo Sow** (guarding hand) on both left and right blocks.

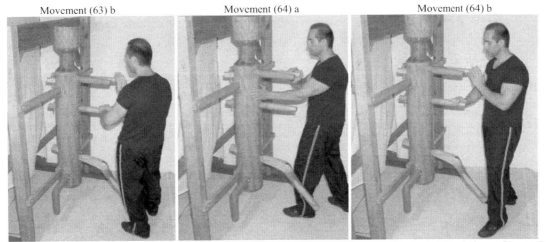

63) B - **Cho Ma** (pivot stance) **Gum Sow** (pressing hand) 64) A - **Seep Ma** (three point stance) **Pock Sow, Chung Die Jan** (slapping hand, low spade palm) 64) B - **Toy Ma** (retreating stance) **gum Sow** (pressing hand)

Pivot right **Cho Ma**, left **Gum Sow** to the top center arm of the Dummy, left hand in **Woo Sow** (guarding hand). Step around the leg of the Dummy with **Seep Ma**. Right hand **Pock Sow** to the outside left arm, at the same time as the left hand strikes the body of the Dummy with **Chung Die Jan**. Retreat back **Toy Ma**, right hand **Gum Sow** to the top center arm, left hand in **Woo Sow** (guarding hand).

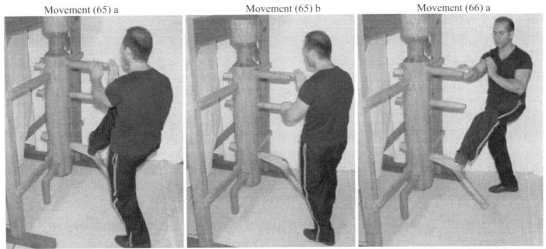

65) A - **Noy Seen Why** (outside step and face) **Pock Sow** (slapping hand) **Woo Sow** (guarding hand) **Die Gyeuk or Teck** (low leg or kick) 65) B- **Cho Ma** (stance pivot) **Gum Sow** (pressing hand) 66) A- **Noy Seen Why** outside (step and face) **Pock Sow** (slapping hand) **Woo Sow** (guarding hand) **Die Gyeuk or Teck** (low leg or kick)

Step around the Dummy with **Noy Seen Why**. Left hand **Pock Sow** to the outside right arm of the Dummy as the right leg simultaneously kicks the knee of the Dummy with the bottom of the foot. Right hand in **Woo Sow**, pivot right **Cho Ma**, left **Gum Sow** to the top center arm, right hand in **Woo Sow**. Step around the Dummy **Noy Seen Why**. Right hand **Pock Sow** to the outside left arm of the Dummy, as the left leg simultaneously kicks the knee of the Dummy with the bottom of the foot, while the left hand is held in **Woo**.

66) A - Cho Ma (stance pivot) **gum Sow** (pressing hand) **67) A - Noy Seen Why** (outside step and face) **Pock Sow** (slapping hand) **Woo Sow** (guarding hand) **Tiu Gyeuk** or **Teck** (instep leg/ kick) **68) A - Noy Jut Gyeuk** (outside jerking leg) **Woo Sow** (guarding hands)

Pivot left **Cho Ma,** right hand **Gum Sow** to the top center arm of the Dummy left hand in **Woo Sow.** Step around the Dummy with **Noy Seen Why,** left hand **Pock Sow** to the outside right arm, right hand in **Woo Sow.** Right foot hooks on the inside of the Dummy's knee as you lean back and jerk the leg backwards, while still maintaining balance on one foot and both hands in **Woo.**

68) B - Cho Ma (stance pivot) **Gum Sow** (pressing hand) **69) A - Noy Seen Why** (outside step and face) **Pock Sow** (slapping hand) **Woo Sow** (guarding hand) **Tiu Gyeuk** or **Teck** (instep leg/ kick) **70) A - Noy Jut Gyeuk** (inside jerking leg) **Woo Sow** (guarding hands)

Pivot right **Cho Ma,** left hand **Gum Sow** to the top center arm of the Dummy, right hand in **Woo Sow.** Step around the Dummy with **Noy Seen Why,** right hand **Pock Sow** to the outside left arm, left hand in **Woo Sow.** Hook the left foot on the inside of the Dummy's knee as you lean back and jerk the leg backwards, while still maintaining your balance with one foot and both hands in **Woo Sow.**

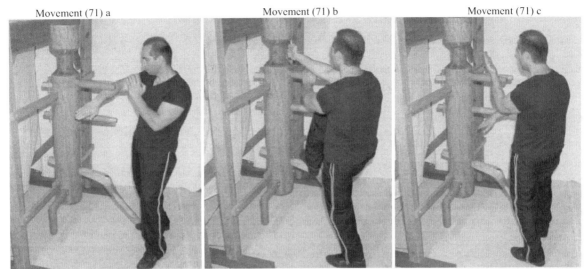

71) A - Toh Ma (step slide) **Bong Sow** (wing arm deflection) **Woo Sow** (guarding hand) **71) B - Pock Sow** (slapping hand) **Foon Non Kune** (phoenix punch) **Cup Yai Sut** (stomping knee kick) **71) C - Soong Ma** (step advance through) **Gung /Jom Sow** (chop /low sweep)

Pivot left **Cho Ma,** block with right **Bong Sow** against the inside right arm of the Dummy, left hand in **Woo Sow.** Without pivoting, block the outside right arm with a left hand **Pock Sow** as you punch with a right phoenix punch to the head. Stomp the Dummy's knee with the right foot. All three movements: **Pock /Foon Non Kune/ Cup Yai Sut** are done simultaneously. Pivot right **Soong Ma,** strike the outside right arm of the Dummy with left **Jom Sow** as the right hand strikes the center arm with **Gung Sow.** All three movements: **Soong Ma/ Gun/Jom** are done simultaneously.

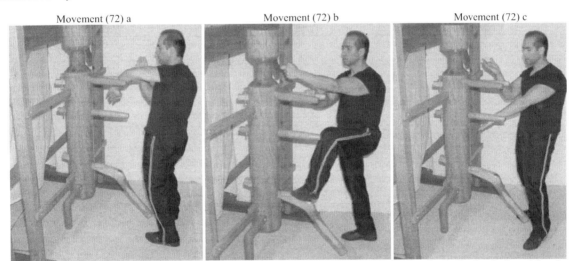

72) A - Toh Ma (step slide) **Bong Sow** (wing arm deflection) **Woo Sow** (guarding hand) **72) B - Pock Sow** (slapping hand) **Foon Non Kune** (phoenix punch) **Cup Yai Sut** (stomping knee kick) **72) C- Soong Ma** (step advance through) **Gung /Jom Sow** (chop /low sweep)

Pivot right **Cho Ma,** block with left **Bong Sow** against the inside left arm of the Dummy, right hand in **Woo Sow.** Do not pivot. Block the outside left arm of the Dummy with a right hand **Pock Sow** as you punch at the head with a left phoenix (without actually connecting). Stomp the Dummy's knee with the left foot. All three movements: **Pock /Foon Non Kune/ Cup Yai Sut** are done simultaneously. Pivot left **Soong Ma,** strike the outside left arm of the Dummy with right **Jom Sow** as the left hand strikes the center arm with **Gung Sow.** All three movements: **Soong Ma /Gum/Jom** are done simultaneously

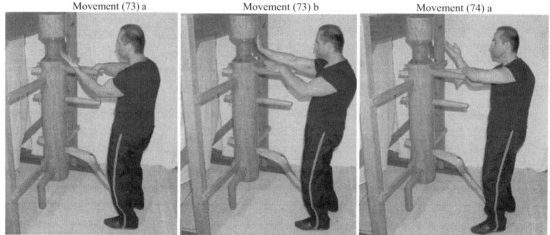

73) A - **Loy Seen Why** (inside step and face) **Loy Kwan Sow** (inside rolling hand) 73) B - **Cho Ma** (pivot stance) **Loy Jut Sow** (inside jerking hand) **Chung Jan** (angle spade palm) 74) A - **Cho Ma** (pivot stance) **Loy Kwan Sow** (inside rolling hand)

Pivot right **Cho Ma**, right hand with two fingers pinched and three fingers closed. **Huen Sow** (circling hand) to the inside left arm of the Dummy as the left hand **Jom Sow's** to the outside right arm. Work for body unity in all three motions. Pivot **Huen /Jom** are all done at the same time. Pivot left **Cho Ma**, left hand **Jut Sow** to the top of the right arm as the right hand strikes the head or the neck of the Dummy. Pivot left **Cho Ma**, left hand with two fingers pinched and three fingers closed, **Huen Sow** (circling hand) to the inside right arm of the Dummy as the right hand **Jom Sow's** to the outside left arm.

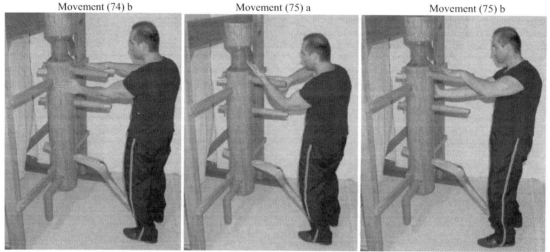

74) B - **Cho Ma** (stance pivot) **Jut Sow** (jerking hand) **Chung Die Jan** (low spade palm) 75) A - **Cho Ma** (pivot stance) **Loy Kwan Sow** (inside rolling hand) 75) B - **Jut Sow** (jerking hand) **Chung Die Jan** (low spade palm)

Pivot right **Cho Ma**, left hand strikes the body of the Dummy with **Chung Die Jan** as the right hand **Jut Sow** to the top left arm. Stay in pivoted **Cho Ma** position, right hand with two fingers pinched and three fingers closed, **Huen Sow** (circling hand) to the inside left arm of the Dummy as the left hand **Jom Sow's** to the outside right arm. Pivot left **Cho Ma**, left hand **Jut Sow** to top right arm as the right hand strikes the body of the Dummy with **Chung Die Jan**.

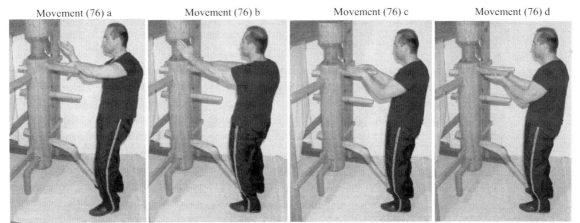

Movement (76) a | Movement (76) b | Movement (76) c | Movement (76) d

76) A - **Cho Ma** (pivot stance) **Loy Kwan Sow** (inside rolling hand) 76) B - **Cho Ma** (pivot stance) **Jut Sow** (jerking hand) **Chung Jan** (angle spade palm) 76) C - **Jing Ma** (center stance) **Soong Loy Jut Sow** (double inside jerking hand) 76) D - **Jing Ma** (center stance) **Soong Pow Jan** (double lifting palms)

Pivot left **Cho Ma,** left hand with two fingers pinched and three fingers closed, **Huen Sow** to the inside right arm of the Dummy. The right hand strikes with **Jom Sow** to the outside left arm of the Dummy, (both done together are called **Kwan Sow**). Pivot to the center and face the Dummy **Loy Seen Why**, right **Jut Sow** to the top left arm of the Dummy as the left hand **Chung Jan** to the face of the Dummy. Facing the center pull in **Soong Jut Sow** to both arms. Remain facing center, push up **Soong Pow Jan** to both arms of the Dummy.

14) Right side set

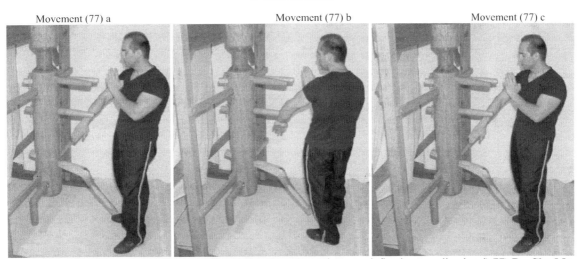

Movement (77) a | Movement (77) b | Movement (77) c

77) A - **Cho Ma** (pivot stance) **Die Bong Sow /Woo Sow** (low wing arm deflection guarding hand) 77) B - **Cho Ma** (pivot stance) **Die Bong Sow /Woo Sow** (Low wing arm deflection guarding hand) 77) C - **Cho Ma** (pivot stance) **Die Bong Sow /Woo Sow** (low wing arm deflection guarding hand)

Pivot left. Right hand strikes the center arm of the Dummy as the left hand remains in **Woo Sow** position, which is right on the center line. Repeat the same move two more times, pivot right simultaneously as the left hand strikes the center arm. This time the right hand remains in the **Woo Sow** position. Then pivot left while simultaneously the right hand strikes the center arm and the left hand remains in **Woo Sow** position on the center.

Movement (77) d   Movement (77) e

77) D - Cho Ma (pivoted stance) **Goon Jee Kune** (ginger fist) **Woo Sow** (guarding hand) **77) E -** In **Cho Ma** position **Jing Jan** (vertical palm)

Remain in pivoted **Cho Ma** position. Right-hand strikes the inside left arm of the Dummy with **Goon Jee Kune** as the left hand remains on centerline in **Woo Sow** position. In **Cho Ma** position, strike **Jing Jan** with the right hand to the face of the Dummy.

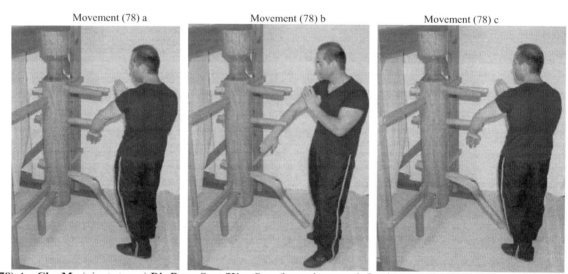

Movement (78) a   Movement (78) b   Movement (78) c

78) A - Cho Ma (pivot stance) **Die Bong Sow /Woo Sow** (low wing arm deflection guarding hand) **78) B - Cho Ma** (pivot stance) **Die Bong Sow /Woo Sow** (low wing arm deflection guarding hand) **78) C - Cho Ma** (pivot stance) **Die Bong Sow /Woo Sow** (low wing arm deflection guarding hand)

Pivot right. Left hand strikes the center arm of the Dummy while the right hand remains in **Woo Sow** position, which is right on the center line. Repeat the same move two more times. Pivot left while simultaneously the right hand strikes the center arm of the Dummy, and the left hand remains in the **Woo Sow** position. Then pivot right simultaneously while the left hand strikes the center arm of the Dummy and the right hand now remains in the **Woo Sow** position on the center.

78) D - Cho Ma (pivoted stance) **Goon Jee Kune** (ginger fist) **Woo Sow** (guarding hand) **78) E** - in **Cho Ma** position **Jing Jan** (vertical palm)

Remain in pivoted **Cho Ma** position. Left hand strikes the inside right arm of the Dummy with **Goon Jee Kune** while the right hand remains on the centerline in **Woo Sow** position. Remaining in **Cho Ma** position, place a left **Jing Jan** strike to the face of the Dummy.

79) A - Cho Ma (pivot stance) **Die Bong Sow** (low wing arm deflection) **Woo Sow** (guarding hand) **80) A - Cho Ma** (pivoted stance) **Gum Jan** (pressing palm) **Woo Sow** (guarding hand)

Pivot left **Cho Ma** with right **Die Bong Sow** to the center arm of the Dummy while the left hand remains in **Woo Sow** position. Strike down with the heel of the hand, **Gum Sow** to the body of the Dummy, left hand remains in **Woo**.

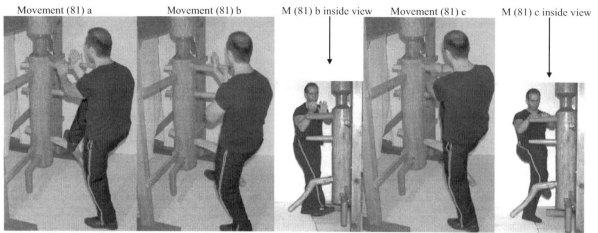

Movement (81) a   Movement (81) b   M (81) b inside view   Movement (81) c   M (81) c inside view

81) A - Noy Seen Why (outside step and face) **Tun Sow** (showing hand) **Pock Sow** (slapping hand) **Tie Sut** (raising knee) **81) B - Woo Sow** (guarding hand) **Jut Teck** or **Gyeuk** (jerking leg kick) **81) C- Soong Lop Sow** (double grab) **Tie Sut** (raising knee)

Step around the leg of the Dummy with **Loy Seen Why** as you block the outside right arm with **Tun/Pock Tie Sut,** all executed simultaneously. With the right knee only blocking the center arm of the Dummy, lean back slightly, and place both hands in **Woo Sow** position right on the center. Strike down with a right **Jut Teck** without contacting the leg of the Dummy. Grab with both hands, **Soong Lop Sow** to the outside right arm as you raise the knee up and strike with right **Tie Sut** connecting with the bottom center arm.

Movement (82) a   Movement (82) b

82) A - Soong Ma (step advance through) **Die Bong Sow** (low wing arm deflection) **Woo Sow** (guarding hand) **82) B - Gum Jan** (pressing palm) **Woo Sow** (guarding hand)

Pivot right and step through **Soong Ma**. As you block with left **Die Bong Sow** to the center arm of the Dummy, the right hand remains in **Woo Sow**. Strike down with the heel of the hand, **Gum Sow** to the body of the Dummy, right hand in **Woo**.

83) A - **Noy Seen Why** (outside step and face) **Tun Sow** (showing hand) **Pock Sow** (slapping hand) **Tie Sut** (raising knee) 83) B - **Woo Sow** (guarding hand) **Jut Teck** or **Gyeuk** (jerking leg kick) 83) C - **Soong Lop Sow** (double grab) **Tie Sut** (raising knee)

Step around the leg of the Dummy with **Noy Seen Why** as you block the outside left arm with **Tun/Pock Tie**, all executed simultaneously. With the left knee only blocking the center arm of the Dummy, lean back slightly, and place both hands in **Woo Sow** position right on the center. Strike with a left **Jut Teck** down without connecting with the leg of the Dummy. Grab with both hands. **Soong Lop Sow** to the outside left arm as you raise the knee up and strike with a left **Tie Sut** connecting with the bottom center arm.

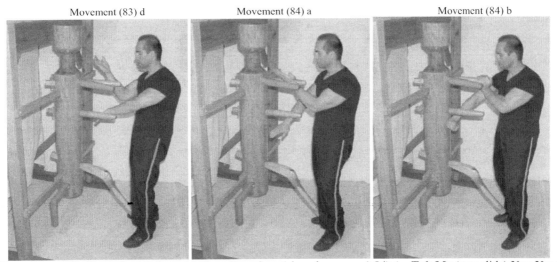

83) D - **Soong Ma** (step advance through) **Gung/Jom Sow** (chop, low sweep) 84) A - **Toh Ma** (step slide) **Noy Kwan Sow** (outside rolling hand) 84) B - **Pock Sow** (slapping hand) **Chop Choy** or **Cho Kune** (low hammer punch)

Step advance **Soong Ma**, left hand strikes the center arm of the Dummy with low **Gung Sow** as the right hand simultaneously strikes the outside left arm with a **Jom Sow**. Step slide **Toh Ma /Noy Kwan Sow**. Left hand blocks the inside right arm of the Dummy with **Tun** as the right hand blocks with **Die Bong Sow** to the center arm. Both are done at the same time. Remain in the same stance while the left hand blocks the inside left arm of the Dummy with **Pock Sow** and the right hand strikes the body of the Dummy with **Chop Choy**. Both are done simultaneously.

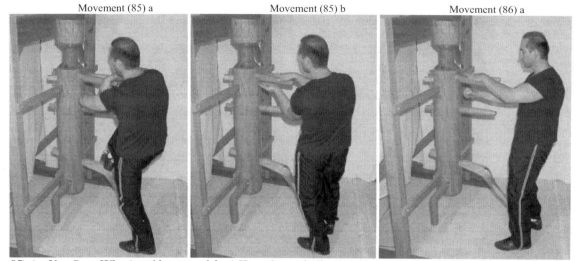

85) A - Noy Seen Why (outside step and face) **Huen Sow** (circling hand) **Fun Sow** (horizontal chop) **Cup Yai Sut** (stomping knee kick)
85) B- Soong Ma (advance step through) **Jeep Sow** (catching hand) **86) A - Cho Ma** (pivot stance) **Jut Sow** (jerking hand) **Choon Kune** (thrusting vertical punch)

Step around the leg of the Dummy with **Noy Seen Why**. Right hand with two fingers pinched and three closed, **Huen Sow** to the outside right arm of the Dummy as the left hand places a **Fun Sow** to the body, while the right leg stomps down on the knee of the Dummy with a **Cup Yai Sut. Huen/Fun Sow/Cup Yai Sow** all are executed simultaneously. Step **Soong Ma,** right hand presses down the top right arm of the Dummy as the left hand pushes up the bottom side. Both attacks are done simultaneously to create a breaking motion. Pivot and face the center of the Dummy, left hand pulls in **Jut Sow** the top right arm as the right hand punches to center without contacting the Dummy, thus creating a **Chey Kune** motion (retracting extension punch).

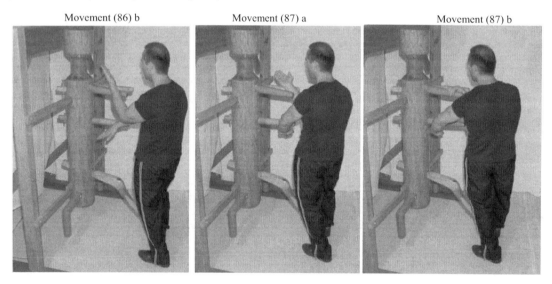

86) B - Soong Ma (step advance through) **Jung/Jom Sow** (chop low sweep) **87) - A Toh Ma** (step slide) **Noy Kwan Sow** (outside rolling hand) **87) B - Pock Sow** (slapping hand) **Chop Choy or Cho Kune** (low hammer punch)

Step advance **Soong Ma**. Right hand strikes the center arm of the Dummy with low **Gung Sow** as the left hand strikes the outside right arm of the Dummy with **Jom Sow**. Step slide **Toh Ma/ Noy Kwan Sow**. Right hand strikes the inside left arm with **Tun** as the left hand blocks **Die Bong Sow** to the center arm of the Dummy. Both are done at the same time. Remaining in the same stance, the right hand blocks the inside right arm of the Dummy with **Pock Sow** while the left hand strikes the body with **Chop Choy**. Both are done simultaneously.

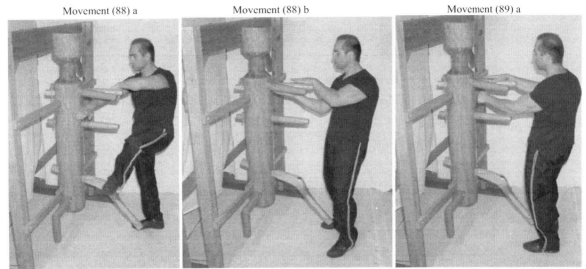

88) A - **Noy Seen Why** (outside step and face) **Huen Sow** (circling hand) **Fun Sow** (horizontal chop) **Cup Yai Sut** (stomping knee kick) 88) B -**Soong Ma** (advance step through) **Jeep Sow** (catching hand)
89) A - **Cho Ma** (pivot stance) **Jut Sow** (jerking hand) **Choon Kune** (thrusting vertical punch)

Step around the leg of the Dummy with **Noy Seen Why**. Left hand with two fingers pinched and three fingers closed, **Huen Sow** to the outside left arm of the Dummy as the right hand places **Fun Sow** to the body. The left leg simultaneously stomps down on the knee of the Dummy with **Cup Yai Sut**. **Huen/Fun Sow/Cup Yai Sow** -- all are executed simultaneously. Step **Soong Ma.** Left hand presses down the top left arm of the Dummy as the right hand pushes up the bottom side. Both attacks are done simultaneously to create a breaking motion. Pivot to face the center of the Dummy. Right hand pulls in **Jut Sow** to the left arm as the left hand punches to center without connecting with the Dummy, thereby creating a **Chey Kune** motion. (Retraction extension punch)

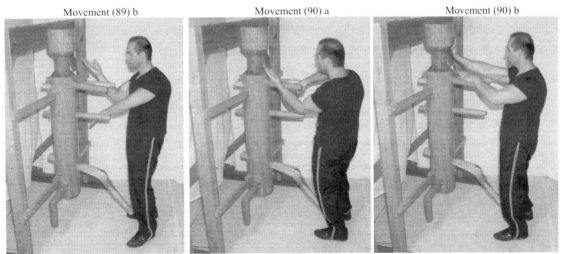

89) B - **Soong Ma** (advanced step through) **Gung/Jom Sow** (low sweep chop) 90) A - **Loy Seen Why** (inside step and face) **Loy Kwan Sow** (inside circling hand) 90) B – **Cho Ma** (pivot stance) **Jut Sow Jing Jan**

Pivot left **Gung/Jom Sow** right hand strikes the outside left arm as the left hand simultaneously strikes the center arm of the Dummy. Pivot right **Cho Ma.** Right hand with two fingers pinched and three closed, **Huen Sow** to the inside left arm of the Dummy as the left hand strikes with **Jom Sow** to the outside right arm, (both done together are called **Kwan Sow**). Pivot to the center and face the Dummy **Loy Seen Why.** Left **Jut Sow** to the top right arm, as the right hand **Jing Jan** to the face of the Dummy.

Movement (90) c

Movement (90) b

90) C - Jing Ma (center stance) **Soong Loy Jut Sow** (double inside jerking hand) **90) C - Jing Ma** (center stance) **Soong Pow Jan** (double lifting palms)

Facing the Dummy pull in **Soong Jut Sow** to both arms of the Dummy. Remain on center and push up **Soong Pow Jan** to both arms. Keep both elbows in while executing the lifting motion.

15) Right side set

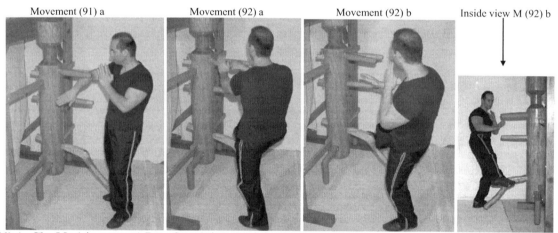

Movement (91) a   Movement (92) a   Movement (92) b   Inside view M (92) b

91) A -Cho Ma (pivot stance) **Bong Sow** (wing arm deflection) **Woo Sow** (guarding hand) **92) -A Noy Seen Why** (outside step and face) **Lop** (grab) **Pock Sow** (Slapping hand) **Mo Yin Gyeuk** or **Teck** (invisible kick or leg -oblique kick) **92)-B Loy Jut Gyeuk** (inside jerking leg)

Pivot left **Cho Ma,** block with **Bong Sow** to the inside right arm of the Dummy, left hand in **Woo Sow**. Step around the leg **Noy Seen Why Lop/Pock/** to the out side right arm, as right leg simultaneously strikes the knee of the Dummy with **Mo Yin Gyeuk**. Pivot the rear foot at a 90° angle as you jerk back with the right toes hooking on the outside of the Dummy's knee by maintaining full balance, while also keeping your rear hand in the **Woo Sow** position.

Movement (93) a   Movement (93) b

93) A - Toh Ma (step slide) **Loy Jut Sow Choon Kune/Ping Choy** (thrusting vertical punch or horizontal) **93) B - Toy Ma** (step slide) **Loy Jut Sow** (inside jerking hand) **Chop Kune/Ping Choy** (thrusting horizontal punch)

Step slide forward **Toh Ma** left hand **Loy Jut Sow** the top right arm of the Dummy, left hand **Choon Kune** to the midsection, but without contact. **Toh Ma/Jut Sow/Chop Kune** are done simultaneously. Repeat the same technique with other hand, in reverse. **Toh Ma** right hand, **Loy Jut Sow** the top left arm of the Dummy, left hand **Chop Kune** to the midsection, no contact. **Toh Ma/Jut Sow/Chop Kune** are done simultaneously.

Movement (94) a   Movement (95) a   Movement (95) b

94) A - Toy Pock Sow (slapping hand) **Mo Yin Gyeuk or Teck** (invisible kick or leg oblique) **95) - B Loy Jut Gyeuk** (inside jerking leg)

Step back **Toh Ma** left block with **Bong Sow** to the inside left arm of the Dummy, right hand in **Woo Sow**. Circle around the leg of the Dummy as you block .**Noy Seen Lip/pock** to the out side left arm, as the left leg simultaneously strikes the knee of the Dummy with **Mo Yin Gyeuk**. Pivot the rear foot at a 90° angle as you hook the left toes on the knee of the Dummy. Jerk back taking care not to lose your balance, while also keeping your rear hand in **Woo Sow** position.

- 309 -

96) A - Toh Ma (step slide) **Loy Jut Sow, Chop Kune** or **Ping Choy** (thrusting vertical or horizontal punch)
96) B - Toh Ma (step slide) **Loy Jut Sow** (inside jerking hand) **Chop Kune** or **Ping Choy** (thrusting vertical or horizontal punch)

Step slide forward, **Toh Ma** right hand, **Loy Jut Sow** the top left arm of the Dummy, right hand **Choon Kune** to the midsection without contact. **Toh Ma/Jut Sow/Choon Kune** are done simultaneously. Repeat the same technique with the other hand in reverse, **Toh Ma** left hand, **Loy Jut Sow** the top right arm of the Dummy, right hand **Chop Kune** to the midsection without contact. **Toh Ma/Jut Sow/Choon Kune** are all done simultaneously.

96) - C Jing Ma (center stance) **Soong Loy Jut Sow** (double inside jerking hands) **96) D - Jing Ma** (center stance) **Soong Pow Jan** (double lifting palms)

Facing the Dummy pull in **Soong Jut Sow** to both arms of the Dummy. Remain on center, push up **Soong Pow Jan** to both arms. You must keep your elbows in while executing the lifting motion.

16) Right side set

Movement (97) a   Movement (97) b   Movement (98) a

97) A -Cho Ma (pivot stance) **Tun Da** (showing hand block hit) **97) B - Cho Ma** (pivot stance) **Loy Jut Sow Choon Choy** (vertical thrusting punch) **98) A - Cho Ma** (pivot stance) **Tun Da** (showing hand block hit)

Pivot left **Cho Ma** left hand **Tun Sow** to the inside right arm of the Dummy as the left hand strikes the outside left arm with **Choon Kune** connecting with the arm. All three motions are done simultaneously, **Cho Ma/Tun/Da Choon Kune.** Pivot right **Cho Ma,** right hand pulls in **Loy Jut Sow** to the top right arm of the Dummy as left hand executes a **Choon Choy** to the midsection. Remain in the same position as you block the inside left arm of the Dummy with **Tun Sow** and simultaneously strike the outside right arm with a **Choon Choy**.

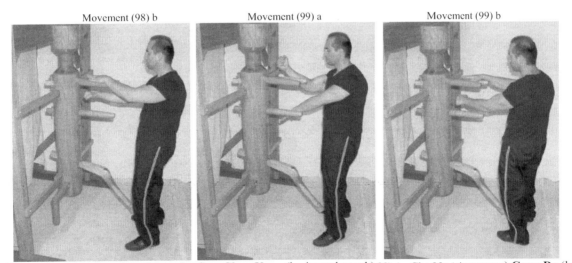

Movement (98) b   Movement (99) a   Movement (99) b

98) B - Cho Ma (pivot stance) **Loy Jut Sow Chop Kune** (horizontal punch) **99) A - Cho Ma** (pivot stance) **Gung Da** (low sweep block hit) **99) B - Cho Ma** (pivot stance) **Loy Jut Sow /Choon Choy** (vertical thrusting punch)

Cho Ma left, as the left hand pulls in **Loy Jut Sow** to the top right arm of the Dummy. Right hand places, without contact, a **Chop Kune** to the midsection. Pivot left **Cho Ma.** Left hand blocks the center arm of the Dummy as the right hand **Choon Kune** connects with the outside left arm. **Cho Ma** right, as the right hand pulls in **Loy Jut Sow** to the top left arm of the Dummy. Left hand **Choon Choy** to the midsection without contacting the trunk.

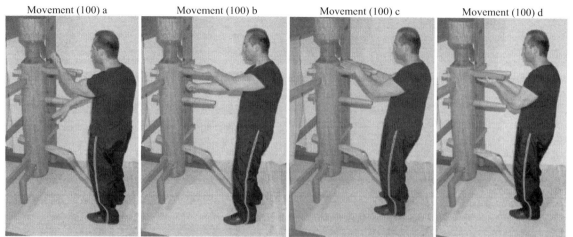

Movement (100) a   Movement (100) b   Movement (100) c   Movement (100) d

100) A - Cho Ma (pivot stance) **Gung Da** (low sweep block hit) **100) B - Cho Ma** (pivot stance) **Loy Jut Sow Choon Choy** (vertical thrusting punch) **100C - Jing Ma** (center stance) **Soong Loy Jut Sow** (double inside jerking hands)
100) D - Jing Ma (center stance) **Soong Pow Jan** (double lifting palms)

Pivot right, **Cho Ma.** Right hand blocks the center arm of the Dummy as the left hand places a **Choon Kune** connecting with the outside right arm. **Cho Ma** left, as left hand pulls in **Loy Jut Sow** to the top right arm. Right hand executes a **Choon Choy** to the midsection of the Dummy without making contact. Facing the Dummy pull in **Soong Jut Sow** to both arms of the Dummy. Remain on center and push up **Soong Pow Jan** to both arms. Keep the elbows in for more power in the lifting motions.

17) Left side set

Movement (101) a   Movement (102) a   Movement (103) a

101) A - Soong Ma (advance step through) **Die Bong Sow** (low wing arm deflection) **Woo Sow** (guarding hand)
102) A - Jing, Ma (center stance) **Biu Jon Sow** (thrusting fingers or hand) **Gung Jing Teck** (lifting front kick) **Woo Sow** (guarding hand) **103) A - Pock Sow** (slapping hand) **Loy Fook Sut** (inside blocking knee)
Woo Sow (guarding hand)

Advance step **Soong Ma** strike the center arm of the Dummy with left **Die Bong Sow,** right hand in **Woo Sow.** Pivot and face the center, block the inside right arm of the Dummy with left **Biu Jon Sow** as the right leg simultaneously kicks the center of the Dummy with **Gung Jing teck**. Left hand remains in **Woo Sow** position. Pivot left, right side hip must align with the Dummy. Block the inside right arm of the Dummy with **Pock Sow** as you simultaneously block the center arm of the Dummy with **Fook Sut**.

Movement (103) b   Movement (103) c   Movement (103) d

103) B - Tun Sow (showing hand) **Bong Gyeuk** (wing leg) **Woo Sow** (guarding hand) **103) C - Juck Teck** (side kick) **Bong Sow** (wing arm deflection) **Woo Sow** (guarding hand) **103) D - Toh Ma** (step slide) **Soong Woo Sow** (double guarding hand)

Facing the Dummy block the inside left arm of the Dummy with right **Tun Sow** as the right leg blocks the center arm of the Dummy with **Bong Gyeuk.** Simultaneously lean back, without moving right **Juck Teck** to the knee. Left hand in **Woo Sow,** step down and slide. Get ready to pivot, both hands in **Woo Sow** right on the centerline.

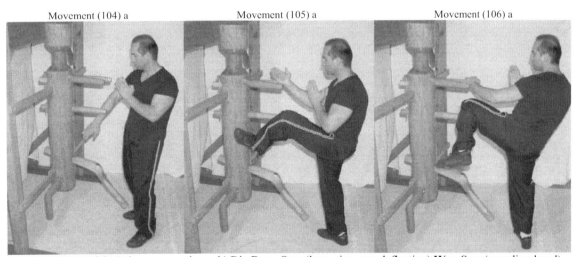

Movement (104) a   Movement (105) a   Movement (106) a

104) A - Soong Ma (advance step through) **Die Bong Sow** (low wing arm deflection) **Woo Sow** (guarding hand)
105) A - Jing, Ma (center stance) **Biu Jon Sow** (thrusting fingers or hand) **Gung Jing Teck** (lifting front kick) **Woo Sow** (guarding hand) **106-A Pock Sow** (slapping hand) **Loy Fook Sut** (inside blocking knee) **Woo Sow** (guarding hand)

Advance step **Soong Ma** strike the center arm of the Dummy with right **Die Bong Sow,** left hand in **Woo Sow.** Pivot and face the center as you thrust the inside left arm of the Dummy with right **Biu Jon Sow** along with a kick to the center, executing **Gung Jing Teck** simultaneously. Right hand remains in **Woo Sow.**
Pivot right. Left hip must align with the Dummy, block the inside left arm of the Dummy with left **Pock Sow** as you block the center arm of the Dummy with **Fook Sut.** Both motions must be performed simultaneously.

- 313 -

Movement (106) b   Movement (106) c   Movement (106) d

106) B- Tun Sow-(showing hand) **Bong Gyeuk** (wing leg) **Woo Sow**- (guarding hand) **106) C- Juck Teck** (side kick) **Bong Sow** (wing arm deflection) **Woo Sow** (guarding hand) **106) B- Toh Ma** (step slide) **Soong Woo Sow** (double guarding hand)

Facing the Dummy, block the inside right arm of the Dummy with left **Tun Sow** as the left leg simultaneously blocks the center arm of the Dummy with **Bong Gyeuk**. Lean back without moving, left **Juck Teck** to the knee of the Dummy, right hand in **Woo Sow**. Step down and slide. Get ready to pivot; both hands in **Woo Sow** right on the centerline.

18) Right side set

Movement (107) a   Movement (107) b

107) A - Soong Loy Jut Sow (double inside jerking hands) **Jing Gyeuk** (front kick) **107) B - Soong Pow Sow** (double lifting hands) **Cup Yai Sut** (stomping knee/ leg)

Facing the Dummy, both hands pull in double **Jut Sow** to both arms of the Dummy as the right leg kicks the body. Remain on the left rear leg, lift up **Soong Pow Sow** to both arms of the Dummy, while the right leg stomps the knee.

Movement (108) a

Movement (108) b

108) A - Soong Loy Jut Sow (double inside jerking hands) **Jing Gyeuk** (front kick) **108) b - Soong Pow Sow** (double lifting hands) **Cup Yai Sut** (stomping knee leg)

Facing the Dummy, both hands pull in double **Jut Sow** to both arms of the Dummy as the left leg kicks the body simultaneously. Remain on the right rear leg, lift up **Soong Pow Sow** to both arms of the Dummy while the left leg stomps the knee.

Sow Sick (1) closing the stance

Sow Sick (2)

SS-1 feet together back straight, bring both palms up near, but not touching the chest **SS-2** drop down **Soong Gum Jan** (double pressing palms) very slowly.

End of the last 48 motions

Extra Ging Lie

Left hand covers the right fist. Step forward with the right foot, as you slide step forward with left foot shoot out left hand over right in a **Biu Sow** motion. Step back as you circle both wrists in **Kwan Sow**. Feet together, retract **Sow Kune** both fists by your side, but without touching the ribs.

Bow, left hand cups the right fist as you nod your head slightly. Eyes are always focused forward on the target.

Finish

Small Joint Lock Manipulations

Most of these locks were used throughout out the book, so I like to show them a little bit closer so you can get a better look and understand the lock and how it should be done to be simple and effective. Most of these locks can be applied to any technique or finish move, whether you want to submit your opponent or simply pop the joint out. Whether it is your wrist, shoulder, joint, ankle, or any body joint, the same exact principle can be applied. Also, they are extremely effective against empty hands, clubs, knives, and with extreme caution, against a gun. Any of these locks can and should be practiced with right and left side.

Wrist lock Outward Motion

(1) (2) (3) (4)

(5) (6) (7)

The technique is only showing against a front choke, it does not mean that this lock will only work against this particular attack. This lock can work against any grab, whether it's a front choke, lapel grab, wrist grab, or any kind of grab with a single hand.

Defense Against Right Hand: cup his hand on top as you squeeze his fingers then rotate his wrist so that his fingers are pointing up. Control his hand and finger as you start pushing his fingers and wrist forward applying pressure, then bring the other hand up and cup the other side of the hand securing it. Start cranking his wrist down with both hands.

Wrist lock Inward Motion

(1)　　　(2)　　　(3)　　　(4)　　　(5)

Same technique can also be applies against many attacks.

From a from choke or any other attack, cup his hand with the left hand. As you start pulling his gripped hand away from the target, start raising the right hand from underneath so you can have two hands against one of his. That way you will have no problem twisting his hand, and from the torque of both hands, he will be forced to fall back or his wrist will snap.

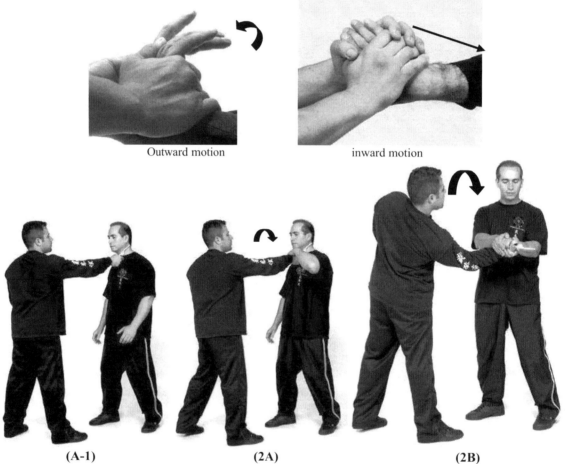

Outward motion　　　　　　　inward motion

(A-1)　　　(2A)　　　(2B)

Defense (1)- This technique can work against a knife or empty hands. Note: **Never execute** defense **(2) below** against a knife if the threat was to the same (LEFT) side, as photo **(A-1)** if the assailant using his right hand, because you can get cut across the neck. Do the opposite if the threat was to the right side.

Left Side Threat Only: Bring the left hand up and control his wrist but not pressed against your neck. Bring up the right hand, pin the other side of the hand, and rotate so that your hip and right shoulder line up with his center. Turn his hand and finger in a circular motion that will force him down from the pressure against the wrist. This defense must be done with speed.

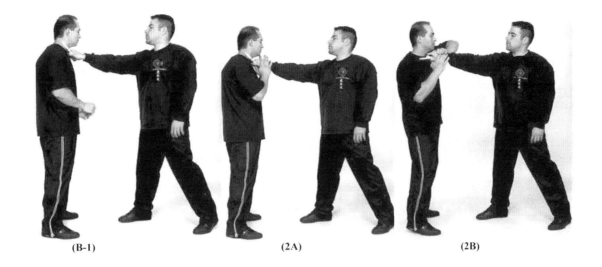

(B-1)   (2A)   (2B)

(3)   (4)   (5)

Defense (2)- This technique can work against a knife or empty hands. Note: **Never execute** defense **(1) above** against a knife if the threat was to the same (RIGHT) side as photo **(B-1)** if the assailant using his right hand, because you can get slashed across the neck.

Right Side Threat Only: Raise both hands at the same time and pin his wrist. Pivot to your right, rotate the left elbow over his right elbow joint as you pin his fingers and wrist, then let the weight of your upper body drop down on his elbow joint forcing him down, so you can get full control of the weapon. The above two defenses are very effective against empty hands. Also as long as you practice them and use caution at first against a weapon, they will become second nature. You don't need to think of which side you should rotate so that you don't get cut. "Practice makes perfect".

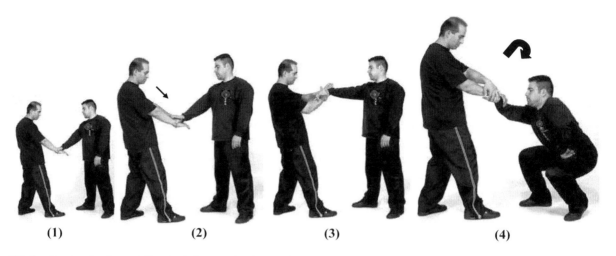

(1) (2) (3) (4)

Wrist Grabs Or Lapel Grab: defense- pin down his hand with your left hand against your right hand. Circle the right hand up while you are still pinning down his hand, clamp the fingers on his wrist and part of his forearm, and push down towards his abdomen. This will force him down on his knees.

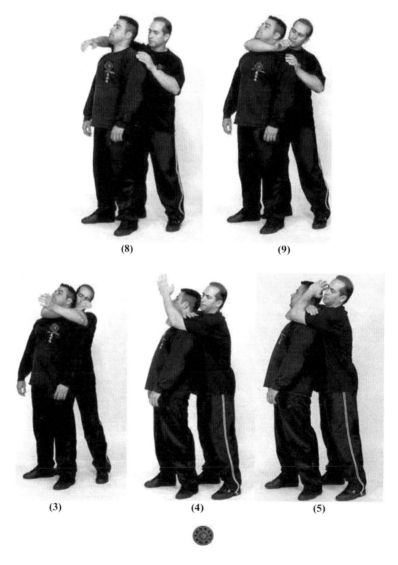

(8) (9)

(3) (4) (5)

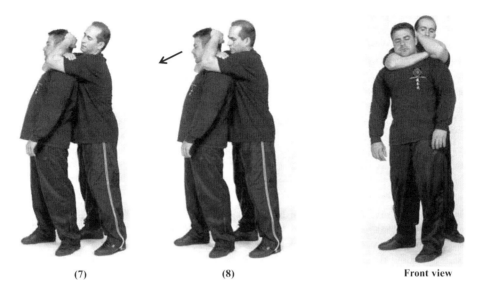

(7) (8) Front view

Applying Rear Sleeper: wrap the right arm around his neck, place the left hand behind his head and over your right hand, as you get full control of his head push forward and down with your left hand. Clamp the right hand on your left biceps. Squeeze, and the pressure from the right forearm and the left hand forcing his head against it cause lights out in less then 3 seconds.

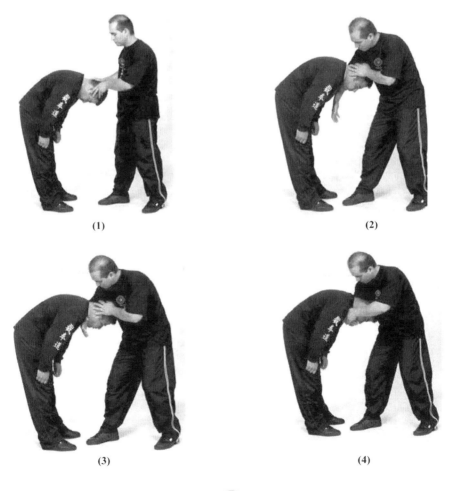

(1) (2)

(3) (4)

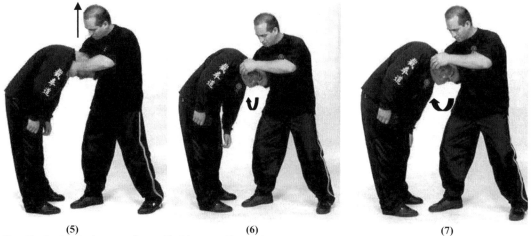

(5) (6) (7)

Front Headlock: this lock normally applied in grappling or in close fighting. Wrap the front hand around his head and neck, and pull his head in under your armpit to secure his head. Grab the right hand with your left hand and jack his head up and back. If for any reason he didn't feel the choke, just rotate his head so that his right face side is in an upward position. If he still doesn't feel it, (its almost impossible for any one to survive both locks), just simply pull him in tight, clamp the right hand over the left forearm and jack his head and neck up.

(1) **Wrist** grab   (2) **cup his hand**   (3) **circle his hand outward while you pin the elbow**

(4)   (5)   (6a)

(4) **Lock the wrist and the elbow,** (5) hit the inside of his elbow joint with the edge of your wrist to cause more damage to the elbow while still holding his fingers in a locked position, (6) open your hand and insert it in between his thumb and the index finger.

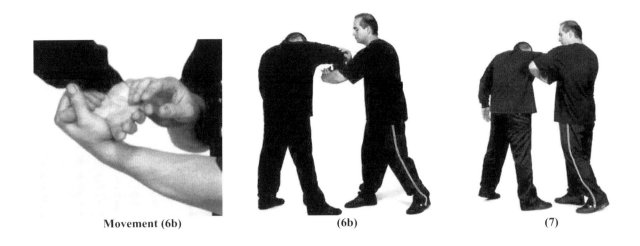

Movement (6b)   **(6b)**   **(7)**

(7) **Circle** his hand inward while pinning down his elbow, place his elbow against your chest or under your armpit as you secure it in a locked position.

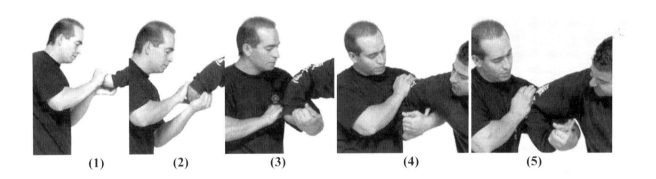

(1)   (2)   (3)   (4)   (5)

Inside View Of Above Wrist Lock Technique

This lock can be applied against any grab, or to any part of the body. Grab his fingers with your right hand, squeeze and rotate his hand so that his fingers are pointing up. Grab his forearm with your left hand controlling his whole arm. You can actually finish him by pushing his fingers and hand towards his elbow joint. That will force him down to his knees. If he didn't feel it, just continue by still controlling his hand and fingers. Raise the left hand and grab his thumb from underneath by only using the inside area between the thumb and the index finger. Circle the hand in towards his ribs, and pin the elbow joint down with your right hand as you jack his hand and wrist up.

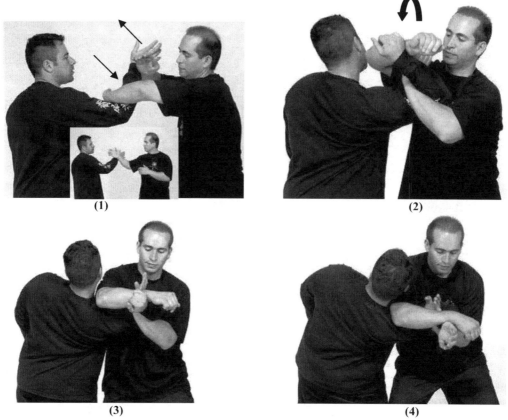

This **Z** lock can work from a block position or a grab. Place the left hand on the inside of his elbow joint as you push forward with the right hand. Circle the left inside both arms, grab the edge of his hand and push him forward with a help of a reverse **woo sow** (guarding hand).

Another option

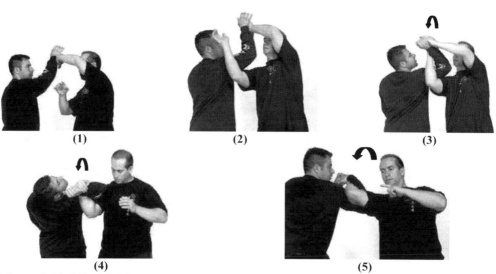

Place the right arm behind his right bicep. As you hook the right hand on his forearm, muscle him down. May the bigger man win. You have to act very fast for this technique to work effectively; because you are in the same position as he is. He can do the same lock to you.

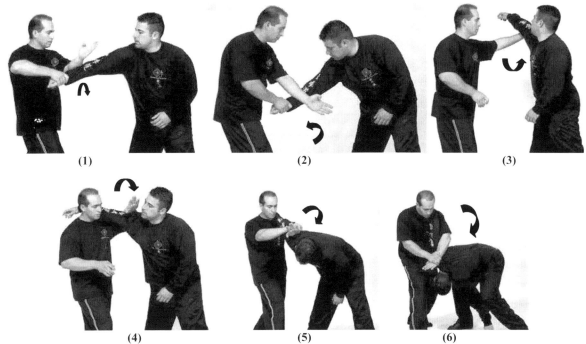

From a blocking position or grab: Circle his arm on the inside all the way around until it lands on your shoulder. Place the right hand over the left and push down against his outside elbow joint while his hand is resting on your left shoulder.
"Note": make sure that you push against the outside of his elbow joint, not the inside, because if you push on the inside his elbow will bend in a natural way and the lock will not work, and you end up head butting each other.

Another option

As you direct his hit or grab, grab his wrist with your right hand and rotate it in a throttle motion as you chop, not using the edge of the hand but using the forearm. It is a bigger surface and much more damaging to his elbow. Execute the chop to the outside of his elbow joint. **"Note"**: make sure that you twist the wrist so that the outside of his elbow joint is facing you, not the inside. Execute all locks with (**L**) **Left** or (**R**) **Right.**

The Arrival!

The Science of St Fighting

Street Self Defense

Hand to Hand Combat

Club Defense

Knife Defense

Gun Defense

NON-SPORT STAGE

Ground Fighting

Sparring & Sport

EMPTINESS

The Non-Thinking Stage!
Your Mind And Body Become One!
You Do Not Hit!

"IT" HITS!

Scientific Street Self Defense

(A)=ATTACKER OR ASSAILANT (D)=DEFENSE = End of the technique
TECHNIQUES CAN AND SHOULD BE EXECUTED LEFT OR RIGHT LEAD.

A JKD practitioner does not hit. "It" hits. "You name it, we use it."
Keep all your techniques simple and direct. Do not use any sophisticated movements. You must respond very quickly and effortlessly to any attack. Treat things very lightly. You must be self sufficient with yourself. This is the only thing that will work in real life situations. That doesn't mean that a JKD practitioner lacks technique because **"I can show you some really fancy movements and feel great and important and all that, but to express myself honestly, that takes lots of practice and very hard work.**

(1)　　(2)　　(3)

(4)

Movement # 1 - (A) Single Wrist Grab (D), strike with front **Choon Choy** (straight vertical punch) to the face, and rear **Ging Teck/Gyeuk** (oblique kick) to front knee, or front **Juck Teck** (sidekick) to the groin. It's not necessary to do all three techniques. Just pick one that will be sufficient at the time. If you put enough power into it, just one move will do enough damage.

Movement # 2 - (A) Single Wrist Grab (D), place your rear hand over his hand. As you pin it down, circle your right hand over and forward to apply pressure against his wrist and force him down.

Movement # 3 - (A) pulls single wrist grab **(D)**. **Juck Teck** (side kick) with the front foot to the ribs, and rotate the hips and rear foot for added power.

Movement # 4 - (A) Double Wrist Grab (D) turn both hands upwards **Soong Tun Sow** (double showing hands), **Lop Sow** (grab and pull) his rear hand as you strike with **Jing Jan** (vertical palm heel strike) under the chin, followed with **Tie Sut** knee to the chest or to the groin.

Movement # 5 - (A) Wrist Grab Hook (D), stop his hook with **Tun Sow** (showing hand), same hand strike the side of his face with **Chung Die Jan** (angle spade palm strike) and rotate the hip for added power.

Movement # 6 - (A) Wrist Grab Hook (D), stop his attack with rear **Tun Sow** or **Woo Sow** (showing hand or guarding). Pass his hand **Gwat Sow** across your centerline in a circular motion. Step slide strike with front **Choon Kune** (straight vertical punch) to the face. Circle his hand out **Huen Sow** (circling hand) to open him up, followed with front **Juck Teck** (side kick to the groin).

(1) (2) right rotation (3) left rotation

Movement # 7 - (A) Rear Arm Lock Left or Right (D), and simply spin or rotate the hips around and execute a **Song Jon** side elbow to the face.

Photo # (4) inside view

Movement # 8 - (A) Full Nelson (D) by rotating the hips and striking with **Sow Jon** (retracting elbow) to the face. Get back on your feet while not losing contact, circle the left hand around his neck, press his head against your body, and turn it upward and sideways at a 90° angle to apply pressure against his neck.

Movement # 9 - (A) Double Lapel Grab (D) and pull in both his arms with **Lon Sow** or **Gum Sow** (bar arm/pressing hand) as you immobilize both arms against your chest. Strike with front hand **Choon Kune** straight vertical punch to the face, knocking his head back.

Movement # 10 - (A) Single Front Choke or Single Lapel Grab (D), and break his hold with rear **Gwat Sow** (sweeping block). Pin the head with your front hand as you continue to control the arm. Strike with the front knee, and **Tie Sut** to the side of the head.

Movement # 11 - (A) Single Front Choke or Lapel Grab (D), and break his hold with **Chum-Q** (bridge block). Rear hand chops across the outside of his elbow joint as the front hand chops on the inside of his wrist, simultaneously causing the elbow joint to snap. Circle his arm out on the inside with rear **Huen Sow** (circling hand), same hand **Lop Sow** (pull, grab) on the inside step slide. Strike with front hand to the face with **Choon Choy,** followed by **Jick Teck** (front kick) to the groin.

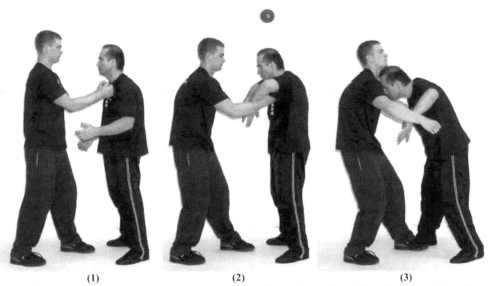

Movement # 12 - (A) Double Lapel Grab (D), and separate his hands on the inside with **Soong Huen Sow** or **Quack Sow** (double spreading hands). Push forward and **Tow Git** (head butt) the face.

(1) (2) (3) (4)

Movement # 13 - (A) Double Lapel Grab (D), push both of his hands to the outside with **Pock Sow** (slapping hand). Pivot out and step forward, striking with **How Choon Choy** (rear cross punch), followed with front **Choon Choy Cheen** (vertical punch) to the ribs.

(1) (2) (3)

(4) (5) (6) (7)

Movement # 14 - (A) Side Chokes (D) with shoulder pinned. With your left hand, pin his hand down against your chest. Strike his triceps upwards with the right arm, followed with a **Gwa Choy** (backhand) to the ribs. Drop down the right knee, and circle the right arm behind his right knee as you continue to control his arm. Flip him up and down on his back. Note: do the opposite if the grab was done with the left hand.

(1) (2) (3) (4)

Movement # 15R - (A) Single Front Choke (D), squeeze his hand with your right front hand as you lean back to create more distance. Lock his wrist with both hands by circling over/down and forward to apply pressure against his wrist.

(1) (2) (3)

Movement # 15 L - (A) Single Front Choke (D), pin the hand with your rear hand. As you get a good grip, place the front hand under his wrist for extra support, and pivot out circling with both hands. That will force him to flip on his back. Lock the wrist.

(1) (2) (3) (4)

Movement # 16 - (A) Double Lapel Grab (D) against the wall, and pin the outside of his hand against your chest with rear hand. Strike with front hand using **Jing Jan** (vertical palm heel strike) under his chin. Wrap the rear leg around his front knee as you push forward with front hand forcing him down to the ground. Note: you will fall down with him because you are both wrapped up. It's okay because his head is going to hit first and you are going to end up on top.

(1) (2)

Movement # 17 - (A) Double Lapel Grab (D) against the wall. Pin both of his hands down against your chest. Strike with front **Jick Teck** (front kick) to the groin, which is simple and direct.

(1) (2) (3)

(4) (5)

(5) (6) (7)

Movement # 18 - (A) Single Lapel Grab (D) pin the hand with both of your hands. Circle the rear elbow in a circular motion as you step forward; drop your elbow against his elbow joint forcing him down. Lock his arm in place. With left foot forward, spin around with the right leg, and drop an **axe** kick to the back of his head.

Movement # 19 - (A) Single Lapel Grab Hook (D), block his attack with rear **Tun Sow** (showing hand). The same hand **Lops** (pull) on the inside as you strike with front **Choon Choy** (vertical punch) to the abdomen. Still having full control of his right arm, pivot in and pass his left hand across his body and trap it over his right hand as you pull in and strike with **Song Jon** (side elbow) to the throat.

Movement # 20 - (A) Single Throat or Lapel Grab / Upper Cut (D) Stop his attack with **Gung Sow** (low sweep block), and **Lop Sow** (grab) his upper cut hand on the outside. Jerk him in as you strike him with front **Jick Teck** (front kick) to the abdomen.

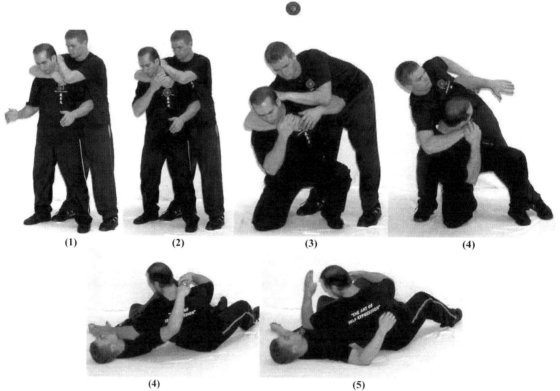

Movement # 21 - (A) Rear Sleeper Hold. It should be executed very quickly. You have less than 10 seconds to react, or it's over. It should be practiced repeatedly. During my many years in martial arts, I have tried many defenses against this technique, and nothing has really worked. Hit the **groin and pull the elbow back; stomp the foot, also hit the face**. When you're in a locked position, it is not that easy. As soon as you get locked, this defense must be executed very quickly. I can almost guarantee that this defense will work; it will loosen him up and give you a chance to breath. However, if you can come up with something that has even better results, don't hesitate to keep practicing and create different techniques until you find something that works well for you. **(D)** Pin his hand with the front hand, drop down on the **front** knee, which will force him to loosen up and fall forward. With the help of an elbow, push him off your back, which will cause him to lose his balance, and will force his head to fall first (where the head goes, the body will follow). Drop his head towards the pavement, and strike the throat or drop an elbow to his face or ribs as he lands on his back.

(1) (2) (3) (4)

(5) (6) (7)

Movement # 22 - (A) Rear Choke (D) with elbow pinned. Pin his hand down as you step to your right or left depending on the attack. Strike him with **Sow Jon,** and rear elbow to the ribs. The same hand drops down with **Chop Choy** (hammer punch) to the groin. While pinning the hand, slip under his armpit and take control of his arm by using both hands. Push his hand down, applying pressure on the wrist as the front hand pins the shoulder to keep his hand in a straight locked position. Step back as you still control his hand, and with both hands strike his face with front kick **Jick teck.**

(1) (2) (3) (4)

Movement # 23 - (A) Rear bear hug **(D)** with arms pinned. Squat down as you push both of your elbows out to loosen him up. Step to the right or the left and Strike him with **Chop Choy** (hammer punch), with either hand, left or right, to the groin.

Movement # 23 A - (A) Rear Bear Hug (D) with arms pinned, squat down with the same motion as above, to loosen him up. Pin the hand. Strike the groin on your way out. Slip under his armpit as you still control his hand, step back to clear the line. You can punch to the back of the head, or elbow to the spine, or even hammer punch to the elbow joint, followed with a **Jick Teck** (front kick) to the face.

Movement 23 B - (A) Rear Bear Hug (D) with arms free. Pin both of his hands against your chest using both of your hands. Strike his face with the back of your head, which will force him back to clear the line as you strike with **How Teck** (back kick) to the groin.

Movement # 24 - (A) Rear Bear Hug (D) with arms free. Simply pin his hands as you rotate the hips around and strike the side of his head with **Sow Jon.** Since you still control the arm, wrap the front hand around his head and turn it at a 90° angle as you push his neck up to apply the pressure for the choke. Note: keep his head tightly against your body in order for the choke to work. Push his body forward as you pull in with right hand in a spinning motion, and make him land flat on his back.

Movement # 25 - (A) Front Pick Up (D) and smash his ears in a clapping motion as you pin the head with both hands, then front head butt to the nose followed by a knee to the groin.

Movement # 26 - (A) High Head Lock (D) left or right, then strike his eyes with **Biu Jee** (finger jab). If that doesn't loosen him up, strike him in the groin.

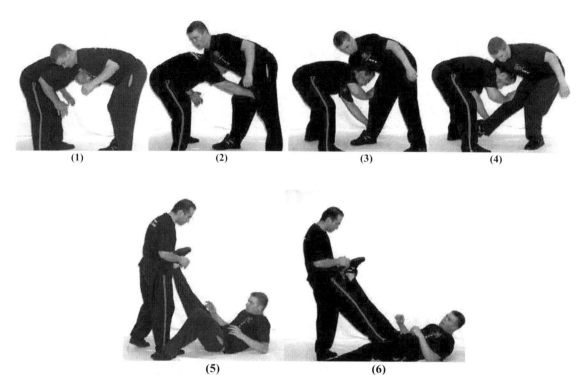

Movement # 27 - (A) Front Headlock (D) hit the groin with an upward right hammer punch. Pin the knee with right-hand as you pull in the leg with the left simultaneously. Stomp the groin as he falls back, controlling his foot. You know that must hurt.☺.

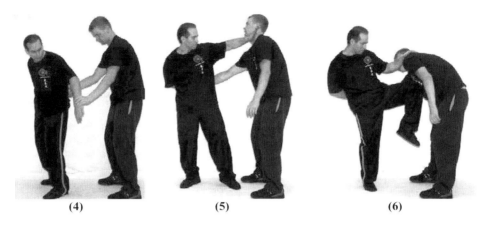

(4) (5) (6)

Movement # 28 - (A) Rear Arm Lock (D) There are a few different ways to handle this attack: **1) How Teck** (back kick) to the knee, **2) How Teck** (back kick) to the groin, or **3)** turn **Fun Sow** (chop) to the neck, pin the shoulder and deliver a knee to the chest.

Movement # 29 - (A) Rear Headlock (D) as he pulls you back, forcing you off balance. Pin the hand, then slip under and strike him with an upper cut to the groin. As you pin his wrist, place the front hand against his shoulder. Pass his head across your Center Line as you push his other hand in a circular motion. The two must be executed together in order to flip him off balance. While he is in a daze, gain control of his hand, grab the head, and knee him in the temple.

(1) (2) (3) (4)

Movement # 30 - (A) Front Headlock With Knee To The Face (D) There are a few ways to stop the knee: **1)** simply strike the groin before he executes the knee to your face. **2) Sup Jee Sow**, **Root Siu Leem Tau** (**X** block or character **10**), or **Soong Chung Die Jan** (double palm strikes) to the hips knocking him off balance.

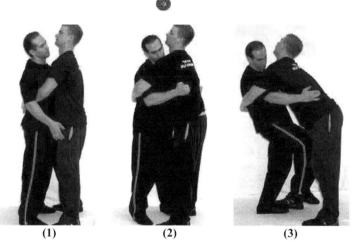

(1) (2) (3)

Movement # 31 - (A) Front Bear Hug (D) with arms pinned. Squeeze or pinch his sides with both hands, then knee him in the groin with front or rear knee.

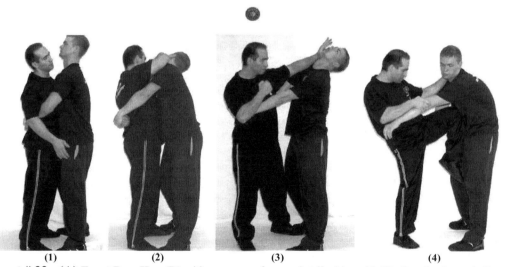

(1) (2) (3) (4)

Movement # 32 - (A) Front Bear Hug (D) with your arms free, and strike him with **Pie Jon** (horizontal elbow) to the face. As his face tilts to the side, follow up with another strike to the face with **Jing Jan** (palm strike to the face), forcing his head back. Then hook the neck and pin the elbow, as you pull him into your strike, **Tie Sut** (raising knee) to the groin or abdomen.

(1) (2) (3) (4)

(5) (6) (7) (8)

Movement # 33 - (A) Rear Bear Hug With Arms Pinned (D). Pin his hand and slip under from either side. In right lead, strike his throat with edge of the forearm. Step behind him and control his neck with the right hand. Place the left hand in reverse **(Woo Sow)** in front of his neck and jerk his head back strike with **Tie Sut** (upward knee) to his spine as you expose his solar plexus. Drop the elbow to the center of his chest.

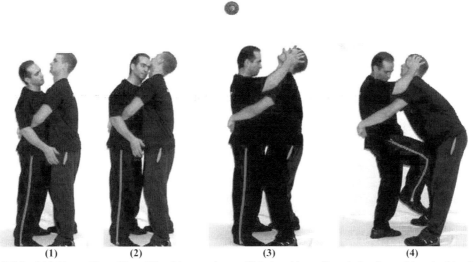

(1) (2) (3) (4)

Movement # 34 - (A) Front Bear Hug (D) with arms loose. Side head butt. Smash the face with a double slaps to the ears, and as you still control his head, knee him to the groin with front or rear leg.

(1)   (2)

Movement # 35 - (A) Head Lock (D). "**You've got to put your whole hip into it. Then snap all your power into the target**". Upper cut to the abdomen. (Facial expression is not an act as he was really hit to demonstrate the effectiveness of a JKD single direct attack right lead from any position.)

Movement # 36 - (A) Head Lock (D) left or right. Strike the groin with reverse **Woo Sow** (guarding hand), which will cause him to loosen up. Strike the side of his knee joint. Slip under his locked arm as you grab his front leg to get him off balance, then elbow the back of his knee as you pull in his leg to force him down face first, smashing into the ground. You must perform techniques simultaneously. As he falls down give him a kick in the rear end.

Hand To Hand Combat

(C) = CLOSED RELATIONSHIP OR SQUARE **(O) = OPEN RELATIONSHIP OR ROUNDED**

<u>Closed</u> relationship is when both fighters are right foot forward or left foot forward and in the same foot position. Same side right-to-right or left-to-left is what is considered close relationship or square.
<u>Open</u> relationship is when both fighters are in complete opposition — one is in orthodox fighting position and the other is in unorthodox fighting position (right to left or vice versa). That is considered open relationship or rounded.

(A) = ASSAILANT OR ATTACK   (D) = DEFENSE **=THE END OF THE TECHNIQUE**

In JKD, you don't change foot position. Your right or left foot is always forward, depending on where you take your power from in the by-Jon position. It does not matter if you are left or right handed, you must put all your power forward. If you want to practice JKD, your power must be forward. Otherwise, you're doing another form of martial arts and you will telegraph your hits. You want to reach your opponent with the least amount of energy as possible. Some might argue that when the power is coming from the rear it's much more powerful. That is how you score a knockout. If you practice right lead everyday, your right hand will become much more powerful than any telegraphic cross. By raising your heel and using a pivoting hip action, you can deliver a very devastating power that is very unlikely to be blocked. If a JKD punch is delivered properly, the opponent should only be able to feel a small wisp of wind then feel the hit. That is how fast a JKD punch should be practiced until you reach your goal.

"Practice makes perfect" in JKD, as in all forms of martial arts. If you're going to practice once a week or every other week, then your cross will be very sloppy. In JKD, you use every part of your body and every aspect of fighting. You will be able to adjust to your opponent, no matter what. First we use our hands, then the feet and the elbows. Knees, head butts, and even biting can be used, but we "don't make it a habit of biting "

Top 50 Guidelines For A Jeet Kune Do Practitioner:

1. BE VERY RELAXED, NOT TENSE.
2. BE READY, BE AGGRESSIVE.
3. HAVE FULL CONFIDENCE.
4. USE YOUR NATURAL INSTINCT.
5. USE NON-TELEGRAPHIC MOVEMENTS.
6. USE NON-SOPHISTICATED MOVEMENTS.
7. PUZZLE YOUR OPPONENT WITH DIFFERENT ATTACKS.
8. NEVER GET INTIMIDATED.
9. DO NOT CONCENTRATE ON BODY SIZE.
10. NEVER UNDERESTIMATE YOUR OPPONENT.
11. TIMING IS KEY.
12. DO NOT LIMIT YOUR SELF TO JUST KICKING BELOW THE WAIST LINE.
13. SIMPLY "EXPRESS YOURSELF".
14. FLOW AROUND YOUR OPPONENT LIKE WATER.
15. EVERY HIT SHOULD FINISH WITH A "SNAP".
16. YOU MUST PUT YOUR ENTIRE HIP INTO IT TO RELEASE THE POWER.
17. BE FORMLESS AND SHAPELESS. BECOME THE OPPONENT'S STYLE.
18. HANDS MUST REMAIN LOOSE AND RELAXED.
19. FIST IS CLENCHED AT MOMENT OF IMPACT OR 2 INCHES BEFORE THE TARGET.
20. SPEED EQUALS POWER.
21. TRAIN UNTIL EMPTINESS. RESPOND WITHOUT THINKING.
22. DON'T GO INTO ANY FANCY STANCES.
23. KEEP YOUR MOVES SIMPLE AND DIRECT.
24. FOOTWORK MUST BE EXECUTED WITH EVERY HIT TO GAIN FULL POWER.
25. A PERSON WITH A WEAPON IS SURELY TO LOSE, FOR HE HAS ONLY ONE WEAPON.
26. YOU HAVE MANY WEAPONS, LIKE HANDS, FEET, ELBOWS, KNEES, ETC.
27. NEVER CONCENTRATE ON YOUR OPPONENT'S WEAPON. "YOU WILL MISS ALL THE HEAVENLY GLORY."
28. NERVOUSNESS BLINDS YOU.
29. ATTACK WITH ALL YOU'VE GOT. NEVER SHORTEN YOUR HITS.
30. ATTACKS MUST FINISH BEYOND TARGET LINE.
31. EVERY PUNCH MUST BE FOLLOWED BY A KICK, ELBOW, OR KNEE, ETC., TO BE VICTORIOUS.
32. BE VERY ALOOF AND DECEPTIVE.
33. ALWAYS ATTACK THROUGH THE CENTER LINE. THAT IS WHERE ALL THE VITAL ORGANS ARE.
34. IN INTERCEPTING, USE YOUR LONGEST WEAPON AGAINST THE NEAREST TARGET: THE KNEE CAP.
35. NEVER PUT DOWN OTHER STYLES OF MARTIAL ARTS.
36. TO EARN RESPECT, ALWAYS SHOW RESPECT.
37. LEARN FROM ANYONE WHO IS WILLING TO TEACH YOU.
38. NEVER TRY TO PROVE ANYTHING TO ANYONE.
39. NEVER GIVE YOUR OPINION UNLESS IT IS ASKED FOR.
40. "EMPTY YOUR CUP TO GAIN TOTALITY".
41. ALWAYS ABSORB WHAT IS USEFUL, THEN REJECT.
42. NEVER REJECT ANYTHING UNLESS YOU UNDERSTAND THE MEANING BEHIND IT.
43. ALWAYS LISTEN. YOU WILL LEARN SOMETHING EVEN IF IT IS JUST ONE THING.
44. A GOOD MARTIAL ARTIST DOES NOT INDULGE IN ANY FIGHTS UNLESS THE FIGHT IS BROUGHT ON TO HIM.
45. A GOOD MARTIAL ARTIST IS ALWAYS IN CONTROL OF HIS EMOTIONS.
46. A GOOD MARTIAL ARTIST ALWAYS AVOIDS FIGHTING.
47. A GOOD MARTIAL ARTIST SEEKS TO DISARM, NOT TO DESTROY.
48. A GOOD MARTIAL ARTIST IS ALWAYS IN CONTROL OF THE FLOW OF THE FIGHT.
49. A GOOD MARTIAL ARTIST NEVER BELITTLES HIS OPPONENT.
50. TRUE MARTIAL ARTISTS KNOW THEMSELVES.

CLOSED RELATIONSHIP OR SQUARE

(1) (2) (3)

Movement # 1- C) (A) Front Jab (D) block or Perry with rear **Pock Sow** (slapping hand) then strike with front **Gwa Choy** (back hand) to side of the head or temple. If he throws a fast jab, then you Perry his punch and counter-attack. But if the attack is committed, then you clamp your block on his wrist at a 45° cutting angle that will not only block his hand, but it will shock his whole posture from the block. If you only block at a 90° angle then you are only blocking his hand. This is okay too, as long as you block the punch.

(1) (2) (3) (4)

Movement # 2- C) (A) Rear Cross (D) block his attack with front **Pock Sow** (slapping hand). Switch to rear **Lop Sow** (grabber pulling) on the outside as you step-slide; not only will you trap his arm, but also his leg (**FIA**). Give him no room for counter-attacks — strike with **Gwa Choy** (backhand) low to the ribs, and continue with a high **Gwa Choy** to the face.

(1) (2) (3)

Movement # 3- C) (A) Front Jab Rear Cross (D) block with rear **Pock Sow** (slapping hand). As you step to the outside of his cross intercept him with a **Biu Jee** (finger jab) to the eyes. Then **Lop Sow** (grab or pull) his rear arm **Choon Choy** or **Choon Kune** (straight vertical punch) to the face with the right lead.

(1)   (2)   (3)

Movement # 4- C) (A) Front Jab Rear Cross (D) block with rear **Pock Sow**, pivot in slightly, block his cross with front **Pock Sow** (slapping hand), and switch to **Cow Sow** (pull back) on the outside. While you still control the arm, **Juck Teck** (side kick) to the ribs.

(1)   (2)   (3)

Movement # 5- C) (A) Front Jab (D) block with front **Tun Sow** (showing hand), step–slide, immobilize his arm with rear **Gum Sow** (pressing hand), and strike with front **Chung Die Jan** (spade palm heel strike to the face) or with a **Choon Choy** (straight vertical punch).

(1)   (2)   (3)   (4)

Movement # 6- C) (A) Front Jab Rear Cross (D) block his front jab with front **Tun Sow** (showing hand). Using the same front hand, block his rear cross with **Pock Sow** (slapping hand). One hand carries two hits. **Biu Jee** or **Biu Sow** (finger jab) to the eyes with front hand. As you **Lop Sow** (grab or pull) with the rear hand to the outside of his arm, step-slide front **Pie Jon** (horizontal elbow) to the side of the head.

(1) (2) (3)

Movement # 7- C) (A) Rear Cross (D) block with front **Jom Sow** (chopping hand) at a 45° angle. Circle his hand on the inside out **Huen Sow** (circling hand), and **Lop Sow** (grab or pull) on the inside strike with rear **Jing Jan** (vertical palm, heel strike) to the face as you control his rear arm.

(1) (2)

Movement # 8- C) (A) Front Jab (D) perry with rear **Pock Sow** (slapping hand). Slip as you push-shuffle counter **Choon Kune** to the ribs, simple and direct.

(1) (2) (3)

Movement # 9- C) (A) Front Jab (D) block with rear **Bong Sow** (wing arm deflection). Switch to front **Lop Sow** (grab) to his outside, step-slide rear **Gwa Choy** (backhand) to the face with rear hand.
NOTE: normally, Wing Chun practitioners do not use reverse **Bong**, but in JKD there are no limitations.

(1)   (2)   (3)

Movement # 10- C) (A) Rear Cross **(D)** block with front **Pock Sow** (slapping hand). Switch to rear **Lop Sow** (grab or pull) to his outside, and rotate the hips for added power as you strike with **Choon Choy** (straight punch) to face.

(1)   (2)   (3)   (4)

Movement # 11- C) (A) Front Jab **(D)** block with front **Tun Sow** (showing hand). Step-slide rear **Gum Jan** or **Sow** (pressing hand), followed by front **Jing Jan** (vertical palm heel block) to the face, or **Choon Choy** (vertical punch).

(1)   (2)   (3)

Movement # 12- C) (A) Front Hook **(D)** block with front **Jom Sow** (chopping block), step-slide to his inside rear, **Lop Sow** (grab or pull), and strike with front **Choon Kune** (straight punch) to the face.

(1)　　　　　　　　　　　(2)　　　　　　　　　　　(3)

Movement # 13- C) (A) Front Hook (D) stop it with rear **Woo Sow** (guarding hand), switch to **Lop Sow** (grab or pull) on the inside step-slide, and **Gwa Choy** (back hand) to the face. **Choon Choy** (vertical punch is also an option..

(1)　　　　　　(2)　　　　　　(3)　　　　　　(4)

Movement # 14- C) (A) Rear Hook (D) block with front **Tun Sow** (showing hand), and guard your head with **Woo Sow** (guarding hand). As you step-slide, strike with front **Jing Jan** to the face as the rear hand re-traps his striking hand on the inside. Switch the rear hand to **Lop Sow**/ front **Fun Sow** (chopping hand) to neck simultaneously. Grab the back of the neck as you still control the arm strike with rear **Tie Sut** (raising knee) to face.

(1)　　　　　　(2)　　　　　　(3)　　　　　　(4)

Movement # 15- C) (A) Front Hook Rear Hook (D) block with front **Pock Sow** (slapping hand) to the inside (same hand blocks his other hook with front **Tun Sow** to the inside (showing hand)). Front hand **Lop Sow** (grab or pull) his rear hook maintaining rear-guarding hand. Execute rear **Jick Teck** (front kick) to the abdomen, followed by front **Juck Teck** (side kick) to the groin or knee.

(1) (2)

Movement # 16- C) (A) Front Hook Rear Hook (D) block front **Jom Sow** to the inside (chopping block), slight pivot out. The same hand blocks his other hook with front **Tun Sow** (showing hand). Keep rear guarding up.

(3) (4) (5)

Pivot into him, drop **Chop Choy** (low hammer) to groin, and high **Gwa Choy** (back hand) to the face. Maintain the rear hand up for extra defense.

(1)   (2)   (3)

(4)   (5)

Movement # 17- C) (A) Back Hand (D) block with front **Tun Sow** to the outside (showing hand). Front **Lop Sow** (grab or pull) and **Ow teck** (hook kick or round house) to abdomen, followed with front **Juck teck** (side kick) to the face as you still control his arm, or roundhouse to the head.

(1)   (2)   (3)

(4)   (5)   (6)

Movement # 18- C) (A) Front Jab (D) block with rear **Pock Sow** (slapping hand), and strike with front **Choon Choy** (straight punch). Then **(D)** blocks with his own **Pock Sow** (slapping hand). Counter with rear **Lop** (grab) then step-slide front **Gwa Choy** (back hand) to the face. Pin the face and introduce your knee to the back of his head (**Tie Sut**). Good night!

(1)   (2)   (3)   (4)

Movement # 19- C) (A) Front Hook, Rear Hook (D) blocks both of his attacks with front **Jom Sow** (chopping block) and front **Biu Jon Sow** (thrusting hand). Then step-slide rear **Pie Jon** (horizontal elbow) to the face, pin the back of the neck, and pull it into your rear knee with rear hand **Tie Sut** (raising knee) to the chest or face as you still control his arm.

OPEN RELATIONSHIP OR ROUNDED

Movement # 1- (O) (A) Front Jab (D) block with front **Pock Sow** (slapping hand). Switch to rear **Lop Sow** (grabbing hand), rotate the hips, and strike low **Gwa Choy** to the ribs. This should be followed with high **Gwa Choy** (back hand) to the face.

Movement # 2- (O) (A) Rear Cross (D) block with front **Tun Sow** (showing hand). Rear **Gum Sow** (pressing hand), step-slide, and strike with front **Choon Choy** (straight punch) to the face.

(1)   (2)   (3)

(4)   (5)

Movement # 3- (O) (A) Both Hands Up (D) breaking down his defense line. Front **Pock,** rear **Pock/Gum Sow** (slap/pin) down. Trap both hands. Strike with **Choon Choy** or **Choon Kune** (straight vertical punch) to the face. This should be done very fast — you must take control and eliminate both of his weapons before he tries to attack.

(1)   (2)   (3)

Movement # 4- (O) (A) Rear Cross (D) block with front **Tun Sow** (showing hand), followed with extra defense line **Pock** (slap) push shuffle forward **Pie Jon** (horizontal elbow) to the body.

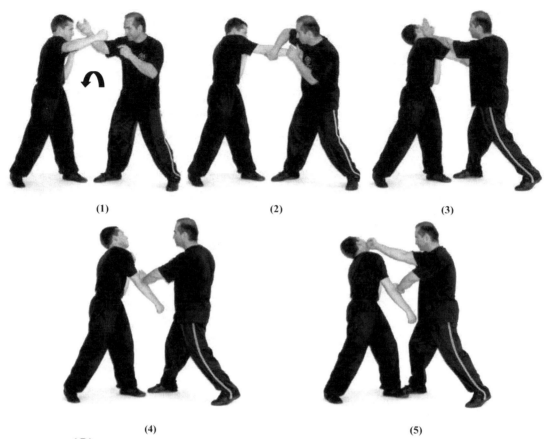

Movement # 5- (O) (A) Rear Hook Or Cross (D) block with front **Jom Sow** (chopping block). Hook the front hand on his elbow joint and circle it out **Huen Sow**. Opening the line for attack, strike with left **Jing Jan** (vertical palm heel strike) to the face, re-trap left **Gum Sow** (pinning hand), and land right **Choon Choy** to the head.

Movement # 6- (O) (A) Front Hook (D) blocks with front **Tun Sow** (showing hand) and maintains left guard up **Woo Sow**. Strike the side of his head by executing a front **Chung Die Jan** (spade palm). Step-slide and **Gwy Jon** (over the top elbow) to the back of the head.

(1) (2) (3)

(4)

Movement # 7- (O) (A) Front Jab Cross (D) block with front **Pock Sow** (slapping hand). The same hand carries the other attack with **Tun Sow** (showing hand block). One hand carries two blocks. **Gum Sow** (pressing hand) with rear hand. As you step-slide, **Biu Jee** (shooting fingers) to the eyes, followed with **Pie Jon** (horizontal elbow) to the chin.

(1) (2) (3)

(4)   (5)

Movement # 8- (O) (A) Rear Cross Front Jab (D) block with rear **Pock Sow** (slapping hand) and rear **Tun Sow** (showing hand block). One hand carries two blocks. **Lop Sow** (grab or pull) with the right hand, **Jom Sow** (chop) with the front hand against his elbow joint forcing him down. While you still control the arm, turn the wrist forward to cause extra pain. Strike **Gwy Jon** (over the top elbow) to the back of the head.

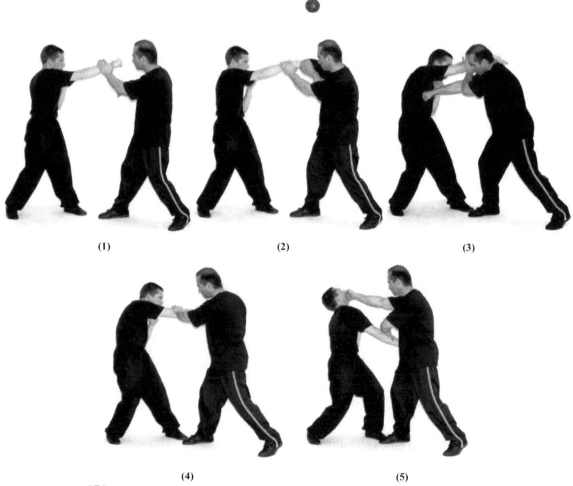

Movement # 9- (O) (A) Rear Cross (D) rear **Pock Sow /Pie Jon** simultaneously (slapping/horizontal elbow). As you smash his knuckles with the elbow, maintain rear hand in guarded position. Step-slide, drop down **Chop Kune** (leak horizontal punch) with front hand to the ribs, and re-trap his elbow with rear **Gum Sow** (pressing hand), followed by a **Gwa Choy** (back hand) to the side of the head.

(1) (2)

Movement # 10- (O) (A) Haymaker (D) Juck Teck (sidekick) to the abdomen. Make sure that you lean back and keep your rear guard up. Rotate the hips and the rear foot for added power. Simple direct, but very effective.

(1) (2) (3)

1) Block with front hand **2)** step forward with right foot, pin with rear hand
3) pin with rear hand strike with the front then slide the rear leg behind your opponent. **<u>Arrows represents footwork</u>**.

(4) (5) (6) (7) (8)

4) As you slide behind him, pull back his head with front hand, then strike with rear hand to the spine **<u>synergistic</u>**.4, 5, 6) Step behind with left foot. As you pin the shoulder with right hand, place the left hand in **Woo Sow** position in front of his neck, and jerk back. 7,8) Controlling the head with the left hand, strike the back of his head with an upward left knee. Switch footwork to right lead, drop the right elbow down to his torso. **(O) (A)** rear cross **(D)** block with front **Tun Sow** (showing hand block), push-shuffle and pin the shoulder with rear hand. As you slide the rear hand down to his elbow, strike with tiger's mouth (**Chung Gang**) to the throat. As you spin behind him, punch the back of the neck/spine as you jerk him back. Place the right hand on his shoulder as you jerk him back with the left reverse **Woo Sow** (guarding hand). As you control the head, **Chum Jon** (downward elbow) to the chest. A lot of footwork is required to do this technique correctly. It doesn't seem very simple, and the reason for that is there are many actual techniques hidden within this big technique. If you break it down to little techniques, they are very simple, all the other techniques are only added on. As you practice, you can start making up your own "add–on" from just simple, little techniques.

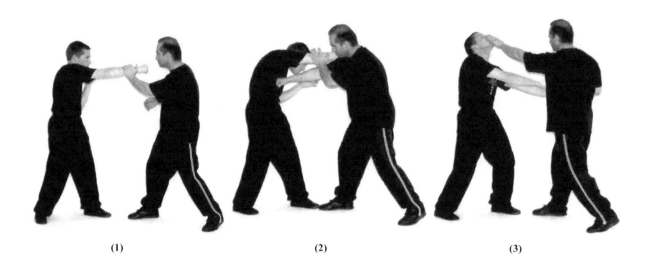

(1) (2) (3)

(4) (5)

Movement # 11- (O) (A) Rear Cross (D) block with rear **Pock Sow** (slapping hand block). Step-slide and strike with front **Chop Kune** (leak horizontal punch) to the abdomen. Push down his rear hand to open up the attack line with rear **Pock.** Shoot forward **Biu Jee** (finger jab) to the eyes with the rear hand, immobilize his front and rear hand with **Lop** and **Gum** (grab/press). Strike with rear kick to the groin with **Moy Yin Teck Gyeuk** (invisible kick), and as you pull him towards you **Juck Teck** (side kick) to the knee maintaining rear guard up.

VARIOUS TAKE-DOWNS CAN BE ADDED TO MOST OF THE TECHNIQUES TO FINISH OFF THE OPPONENT !

1) Side hack-down   2) Rear leg hook take-down   3) Front leg take-down   4) Oblique take-down

5) Front side kick take-down   6) Rear round house kick take-down   7) Sweep-down

(1)

Place the right or the left leg behind his right or left leg, depending on the position of the attack. Place the same-side hand against his chest as you pin the other arm or the shoulder. Kick back up as you push down with the same-side hand. This particular take-down is heavily used in **karate**. Right to right, left to left. If partners are on the same side, this take down is efficient, but it has its downfalls. Your opponent can take you down as well. He is in the same position as you. There must be no delay when executing the take down because if he is stronger than you, you're in trouble. Before executing, you must attack first to loosen him up, and then take down. Otherwise, it is not going to be in your favor every time.

(2)

This take-down is also efficient, but it must be executed with a push as you wrap your leg around his leg and place your other hand against his chest. As you pull him in with your leg, you must push with your hand at the same time and remain balanced. If you don't, you will end up on top of him and that is something you don't want to do. After plenty of practice, this take down will work very well. The worst scenario possible would be losing your balance and he takes you down first. Through training, practice, and using your natural instincts you will be able to maintain your balance.

(3)

I do not use this take-down a lot — the reason being that unless he is in a standstill position and his legs are both apart or the other one is kicking, then it is very difficult for anyone to execute this take-down. If he or she is in a by-Jon position, forget about the take-down all together, because it's not going to work. Some martial artists do keep their whole posture exposed and both legs apart; in these instances, this take-down will work. To execute it correctly, again, you must place your other hand against his chest as you grab his other hand. Place either leg between his legs then kick back as you push forward in a **synergistic** attack.

(4) (5)

4/5) These are my favorite take-downs. They are very simple and direct. After his attack, you step to the side of your opponent as you immobilize his arm, shoulder, head or hair — whatever is available at the time. Kick his leg forward with an oblique kick or side kick to the back of his knee; it will force the lower half forward as the top half gets jerked back from the impact. He will not know whether he is coming or going. No matter how strong the person is, he will go down. Not much balance or effort is required.

(6)

Another favorite of mine uses the total flow of energy and deception. This take-down is heavily used in up-close fighting and hand immobilization attacks by flowing from hand-traps to take-downs. This take-down is executed by kicking with a roundhouse kick or hook kick with the rear leg across the back of the knee. From the impact that will force him up, he will land on his back without even expecting it. Or simply place the rear leg behind his front leg, place the front hand in front of his neck, and grab the hand or shoulder as you simultaneously kick up the back of the knee and push down against his neck. This will force him down.

(7)

This take-down is to be used with caution. You have to be in reach range, and should be executed with **speed** — if not, you will lose balance, your back will be turned to him, and will be open to an attack. From a by-Jon kneel-down, and with front leg, spin on the front knee with a rear kick against the back of his knee. As you lean back, keep your head away from his kicking range, just in case you did not score.

Blocking Against Kicks

My number one technique against a kick is to simply just get out of the way and just let it pass by. I would try my very best not to block a kick. You don't want to be in the way of a kicker. Some martial arts styles depend heavily on kicking, and so their two weapons are extremely powerful. Why take the chance of blocking? That's why footwork is very important in JKD. You must be very fluid on your feet. Advance, retreat, move side–to-side, even circle to get out of the way before you get hit. You must be able to take away their weapon or weaken it in any way possible. Some of these techniques will work against a good kicker. Because JKD uses hands, feet, elbows, knees, and head butts, you have an advantage over a kicker. That's why training on a wooden dummy is very important: it toughens up your hands and legs, and turns your block into a strike.

1) Stop kick against a front kick   **2)** Shin blocking against a low round house or hook kick

1) Rear- or front-kick attacks can be intercepted by a JKD stop kick, using the bottom of the foot against his shin.
2) Raise the front leg in a bent position against a rear roundhouse kick.

1) Rear shin blocking against a low roundhouse or hook kick   **2)** Invisible/oblique kick against a rear front kick

1) Raise the rear leg half way up against roundhouse kicks. **2)** Intercept his rear front kick using the bottom of the foot.

(1) (2) (3)

Against a roundhouse kick, rear **Woo Sow** guarding or double **Jom Sow** (chopping hands), or a single hand against a high roundhouse or hook kick.
You must strike the leg with your block at a 45° angle to make it more effective.

(1) Inside view don't switch position   back view (2)   (3)

(4)   (5)

Use a **Pock Sow** (slapping hand) against a high kick or simply absorb the kick. Then circle the leg with the rear arm as it lands against your body. Place your foot behind his other base leg, sweep it out from under him, and stomp the groin. Then, if that isn't enough, kneel down show and your respect. I think that will hurt even more!☺

(1)

(A) Against A High, Kick (D) Perry the kick with the front **Pock**. Then intercept with front sidekick to his groin.

(1)　　　　　　　　　　(2)　　　　　　　　　　(3)

Initiate the attacks from a relaxed standstill position. Shoot forward thru the center or to his outside with a finger jab to the eyes or a straight punch to the face. It is like a fencer's movement. Just sprint forward and land on the target using push-shuffle footwork.

(4) (5) (6)

Follow up with a cross; grab uppercut to the body, and an elbow to the head. Give him no room for additional kick — stop him before he starts.

(1) (2)

Initiate the attack by side kicking the knee. Follow up with a hook kick to the back of the head. Surprise him with your own kicks.

Club Defense

When defending your self against a club attack, JKD attack by drawing (**ABD**) and timing are the most important principles when facing an opponent with a club. Never block the weapon; always the source. Stop your opponent's hand and arm before they can strike you. Do not try to hop around: you will lose concentration. When facing an opponent with a very long reach he can hit you from a long distance. He doesn't need to be very close to strike. Your biggest problem is reach, and that is why timing is key. If your opponent is fully committed to the attack and you take it seriously, you can always stop it from hitting you, but if he is swinging and out of control, then you are in trouble. Footwork, timing, and speed will save you from being hit. That's why advance, retreat, side-to-side footwork, and pivoting play a big part against a club - or any opponent for that matter. For example, if your opponent swings with full commitment, then you can retreat or move sideways to defend against the attack, but you must advance very quickly to stop your opponent from returning to position. In almost every club attack, whether it comes from the side with a haymaker or over the top, you must be very meticulous in your counterattack. Let it pass you by.

"**Don't charge without thinking. You have to listen to his movements !**

Most of these techniques will work against an opponent who gives you full commitment, but you must make him commit. If you're ever in a situation where he is just going to swing, it doesn't matter how he hits you, as long as he scores and does the most damage to you that he can. It's up to you to make him change his method of attack. You have to be very deceptive and make him do something that he did not intend to do by committing himself. Then it is all over for him.

A=ATTACK OR ASSAILANT; D= DEFENSE THE END OF THE TECHNIQUE

There's no certain way of blocking the source, as long as you stop it from hitting you. Use the most scientific block available to you at the time of the attack.

NEVER BLOCK THE WEAPON THIS WAY

BLOCK THE SOURCE

PASS THE WEAPON OR SIMPLY GET OUT OF THE WAY

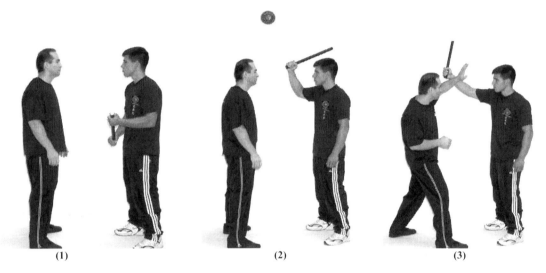

(1)　　　　　　　　　(2)　　　　　　　　　(3)

Movement # 1 - (A) Over The Top: full commitment. **(D)** Step forward and block the source with a rear **Fack Sow** (high block), blocking the inside of the attacker's arm. A good JKD block should feel like a strike.

(4)　　　　　(5)　　　　　(6)　　　　　(7)

Pivot at a 25-degree angle. **Lop** (grab) the wrist and strike with a **Choon Choy** (straight punch) as your rear hand wraps his elbow. While your front hand pins his shoulder, apply pressure to release the club, then **Tie Sut** (knee up) to the groin as you push his head back, forcing him to lose balance and his control of the club.

Right hand is ready to strike at moment of impact or simply lock the elbow.

Movement # 2 - (A) Committed Hook. (D) Step forward and stop it with a rear **Woo Sow** (guarding hand). The rear hand wraps around the elbow as the front hand pins the shoulder. This is followed by a **Gwy Jon** (over the top elbow) to the face.

Movement # 3- (A) Wild Swing. (D) Simply step back as it passes by, then step slide **Juck Teck** (sidekick) to the midsection. **Note:** one kick might not be enough to knock him down, but it will be a good strike to slow down his attack. Additional techniques can be used against this attack to guarantee full defeat, such as a backhand to the head or a spinning back kick to the head.

Keeping your defense simple and effective is very important when facing an attacker with a weapon. When proper timing, power, and speed is executed you should not need more than one or two hits, and it will be over. No matter what kind of attack it is.

Movement # 4 - (A) Wild Swing. (D) Retreat, step forward, and **Juck Teck** (sidekick) to the face. With proper **pivoting** and body **alignment** you will be right on target.

Simply intercept his emotions and take him out before he does. Use **Jick Teck** (side kick) to the knee, or **Ow Teck** (hook kicks) to the back of the knee, but stay very alert. Just that strike might not be enough.

(1)   (2)   (3)

Movement # 5- (A) Committed Backhand. (D) Timing is key against this attack. Don't block too soon or halfway through the attack. Block it with a front **Tun Sow** (showing hand).

(4)   (5)   (6)

Step slide **Gum Sow** (pressing hand) with a rear hand **Chung Jan** (spade palm heel strike) to the face. Pivot outward with a **Lop Sow** (grab), circle the left hand up, and pop the elbow. Then sidekick the back of the knee as you control the wrist and the elbow.

(1)   (2)   (3)

Movement # 6- (A) Committed Over The Top. (D) Step forward and slide. Meet (a) with a rear **Woo Sow** (guarding hand) followed by a **Lop, Jick Teck** (grab, front kick) to the knee.

(4)

Switch to a **Lop Sow** (grab, pull) and step on his instep with your front foot as you deliver a **Choon Choy** (front punch) to his face, knocking his head back.

(1)　　　　　(2)　　　　　(3)　　　　　(4)

Movement # 7- (A) Committed Over The Top. (D) Block it with a front **Tun Sow** (showing hand). As you pull his arm down, switch the **Tun Sow** to a **Gum Sow** (pressing hand) and press down with rear hand as the front hand strikes under the chin with a **Pow Jan** (lifting palm).

(5)　　　　　(6)　　　　　(7)　　　　　(8)

As you continue to immobilize the hand, deliver a **Pie Jon** (horizontal elbow) to the face. Wrap the head with the right hand still controlling the hand with the weapon, and in a simultaneous movement push his head past your centerline. Then switch hand on the inside, from left to right.

(9)

Maintaining full control of his arm, grab the inside of his wrist and the biceps so the inside of his arm is facing the sky. Strike the outside of his right elbow at the joint, causing it to snap like a stick.

(1) (2) (3) (4)

Movement # 8- (A) Committed Hook. (D) Stop it with a rear **Woo Sow** (guarding hand). As you circle and wrap his elbow controlling the arm, deliver a **Pie Jon** (horizontal elbow) to the face.

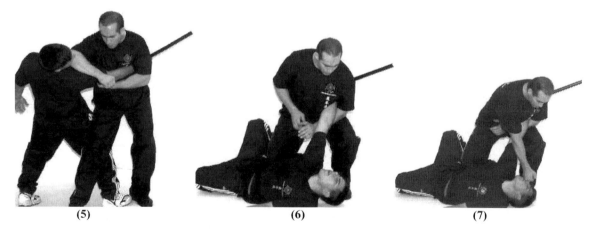

(5) (6) (7)

Place your front foot behind his front foot and hack him down. As he lands on the ground, drop your front knee into his ribs and lock the arm. Then punch him in the face, maintaining full control of his arm.

Movement # 9- (A) Committed Backhand. (D) Block it with a front **Tun Sow** (showing hand). Then switch to a **Lop/ Fun Sow** (grab, chop) to the throat by stepping behind his front leg. Kick the back of knee joint forcing him down (to do the attack effectively you should pull back on his shoulder as you kick the leg), and the impact of the simultaneous movement will force him down flat on his back.

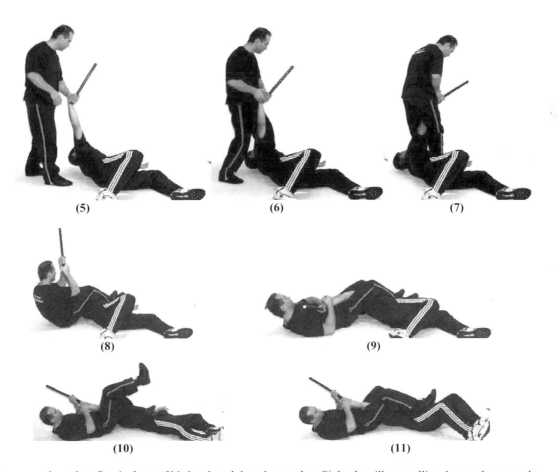

Place your front foot first in front of his head, and then the rear leg. Sit back, still controlling the arm between the knees. Crank his elbow back into a locked arm bar position. From an arm bar lock, raise the leg up and drop the heel into his groin.

(1)   (2)   (3)   (4)

Movement # 10-(A) Committed Over The Top. (D) Stop it with a front **Tun Sow** (showing hand block) high block. Then step slide and pin the hand with the weapon as you strike his throat with your forearm. Step behind him and punch his spine with the left hand as you still control his head.

PHOTO # (4) BACK VIEW   (5)

Jerk the head back against your chest in a tight grip position. Drop a **Chum Jon** (downward elbow) to the chest or throat.

(1)   (2)   (3)   (4)

(5)

Movement # 11- (A) Wild Swing (D) bob and weave to the outside, push shuffle and execute a rear cross to his ribs. Pin down his elbow with rear hand as you deliver a front vertical punch to the face followed with a **Owe Teck** (roundhouse kick) to the ribs, causing him to drop the weapon.

(1) (2)

Movement # 12- (A) Pinned To The Wall, pressing weapon against the throat. **(D)** Simply give a front kick to the groin.

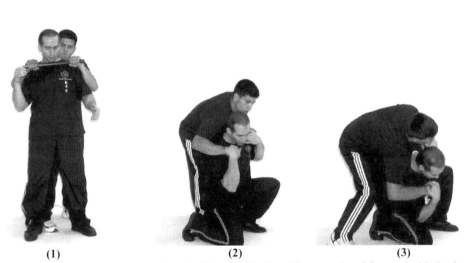

(1) (2) (3)

Movement # 13- (A) Rear Choke using the club. **(D)** Pin the club as you kneel forward with the **front leg** and lean. That will make him lose balance, and cause him to loosen up. Then flip him over onto his back.

(4) (5) (6) (7)

He will land head first which will cause him to be unconscious. Strip the weapon away, strike the head with an elbow followed with a smash to the face using his own club.

   (1)   (2)   (3)   (4)

Movement # 14- (A) Committed Hook. (D) Push shuffle and meet his attack with rear **Woo Sow** (guarding hand). Pivot, face him, and grab the wrist. Then strike under the biceps and slip the rear arm behind his elbow as you place the club behind your head.

   (5)   (6)

   (7)   (8)

Pivot and turn inward, forcing his body down. Controlling the arm, deliver a **Choon Kune** (straight punch) to the back of the head followed with a knee to side of the head. Then press his arm tight against your body, and turn his wrist out so that the fingers are pointing at his head. Put him in agony by controlling the arm very tight against your chest and pressing down on his fingers and wrist, locking the whole arm in place. One wrong move by him will cause the wrist and the elbow to snap.

Knife Defense

When facing a person with a knife, it's to be treated lightly but taken seriously. Here is why:
"Don't concentrate on the finger or you will miss the universe." If you only concentrate on his weapon and get threatened by it, automatically you will lose. You must not just focus on the knife, otherwise you will not to able to execute your techniques by targeting other areas. The knife is only an image, destroy the image, and you will win.

The threat is always either to the front, side, or back and can be treated lightly, unless the person has full control of one of your hands or you have been pinned against the wall - then it's treated very seriously. The first thing you can do is run and leave him standing there. This is using **"The Art of Fighting Without Fighting the fight."**

If you're very confident, you can strip the weapon out of his hand before he can blink an eye. In practice, you should always use plastic or wooden knives to prevent any accidents. I know a lot of people like to use live weapons, but I don't recommend it. If you are ever in a real life situation, then you apply the same techniques you have practiced to the real weapon. All these techniques I will demonstrate are very effective and will work every time if practiced and applied correctly. Remember, you must strip the weapon every time, and always push the knife away from your body not into it.

A=ATTACK OR ASSAILANT D=DEFENSE - ● =THE END OF THE TECHNIQUE

STATIONARY ATTACKS

(1) (2)

MOVEMENT # 1- (A) Threat To The Front (D) both hands come up at the same time, one pushes the outside of the hand in and the other pins the inside of wrist.

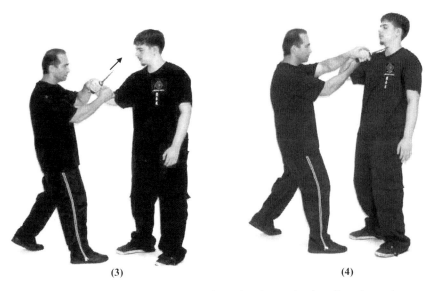

As you control the hand and the wrist, jam the knife into the throat, by bending the wrist towards his face.

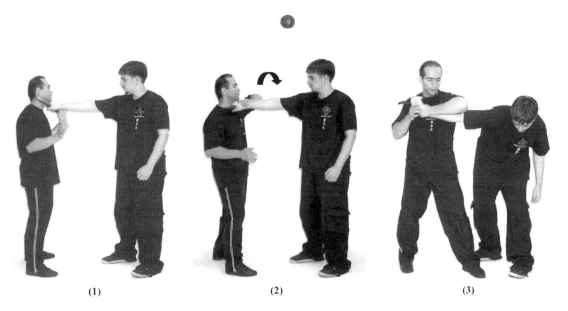

Movement # 2- (A) Threat To The Right Side Of The Neck (D) remember to pivot in and not out - the knife will cut you if you pivot out. Your left hand pins the wrist with the weapon. As you pivot, throw your elbow over his elbow for the lock as you control the weapon with both hands. Make sure you rotate the wrist so that his elbow joint faces the ceiling, to make the lock work. If you don't, then his elbow will bend a natural way and the lock or break will not work.

(4) (5)

Apply more pressure against the elbow until he releases the knife. Strip the weapon.

(1) (2) (3)

Movement # 3- (A) Threat To The Left Side Of The Neck (D) both hands shoot up from underneath the wrist. Then you control the hand, pivot out, and twist the wrist by pinning the fingers with the left hand and the inside of the wrist with the right hand. You can strip the weapon by applying pressure on the wrist after forcing him down.

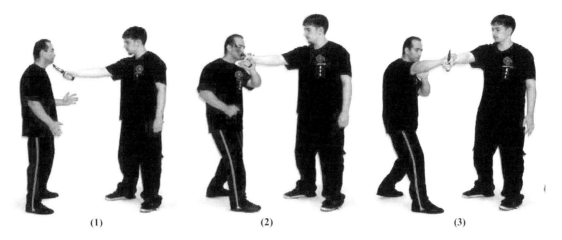

(1) (2) (3)

Movement # 4 – (A) Threat To The Front (D) push **Pock Sow** (slapping hand) with the rear hand, then switch to **Lop Sow** (grab, pull) get very good control of his arm.

(4) (5) (6)

Lop/Choon Kune (grab/straight punch) to the ribs, then pin the shoulder with the rear hand and kick Down his knee with an oblique kick as you jerk the shoulder back. Both motions must happen simultaneously causing him to collapse.

(1) (2) (3) (4)

Movement # 5- (A) Threat To The Left Side Of The Neck (D) both hands sneak up and control the wrist as you push away from your neck and slice across his neck in a circular motion.

(5) (6) (7) (8)

As you apply pressure on his wrist, slice across his abdomen in circular motion. That was vicious! Then hammer punch the back of the neck followed by a **Jick Teck** (front kick) to the face.

(9) (10) (11)

Pin the back of the neck as you push with your other hand to flip him over on his back. Strip the weapon.

Movement # 6- (A) Threat To The Right Side Of The Neck (D) push with your left hand and pull in with your right, jam the knife into his throat then circle his hand under and slice across the abdomen.

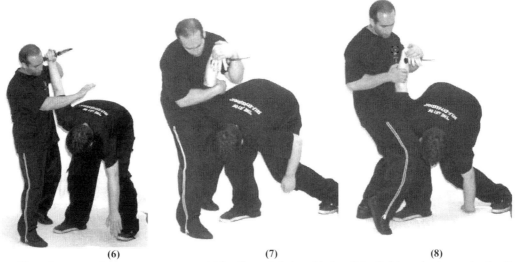

Lock the elbow by wrapping your arm around his elbow joint and bring it in tight against your body. Push the fingers down towards his back and that will apply pressure on the wrist. While applying pressure, front knee to the face.

Movement # 7- (A) Threat To The Back Of The Neck With Hand Pinned (D) step out with the right foot as you sneak the right hand up and pin the hand with the weapon; this must be done very fast as you slip under his armpit. With control of the hand, jam the knife into his abdomen using the right hand. Control with both hands and lock the wrist by pushing the fingers at a 45-degree angle. Note- if you get good control of his hand with the weapon you can also strike the groin as you slip out - that will cause him to loosen up.

Sneak the right hand and pin his hand with the weapon as you strike the groin with the left hammer punch. Pivot out as you control the hand with the weapon with both of your hands.

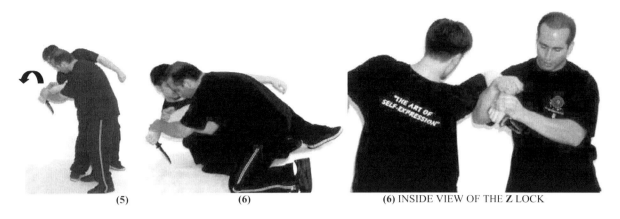

(5) (6) (6) INSIDE VIEW OF THE Z LOCK

Movement # 8- (A) Threat To The Back Of The Neck Hand Pinned (D) pin the hand with the knife as the other hand slips behind his wrist. Push it away and place the right hand behind the triceps as you push with your left hand creating a z lock. That will cause him to either fall down or the shoulder will pull out of the socket.

(1) (2) (3)

Knife

(4) (5)

Movement # 9- (A) Threat To The Front (D) Soong Pock Sow (double slapping hands) simultaneous attack. Your left hand pushes the outside of his hand and knuckles as the right strikes the inside of the wrist, forcing the knife out of his hand.

Movement #10- (A) Threat To The Front With Your Hand Grabbed (D) your other hand comes up, pivot at 90 degrees and push the hand with the knife across his body, trapping it.

Circle your elbow over his elbow joint and as you bend the hand, pull his arm tight into your body controlling the whole arm. Apply pressure against the elbow and the hand, and then strip the weapon as you execute a rear knee to his face.

LUNGING IN ATTACKS

(1)　　(2)　　(3)　　(4)　　(5)

Movement # 11- (A) Attack Comes Straight In (D) pivot out at a 25-degree angle and block with left **Die Bong Sow** (low wing arm deflection). Then **Lop Sow** (grab, pull), **Gwa Choy** (back hand) to the ribs, followed by a backhand to the face. Note - make sure you lop and strike at the same time with a little jerk with your **Lop** for added torque and power.

(6)　　(7)　　(8)

Pin the face as you control the hand with the knife. Then kick the back of his knee with an oblique kick. As he falls back, meet his elbow with your knee, causing it to snap at the joint.

(1)　　(2)　　(3)　　(4)　　(5)

Movement # 12 - (A) Hook With An Arm Grab (D) block with left **Tun sow** or **Woo** (showing block or guarding block) and pivot at a 90 degree angle by trapping his elbow joint between your ribs and your arm. Pivot back to position and face him, circle the hand under his armpit, and pin the shoulder with the right hand. As the left hand clamps on the right wrist, push his arm up towards the ceiling to make him release the knife. That will also snap the elbow at the joint.

Movement #13- (A) Straight In (D) step out of the way to your left (his outside) and block with a low **gung sow** (low sweep block). Turn and face him, immobilize his hand with rear **Gum Sow** (pressing hand) as you strike him under the chin, with rear **Chung Jan** (angle spade palm strike). Re-trap by grabbing the hand with the weapon as your left hand **Fun Sow** (chops) his throat.

Movement #14- (A) Straight In (D) pivot in at a 25-degree angle, block with rear **Die Bong Sow** (low wing arm Deflection)

Lop (grab) with the front hand, get good control of the hand and strike with rear **Gwa Choy** (Back hand) to the side of the head. You can take it even further. Pass his hand across your body with Cautious **Gwat Sow**. As you pass, switch the hand to a grab and strike his face with a **JKD** vertical punch **Choon choy.** Note -you can stop at movement **(2)** or you can kick low or break the elbow, but to add to the technique you can pass it across your body. You have to be very cautious. Normally you don't pass a sharp object in front of your body. You always want to be on his outside, but movement # 3 and 4 are executed only if you strike first. That will make him very loose, so it is much easier for you to pass a weapon with confidence.

(4)   (5)   STRIP THE WEAPONS

Switch to **Lop Sow** (grab, pull), **Gwa Choy** or **Choon Choy** (straight punch) to the face. Always strip the weapon.

(1)   (2)   (3)

Movement # 15- (A) Straight In/Threatening (D) deflect the hand with **Noy Huen Wan Teck** (outside crescent kick). While deflecting the hand down, **Ow Teck** (hook kick) to the face. This technique is normally executed with speed at the moment of attack as he is still in kicking range and he is unaware of your defense. If he is coming in with power and speed then you must apply other applications to the same attack.

(1)   (2)   (3)   (4)

(5)   (6)

Movement # 16- (A) Straight In (D) block his hand with rear pock **sow** (slapping hand), switch to **Lop** (grab) **Ow Tech** (round house) to the ribs. While still in good control of his arm **Juck Teck** (side kick) to the knee.

(1) (2) (3)
(4) (5) INSIDE VIEW OF PHOTO (5)

Movement # 17- (A) Over The Top (D) block his hand with front **Fack Sow** (high block). Place the rear hand on the inside of his elbow joint. Simultaneously push with your right forearm and pull in with the left hand locking the arm into a **Z** lock. If he still doesn't feel it, simply push down further, that will pop the shoulder out of the socket.

(1)   (2)   (3)   (4)

Movement # 18- (A) Over The Top (D) step forward, and meet his attack with front **Biu Jon Sow** (thrusting hand). With speed switch to rear **Gum Sow** (pressing hand), then strike with **Chun Jan** (spade palm strike) to the face.

(3)   (4)

Re-trap, pin the shoulder, grab the hand with the knife and pull back. Then **Moy Yin Gyeuk** (invisible kick) to the back of the knee. All motions must happen at the same, which will cause him to collapse on impact.

(1)   (2)   (3)

(4)   (5)   (6)

Movement # 19- (A) Front Hook (D) stop his attack with front **Jom Sow** (chop block), guard his hand by controlling it with **Lop Sow** (grab, or pull) as you switch the front hand to a **Gwa Choy** (back hand) to the side of his face. **Lop** (grab) his front hand and finish him with an **Ow Teck** (hook kick) to the abdomen, or **Juck Teck** (side kick to the head).

Movement # 20- (A) Upward Lunge (D) step in and block his attack with **Sup Jee Sow** (x block). Circle his hand and pivot inward towards his body so that your hips line up with his. Place the shoulder under his elbow joint, and turn and face the opposite direction. With both hands controlling his hand, pull down the hand with the weapon as you push up with your shoulder. Apply pressure on his elbow joint and pop the elbow.

Movement # 21- (A) Right Hook (D) step in and meet his attack with **Soong Jom Sow** (double chopping block). Turn and face him and circle the rear arm around his elbow joint. As you pin the shoulder with the front hand, lock the elbow by pulling in towards your chest with the rear hand and pushing his shoulder back with the front hand. Note - make sure that his arm is trapped at least half way in. Also use your forearm to jack up his elbow for more surface power.

Pin the back of the head with the front hand and pull it down to your knee. Smash his face.

Movement # 22- (A) Front Back Hand (D) block with front **Tun Sow** (showing hand), **Lop** (grab), and **Jom** (chop) the elbow. Then take him down. Get good control of his arm and pin him down.

Place yourself in front of his body and fold his fingers back as you pin down his shoulder with your elbow. Lock the arm by pushing back on the elbow joint and the fingers causing his wrist, elbow, and shoulder to lock. Strip the weapon.

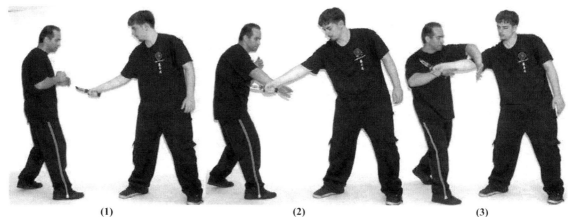

(1)　　　　　　　　　　(2)　　　　　　　　　　(3)

Movement # 23- (A) Straight In (D) step slightly to his outside and block with **Gung Sow** (low sweep block). Place the rear hand on the inside of his elbow joint and push with the right hand into him as you trap his elbow.

(4)

Jam the knife into his throat. A good martial artist will try to get control of the weapon without hurting anyone, but sometimes, you have to do what it takes to save your own life.

(1)　　　　　　　(2)　　　　　　　(3)　　　　　　　(4)

(5)

Movement # 24- (A) Right Pin Against a Wall (D) raise the left and control the hand with weapon. Grab with your other hand to get full control, and twist his hand out in a circular motion, which will cause pain to his wrist and elbow joints. Maintaining full control of his arm, strike him with **Soong Jon** (horizontal elbow) to the face.
As he gets knocked down, finish him with a straight punch to the side of the head

(1)　　　(2)　　　(3)　　　(4)

(5)　　　(6)

Movement # 25- (A) Right Pin Against a Wall (D) pin the hand with the knife. As you pivot in, locking his elbow, turn the hand with the knife in so it's now pointing at his head and locking the wrist. Strip the knife.

(7)   (8)   (9)

As you control the arm, place the edge of the knife against the inside of his elbow joint, pull in. Place his elbow against your chest and press back with his wrist. This will hurt.

(1)   (2)   (3)

Movement # 26- (A) Hand Grab And Lunging In Attack (D) with speed, pivot in and block with rear **Die Bong Sow** (low wing arm deflection). Free the grabbed hand. Grab and get control of the hand with the weapon.

(4)   (5)

Control the hand with the knife **Lop** (grab) and **Fun sow** (chop) to the throat. Lean back **Juck Teck** (side kick) to the back of his knee to knock him down. Note- make sure that you pull your knee back to generate power and to create distance to deliver the most power into one spot.

SIMPLE AND DIRECT!

(1)　　　　　　　　　　(2)

Movement # 27- (A) Lunging Attempt (D) Juck Teck (side kick) to the abdomen.

Note" - executing the sidekick, you must lean back and remain low. You want to be as far as you can from his reach just in case enough damage wasn't done. This will enable you to follow up with extra techniques if needed.

Gun Defense

(A)=ATTACKER OR ASSAILANT (D)=DEFENSE. ⬤ = END OF THE TECHNIQUE
First, you should always practice with wood or plastic guns - never with real weapons to prevent any accidents.

Several things should be considered when facing an opponent with a gun. He should be treated much more seriously than a person with a knife, club, or empty hands. You have very little time to respond, and need a lot of confidence to execute the move correctly. One mistake can mean the difference between life and death. Confidence, speed, and coordination are depended on heavily. Every single technique should be executed properly, and practiced over and over until the move becomes part of you. In real situations you don't have enough time to say 'maybe I will push it out of the way, or maybe I will strip the gun this way.' If you do you have already lost.

However, remember that someone with a gun has only one weapon, and he's very concentrated on that weapon. You have many weapons, like hands, feet, elbows, knees etc. If you use them to their maximum, you will be in better position over the person with a gun. These techniques will **only** work in **up close** threatening situations. They absolutely **will not work** from a distance. You see you might be able to take a little cut here and there, or get hit with a club, or get punched, but no one can take a bullet.

The weapon must be **stripped** from the assailant every time after the technique is executed. Especially guns - never think for one moment that you can hit someone and assume that you don't have to strip the weapon away. You want to finish him and finish him fast. Extra strikes can be added to these techniques. Always get full control of the arm or the weapon, then strike. It can be a knee, kick, punch, elbow, or what ever is available during the execution of the technique. **Do not** indulge in any unnecessary movements. The less done the better. The faster you strip the weapon or control the arm the better.

Distraction is very important against your assailant. You have to be very deceptive by allowing him to think you are scared, and that you can't defend yourself. The best way is to get his mind off the weapon and more concentrated on you. Ask him questions, like 'what do you want? Do you want my wallet? Why are you trying to hurt me?' Etc… You must distract him to make the technique more effective. While he is answering, execute the technique.

(1)   (2)   (3)

Movement # 1- (A) -Pointing At –Midsection (D) all blocking, stepping, pivoting must happen at the same time.
Step to the left side and pivot the upper body at a 35-degree angle to get off the fire line. Push the assailant's hand with your left hand, grab underneath the barrel with the right hand. As you get full control of his hand and the gun, circle up pointing the gun at the assailant's midsection leaving his finger in the trigger and causing the gun to fire. Something you didn't intend to happen but it happens.

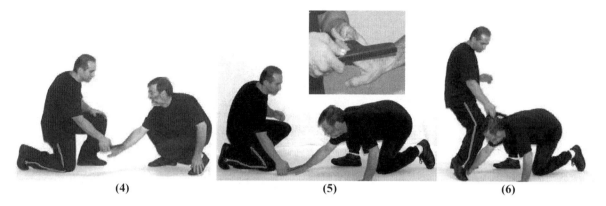

(4) (5) (6)

If the gun didn't fire, try trapping the finger inside the trigger. Apply pressure pulling the gun down. That will force him to go down or the finger will break inside the trigger. Take him down to the ground using the gun. Then strip the weapon. Either a knee to the face or a punch to the head will do very good damage.

(1) (2) (3) (4)

Movement # 2- (A) Gun Pointing At Head- (D) duck down and reach up with both hands at the same time. Pin the wrist with both hands as you circle your elbow over his elbow still controlling the arm. Apply pressure, causing him to release then strip the weapon.

(5)

FRONT KICK TO THE FACE CAN BE APPLIED AFTER YOU STRIP THE WEAPON.

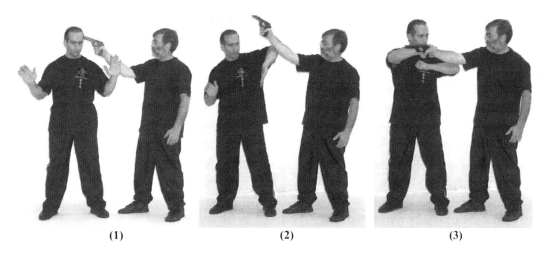

(1)   (2)   (3)

Movement # 3- (A) Left Side Threat. **(D)** Deflect his arm with your own **Bong Sow** pull **Lop Sow.**

(4)   (5)   (6)   (7)

Lop /Fun Sow or Gwa Choy (grab/chop or back hand) to his throat or the face as you control the hand with the gun. Pin the shoulder and sidekick down the back of the knee forcing him back. As he falls back meet him with a knee to the back of the head.

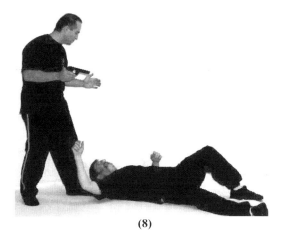

(8)

Take full control of the weapon, stomp the face.

Movement # 4- (A) Right Side Threat (D) pivot out and face the assailant blocking his arm with **Woo Sow** (guarding hand). **Lop (grab)** the wrist **controlling the arm** /**Jom Sow** (chop) the elbow. The chop in this defense is mainly used to break the elbow. You must pull in his wrist and turn it up so that his knuckles are facing the sky. That will force his elbow to lock so it will be much easier for the break. Compare it to a motorcycle throttle - it's the same motion.

If the break does not happen then the pressure from the blow will force him down. That will give you a very good opportunity to strip the weapon. Execute a rear front kick to the ribs.

Movement # 5- (A) Threat To The Back Of The Head (D) pivot out and deflect his arm with **Fack Sow** (high block) on his outside. **Lop Sow** (pull or grab) his wrist as you chop his elbow joint using the forearm for a stronger break.

Apply pressure on the elbow forcing him down. Maintain full control of the arm, strip the weapon.

Movement # 6-(A) Threat To The Back Of The Head (D) pivot in to his inside with **Fack Sow** high block)

deflecting his arm. Right hand pins the shoulder as the rear hand circles underneath the elbow joint, trapping the hand with gun under the armpit. Note: make sure that when locking the elbow you're right on the center of his arm. The closer you are to his body the better, that way you will have very good control of the arm and

the weapon. On the other hand you don't want to be too far out because the gun barrel will be too close to your side.
If you are in closer to him and he decides to fire from the pressure on his elbow, it will not hit you.
Circle on the inside, and pin the shoulder with the front hand as you wrap the elbow and lock it. If the lock is applied correctly, the assailant will not have enough strength to pull the trigger because his elbow will be separated from the joint. To apply proper pressure on the elbow you must push down with front hand against his shoulder and push up the rear forearm against his elbow joint. Raising the rear heel for extra torque will be ideal. If he tries to struggle a good knee to the groin will be very efficient.

(1)   (2)   (3)

Movement # 7-(A) Threat To The Back Of The Head (D) pivot outside **Fack Sow** (high block) deflecting his arm. Grab the wrist with the front hand and place the rear hand on the inside of the elbow as you push and pull in **Jut Sow** (jerking hand) at the same time.

(4)
Smash the face with his own weapon.

- 414 -

(1)   (2)   (3)

Movement # 8- (A) Side Threat (D) left **Bong Sow** (wing arm deflection block) **Lop Sow** (grab, pull) with the right hand and juck **Teck** (sidekick) to the knee. That will force his body forward for the backhand to the ribs while controlling the arm.

(4)   (5)   (6)

As you **Lop Sow** (pull, grab) **Gwa Choy** (back hand) to the ribs followed with a backhand to the head.

(7)   (8)   (9)

As you still immobilize the hand **Ow Teck** (hook kick) to the abdomen **Juck Teck** to the knee, then strip the weapon. Note - make sure that the weapon is not pointing at you when you side kick to the knee. You should have full control of the arm at all times.

(1)   (2)   (3)

Movement # 9- (A) Threat to The Back Of The Head (D) pivot inward facing him as you guard the hand pull into **Lop Sow.Choon Choy** (grab/straight punch) to the face.

(4)

Keep full control of the hand with the weapon. **Lop /Jick Teck** (grab/front kick) to the groin.

(1)   (2)   (3)   (4)

Movement # 10-(A) To Mid Section (D) pivot out a t a 35-degree angle (push grab and pivot) simultaneously. Getting full control of the hand, turn and face him. As you support with other hand, point the gun at the Face. Apply pressure to the wrist to strip the weapon. Note- when you pivot and grab you must grab and trap the thumb and part of the gun. If you don't he will slip out.

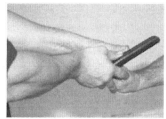

Movement # 10, trapping the gun and the hand

(1)　　　　　　(2)　　　　　　(3)　　　　　　(4)　　　　photo (4) back view

Movement # 11- (A) Under the Chin (D) pivot into his inside push his hand away from your face with **Woo Sow** (guarding hand). Place the right hand on the inside of elbow joint as the left hand hooks on his wrist. Simultaneously pull in and push out - that will force him down or his shoulder joint will dislocate. Always strip the weapon.

(1)　　　　　　(2)　　　　　　(3)　　　　　　(4)

Movement # 12-(A) Threat to the Head (D) deflect his arm with the front hand as you step forward **Lop Sow** (grab, pull) **Choon Choy** (straight punch) to the ribs. As you control the hand **Jeep Sow** (break the elbow), pull down his hand as you push the elbow joint up. That will cause the elbow to snap.

(5)   (6)

Added movements: oblique kick to the knee or, roundhouse kick to the abdomen.

(1)   (2)   (3)

Movement # 13- (A) Threat To The Left Side Of The Head (D) turn and face him by deflecting his hand with **Woo Sow** (guarding hand). **Lop** (grab) with the left hand as you strike with **Pie Jon** or **Song Jon** (horizontal or outward elbow) to the face.

(4)   (5)

Lop (grab) front **Jick Teck** (front kick) to the groin to loosen him up. Step slide **Choon Choy** (vertical punch) to the face. Control the arm.

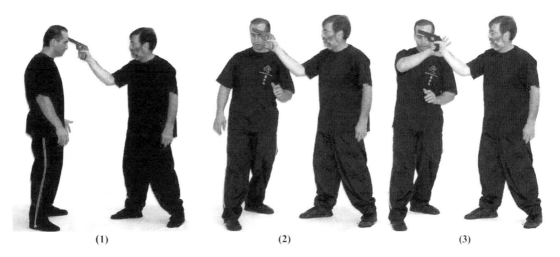

(1) (2) (3)

Movement #14- (A) Front of the Head (D) pivot out, getting out of the fire line. Grab with right hand controlling his hand.

(4) (5) (6) closer view of photo (6)

Lop Sow (grab or pull) the hand with the weapon as you strike his ribs with **Gwa Choy** (back hand). Place the left hand on the inside of his elbow joint and push with the right towards his face smashing his face with the gun. Simple, direct but damaging.

(7) (8) (9)

Pass the gun thru the center in a circular motion. Make sure that the barrel is pointing downward and lock his wrist as you strip the weapon. Normally I do not pass any kind of weapon in front of me, but you should be able to do it if you applied the previous techniques correctly and with power. That should've left him in no position to do anything.

Final reminder - always strip the weapon because you don't want to take any chances.

Scientific Ground Fighting

I don't like to call "Ground Fighting" Grappling because in ground fighting, the way I teach, there are no rules. Everything goes. Another major reason is the word `**Martial,** which means **warlike; fond of fighting.** When grappling is used in the ring as a **sport**, there are many rules and regulations to follow such as: no eye jabs, no hair pulling, no biting, no small joints manipulation, no closed fists, no strikes to the groin, no kicking to the face, no knee shots, no head butts to the face, no pinching, no throat shots, no kicking to the spine, no elbow strikes, and no dirty fighting. When **Martial Arts** (all combative forms, like Jeet kune do, karate, judo, gung-fu, aikido, Ju-Jitsu etc....are treated as a sport, you will develop weakness in your defense against your attacker and all your weapons will be stripped way from you. It is like sending a soldier to war with a big gun, but without ammo.

Like I mentioned before, to be a good JKD practitioner, you must be open-minded and learn all ranges. The way I like to teach is more of a fighting approach and not a competition approach. Besides when facing an opponent that weights 275 lbs and is 6'5", who wants to be grappling with him? Let me assure you, you will lose if all of your weapons are taken away. Most real fights end up on the ground, so ground-fighting techniques are extremely useful, but you shouldn't just grapple, you must be a complete fighter to survive on the ground. And a good JKD fighter finishes the fight before it gets to the ground. In addition, you can apply all your techniques on the ground the same way as you would standing up.

"In sports, there are rules and regulations, but in real fighting, you better train every part of your body to it's fullest and Be prepared for what ever needs to be done and what ever works to WIN.

Having second thoughts?   Become his best friend and pose with him   or- Just do it, and be a Martial Artist

I definitely don't want to be grappling with this man, he is too big! Besides, he studies martial arts and is a weight lifter as well as being extremely powerful. There are few options, you can use, you can ask him to train you, or just become his best friend like I did. Or you can use all of your weapons to their maximum capacity, and use every range of combat without being limited to just grappling range. Then you will have a better chance against this man.

There are many ways you can defeat a man this size. If you are confident about yourself and use every part of your body -you will have a very good chance of taking him out.

Your opponent is facing you, ready to charge in. He is not striking, nor is he committed to any attack. He just wants to knock you down like a charging bull.

Defense: Execute a roundhouse kick to his front knee knocking him off balance. That will give you a better opportunity to shoot in and wrap both arms around his waist in a tackle. But don't just lie on top. Make sure you finish him by applying closed fist to the side of the head or knees to the spine. That is the only way you're going to keep him down.

Another way is as he charges in, push his face with the front hand as the left hand wraps around his head. Apply the front head lock. Make sure you view small joint manipulation for proper execution of the front headlock.

There are two ways to stop this guy from taking you to the ground. As he attempts to shoot in at you, push his head to the outside with the rear hand. As you place or strike with open ridge hand against his throat, you can either twist his head and jack it up which it will be very devastating, or you can just place your chest tight against his head, and strike under his chin or throat using the forearm. Grab the right hand with the left hand and jack him up by applying pressure against his neck.

(1) (2) (3)

If he charges in and catches you by surprise, and you have no time to strike or get him in a front headlock, then just let your upper body weight rest on his head slowing down his attack when he goes in to grab you for a takedown.

(4) (5)

Wrap the left arm around his neck. As you place the front foot behind his front leg, get good control of his head and neck and force him off balance. Turn your upper body in clockwise rotation as you control his head. Flip backwards landing on your feet and back - make sure that you never let go of his neck while falling back. Maintain full control of his head and neck throughout the whole technique as you apply a reverse choke and a bar arm lock.

(1) (2) (3)

Another way of getting him off you is to step back a few steps depending on how hard and fast he is coming in. Just clear enough distance between you and him as you push his head down, throwing him off balance. Execute a rear knee to the side of the head, getting him dizzy, then step back with the rear foot as you front kick him to the throat just in case he didn't feel the first hit.

If still more is needed, step down with the front foot and knee him right in the kisser. Push his head back to clear the line, and execute a front vertical punch to the side of the head

Push down against his knee joint with the left hand, as you pull his front leg off the ground. Both the push against the knee and pulling back must happen simultaneously, but make sure that you do all the strikes first before you execute this technique. He is too big and he might just knee you in the face while you're trying to lift his leg up. After he falls back, get good control of his leg, stand up, and stomp down his groin using all of your weight.

Here, your opponent knocks you down. As he tries to reach you for more attacks or gets on top to pin you down, intercept him with a front kick to his groin as you wrap the left leg behind his front leg. Kick him back off balance. Make sure that you place the left leg behind his right leg in a hook position and push against his groin with the right leg at the same time.

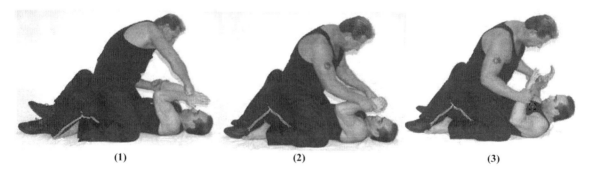

In this series, he gets you down on the ground as he kneels down by placing all of his weight on your stomach and chest and ready to strike you to the face. Bring both hands up and protect your face from any straight blows to the center of your face. He grabs both of your hand trying to clear the path so he can strike. Turn your hand outward to loosen him up, and then jack the lower part of your body up, knocking him off balance. As he tries to regain his position, grab his right arm with both hands and slip under his armpit as you place his arm on your right shoulder. Push down with both hands against his shoulder, slightly locking his arm in position until he taps out.

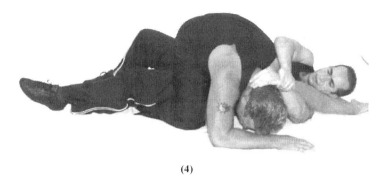

(4)

Make sure that both hands are pressing against his shoulder and the back of his elbow joint. Also make sure that it is facing up not down, because if you don't, then his elbow will just bend in a natural position and he will not feel the lock.

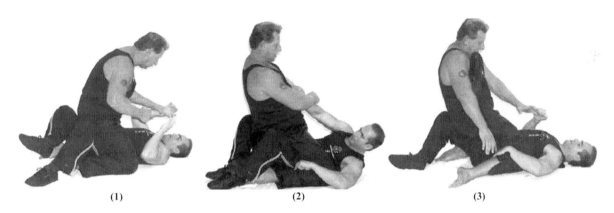

(1)   (2)   (3)

Variation: He knocks you down and he kneels on top of you with all of his weight. Wrap your left arm around his right knee and push him back with right arm to clear the distance between his chest and your left leg.

(4)

Place the left foot on his chest as you push him back but maintain control of his leg. As he leans back, place the right hand against his left knee and wrap the left arm around his right calf and push his knee back. This might not be the best lock available but it will definitely get him off you.

Variation: He is on top of you, ready to knock your lights out, and he might think that you're defenseless but he's wrong. Like I said before, you can apply the same techniques on the ground as you have standing up - there is no difference. Block on his inside with your left block of any kind as you wrap around his elbow joint locking his arm. You can execute a punch to his face, or just simply grab the back of his head with the right hand as you still immobilize his arm. Jerk him in tight against your body and show him some love by biting the side of his neck. **"If you're in a close quarter and wish to survive and NOT get tapped out, what do you do?** You bite, Scratch, finger jab, pull the hair, pinch, fight dirty.

He is ready to get you in a side mount, pin his left arm against your chest, raise the left leg and place it on the side of his neck. Drop your leg down, getting him in a leg choke by squeezing against his neck and using the back of your thigh and the back of the calf. Apply it like a pair of closed scissors. Make sure that you straighten up the right knee and place it against the right side of his face so that he doesn't have room to escape.

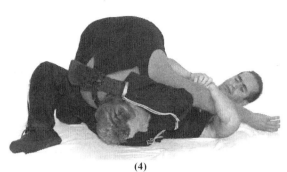
(4)

Squeeze his neck tighter against the back of your thigh, straighten his arm out and lock his elbow, giving him no room to escape.

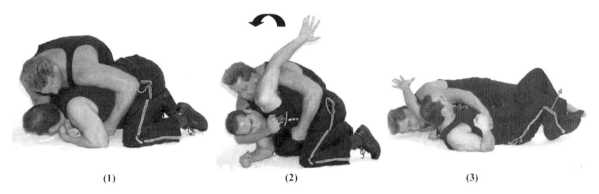
(1) (2) (3)

He's in a side, kneeling down position. Wrap the arm around his side and rotate your body in a circular motion, flipping him on his back. As he lands on the ground strike him in the groin so he stays down.

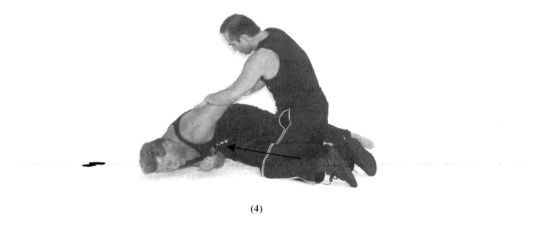
(4)

Rotate your body in a kneeling position and get control of his arm by pressing down on the elbow joint with left hand, and by controlling the wrist with the right hand. Knee him to the face.

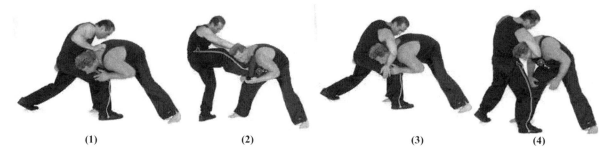

As he charges in anchor the ball of the rear foot into the ground and push him back. Grab the back of his head with the front hand and pull him in as you front kick him to the throat or the face. Wrap the front hand around his head and lock him into a front headlock position.

Both partners in kneeling position with both hands on each others shoulders. Either partner can slip in the left hand across the side of the face. Place the edge of the hand against his Adam's apple. As you circle around his neck, turn it so that his face is in a horizontal position. Press his head against your chest as you jack up his neck - that will make him tap out and will leave him no choice.

Both partners are struggling for a take down or a lock. Either partner can slip down and wrap both arms around the waist. Surge forward with both feet knocking him back. Make sure that you keep your head behind his shoulder and body tight against his body, so that he's not in striking range of your head. Push down with your left hand and strike repeatedly with closed fist to the head.

As you attempt to shoot forward, make sure that both hands are in front of you for a guard - just in case your opponent attempts to knee you in the face. Block his knee with an **x** block. Grab his front knee with both arms and lift him off balance for the flip. Make sure that you are not standing directly in front of his leg, and make sure that you step to his inside. If you don't as you try to attempt to lift his leg, he can kick you straight in the groin and you will be helping by lifting his leg up.

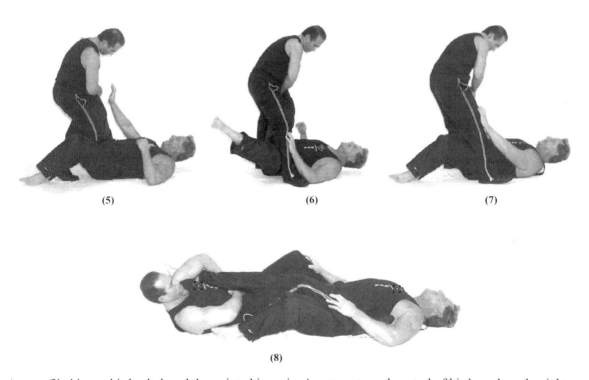

As you flip him on his back, kneel down into his groin. As you get good control of his leg, place the right foot on the side of hips and lean back and place the right legs on top of his chest to help pin him down. Get good control of the leg by wrapping the left arm around his ankle and calf area, and place the right hand behind the calf simultaneously. Jack the leg upward causing enough pressure against his knee and ankle area that he will tap out or the ankle will be permanently damaged.

(1) (2) (3) (4) (5)

I attempt a roundhouse kick to his ribs. He grabs my leg as he takes me down on my back and pins me down with his front hand. I sneak my left leg straight through his centerline as I pin down his arm against my chest. If he slips his head to the opposite side, I place the left foot under his chin and push up, as I still control his hand against my chest. That will give me a better position because I get control of him.

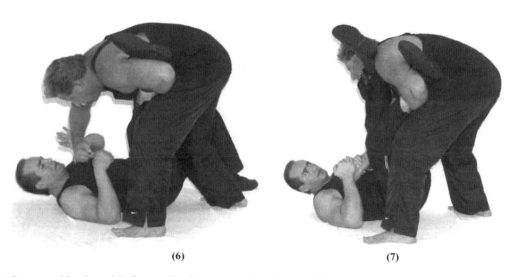

(6) (7)

He gets loose and back on his feet and strikes at my face. I parry his fist across, wrap both arms around his hand and pin it again against my chest. I throw the left leg over his right elbow joint as I push against his throat with top of my foot. Any movement by him will cause instant tap out.

He charges in and hangs on, and when it becomes a brawling match, there are many ways you can end the fight quickly. You can strike to the throat, knee to the groin, head butt to the face, finger jab to the eyes, or even pinch his sides and he will let go quickly. You can wrap the left leg around his front leg and the left arm around his elbow joint and push back with the right hand against his throat or shoulder knocking him down. As he falls back, catch him on the way down by hanging on his arm. As he hits the ground, drop the right knee against his right rib and clamp the left hand on the inside of your elbow joint as the right hand pushes up for extra strength against the left hand. The applied pressure from both attacks will cause his elbow joint to snap.

(1) (2)

He charges in trying to grab you, go on the inside of his arms. Push against his left shoulder with the right hand spinning him around.

(3)   Back view   (4)

Grab his head with a rear headlock /choke and jerk him back getting him off balance. As he falls back, punch him to the spine with the left hand followed with a knee to the center of the back. No matter how strong and big he is, he's not getting back up.

(1) (2) (3) (4)

From a charging in position he gets you in a front headlock. Strike with the forearm upwards to his groin. That will force him to step back as you slip out. Note: Make sure that you don't allow him enough time to squeeze your head - strike as soon as he grabs.

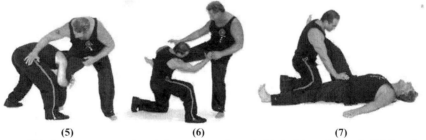

(5) (6) (7)

Wrap both arms around his knee area as you kneel down on one knee to his inside and keep in tight against his leg to avoid any kneeing to your face. Strike his groin with an open palm. As he leans back, pick him up on one leg and push him back, dropping him on his back.

All fights that I have witnessed start with a shove. As he places both of his hands on your shoulders or chest, circle the left hand over his right and left arms. As you grab the side of his left hand, push down with both of your hands against his wrist.

Or from the shove, circle the left arm on the inside of his left arm, and place his hand on your left shoulder. Grab your own hand with the right, and press down against his elbow joint see photo **(A)**.

Another option- from the lock, slide both hands back along his arm, and clamp on his hand. Control it with both hands and press forward against his wrist. Circle the left elbow over his right elbow joint by stepping forward. Push down against his wrist locking the wrist and elbow. Make sure that you rotate his arm so that the outside of his elbow joint is facing the ceiling. Otherwise, his elbow will bend in a natural position. As you still control his hand and wrist step back and execute a front kick to his face.

(1) (2) (3)

From a shoving attack, grab the back of his neck with both hands and bring him in into your head butt. Step back and finger jab him into the eyes blinding him even more. Grab both of his wrists and jerk him inward as you meet him with a front kick to the groin.

(4) (5)

Grab the back of his head and jerk it down as you knee him to the face. Rotate the hips to gain distance, and side kick his knee down collapsing it.

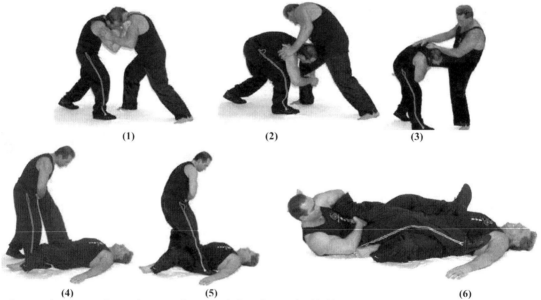

(1) (2) (3)

(4) (5) (6)

He grabs your head to push you down on the ground. Step forward with his momentum and wrap the back of his front knee with your left arm and lift him off the ground down on his back. Sit back, place the right leg over his right knee joint, and get good control of his foot. You also heel kick him to the groin while you're on the ground - don't hold anything back!

From a ready fighting position, he's ready to take you out. Do not be intimidated by his thick neck and size. He steps forward so intercept him with a sidekick to the throat, knocking his head back. Make sure that you pivot the rear foot and rotate the hips for extra power.

In case he didn't feel the kick to the throat step forward and open up on him with a left cross, right cork screw to the side of the head, left cross again, and right elbow. Pass the right hand under his elbow and smash his face with an open palm as you immobilize his arm. If you need to add kicks and knees to finish the job, just do it and don't let any rules stand in your way.

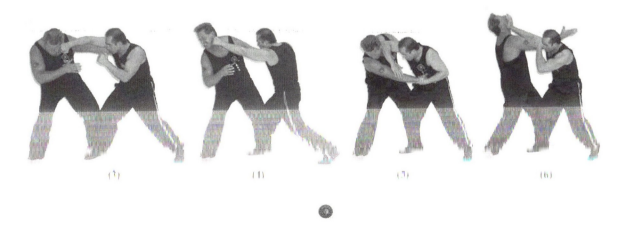

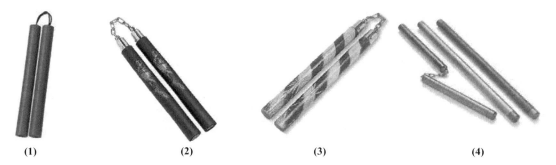

1) Foam with a cord attachment. 2) Foam with ball bearing and chain 3) Wood with ball bearing and chain 4) Aluminum and it can be used as a club.

Nunchaku

  The nunchaku comes in many different styles. Some are made out of foam with a cord connecting the two sticks. Some are made out of foam, wood, or aluminum with a chain and a ball bearing swivel connection. The nunchaku are mainly used for demonstration purposes. **They are illegal in some states, so it's not advisable to walk around the street with them.**

  What the nunchaku will help the practitioner develop are speed, coordination, and whipping power. It is just an **extension of your hand.** If you take away the weapon, nothing should change as far as speed and whip power. Every single movement with the nunchaku represents a technique, whether it is a block or a strike. That is another reason why I teach it. The nunchaku is an exercise to help maintain your speed and coordination. You must practice it periodically to get good at it. Then you can apply it to a real life situation. The demonstration will only help you follow along but it is up to you to get better at it, and get faster, and to be creative with it.

  There is no particular way to practice the nunchaku or a certain opening. Each person should have his or her own unique way of doing it. The way I do it is not necessarily the same way another person would do it. That is why it is not a form or a kata. Some schools might make it a kata or form, but I don't, so it is up to you to practice it any way you like.

  The nunchaku will also help build your right lead tremendously as far as the hammer principle, straight punch or block counter. It forces the hand to remain in a vertical punch and to retract back to position if you don't bring it back, because then the nunchaku will just dangle. It will not have any whip power. When you tuck it under your armpit it's also forcing your elbow in to protect your ribs - otherwise you will lose it. The distance between the armpit and the fist when you are holding the nunchaku in position is a perfect distance for a punch without the nunchaku. You will not be too far out or too far in.

  After practicing the nunchaku religiously, your right hand punch becomes like an elastic band - it will be **"felt before it's seen."** The nunchaku exercise that has been demonstrated here is not so much for you to follow step by step; it's only to have you pick and choose the technique you like to get good at. I don't expect you to do the same as I do, because it's not a rehearsed routine. Just pick it up and make up your own routine.

  I also highly recommend that you start with the foam with cord attachment nunchaku to prevent any injuries. As you get good at it then you can move up a step to foam with ball bearings and chain, then to wood or aluminum. Some practitioners like to do it in a By-Jon stance, while some like to do it in natural stance. You can add footwork to it and acrobatic techniques. Try to make it very loose and alive.

Examples of nunchaku applications

Proper distance for a JKD hand positioning to deliver the right lead punch

Block hammer principle punch, or block straight vertical punch

Rear hand on guard, front hand executes a front vertical punch /pin down horizontal elbow strike

Low sweep block open or closed hand   upward elbow and strike the person behind you

Perry Left horizontal elbow strike/ front pinning down block, rear hand on center

Follow Along Only
Natural Stance or a By-Jon Position.

Nunchaku by your side, bring it up with right hand to left hand. Grab each end of the nunchaku and open so that the chain is exposed. Bring left back to right and close. Grab with the right hand and only release one section of the nunchaku down.

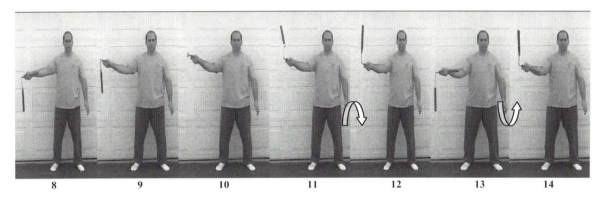

Circle forward and back in a circular motion as many times as you prefer. Then switch to the next move.

Tuck under your armpit. Then release upward and over the right shoulder. Grab it from underneath your right triceps and pull it out with left hand over the left shoulder. Repeat many times.

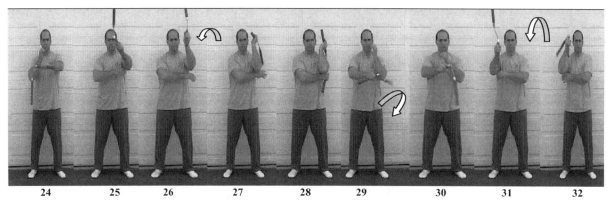

Throw it over the left shoulder as you grab it from underneath your left triceps; pull it out with right hand over the right shoulder. Repeat many times.

Throw it forward with right hand in punching motion. Tuck under the right armpit release and pass it across the center to the other side from underneath the left elbow. Grab it with the left hand

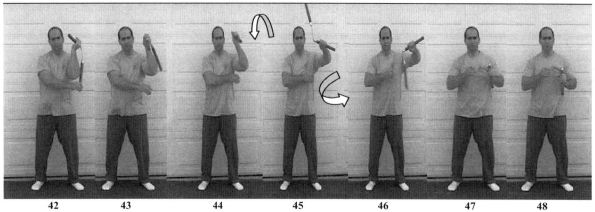

As you grab it with left hand throw it over the left shoulder forward and tuck it under the left armpit.

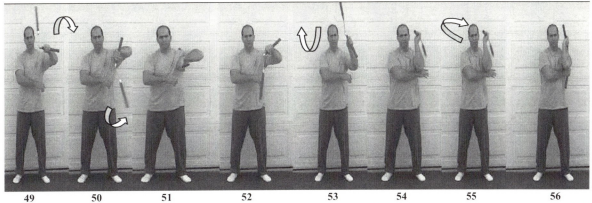

Release and throw it forward and let it swing down, as it hits the arm pit not tucking it throw it back up and over the left shoulder as you grab it with right hand from underneath the left elbow.

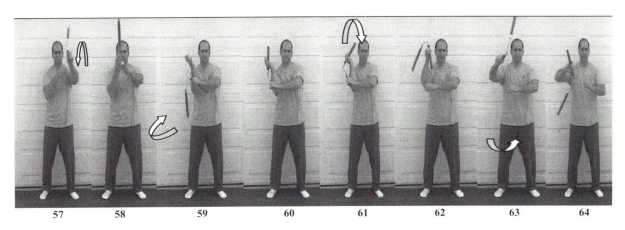

Throw it up and let it pass the center as it circles under the right elbow, grab it with right hand. Throw it forward and over as you tuck it underneath the right armpit.

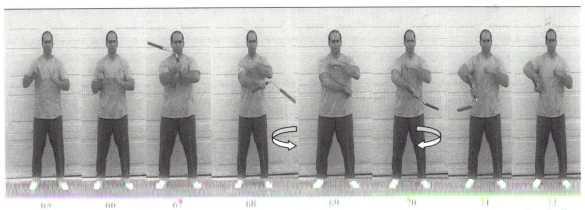

As you grab under, pass it across the center, let it hit left side as you let it pass the center to the right side to side circling.

Repeat side to side many times; throw it up and over the right shoulder as you grab it from under the right elbow.

Grab, pass across and around the neck and grab it with left hand. Pull it out with left hand as you let it hit under the arm pit.

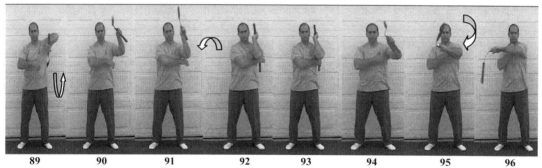

Throw it back up and over the left shoulder. Grab it with right hand from under the left elbow. Throw it over with left hand and pass the center.

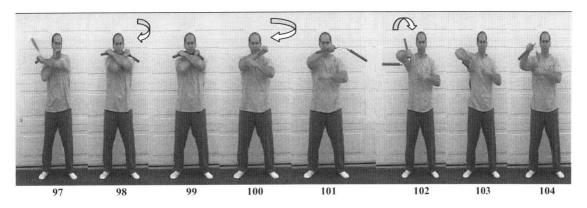

As it passes across to the other side circle it around the neck as you grab it with right hand. Pull it out with right hand, pass the center and let swing underneath the right armpit.

As you grab with left hand from under the right elbow, throw it back forward and over under the groin area without hitting. As it passes grab it from the back with left hand.

As you pull it out pass it to the right hand as you circle up and over the right shoulder. Grab from under the right elbow with left hand.

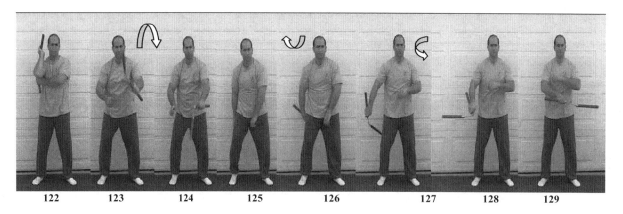

As you grab pull it out with left hand upward and downward under passing the groin area, grab it with right hand and pull it out and pass it around the hips to the other side.

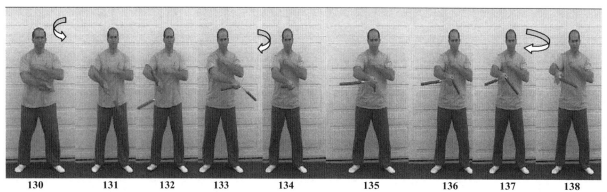

Swing side to side as you get a good smooth swing, and let roll around the hand as you grab the other side of the handle. Then you roll the nunchaku around the left handle which becomes he right handle.

Repeat it many times, rolling it around the hand, right to left with speed.

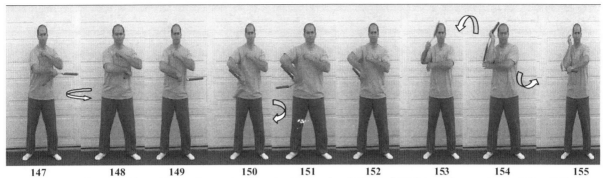
As you swing side to side throw it up and over the right shoulder, and pull it out with left hand from underneath the right elbow.

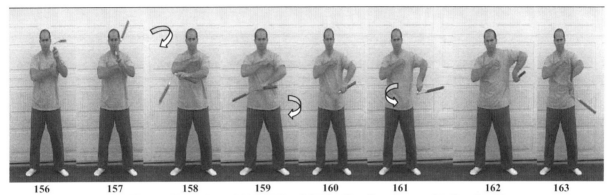
Pass it across the center and let it hit the right hip. Pass it again around to the other hip.

Swing side-to-side get a smooth flow. Start the rolling around the left hand, same as the right hand above. Left to right, right to left.

172 173 174 175 176 177 178 179 180
Roll around side-to-side, but it must roll over the hand. It rolls around the hand as you grab it with the same hand that the nunchaku been rolled on.

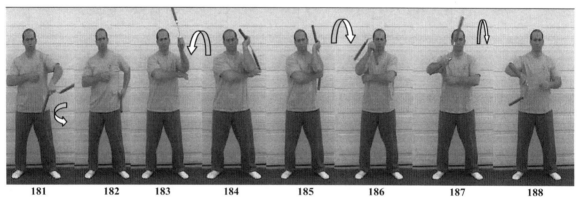

181 182 183 184 185 186 187 188
Rolling to the left hip, throw it up and over the left shoulder. As you grab it from under the left elbow with right hand, pull it out and let it swing.

189 190 191 192 193 194 195 196
Throw the nunchaku around the right hand up and over in a front circling motion and grab the other handle of the nunchaku becoming upside down.

As it swings upside down stop it with left hand on the centerline. Give it a toss with left hand around the right hand and let it roll around the hand.

Grabbing the opposite side, pass down and up around in rolling motion around the right hand. Grabbing the left handle.

Pass across the center in an **X** motion. Pass to the left then bring around to the right side.

As it comes around the right side throw it from under the hand around backwards as you grab the other handle.

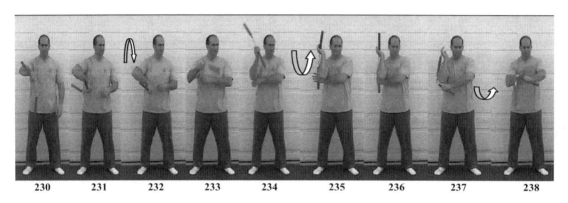

Let it swing down under the right armpit, swing it back up over the right shoulder, grab it with left hand, pull out.

As you throw it forward flip the hand so the nunchaku is held upside down with left hand. Give it a little toss around with the left hand so it rolls to the other side. The left handle becomes right.

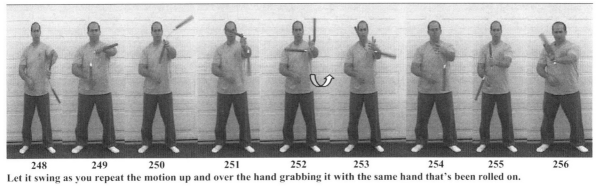

248 249 250 251 252 253 254 255 256

Let it swing as you repeat the motion up and over the hand grabbing it with the same hand that's been rolled on.

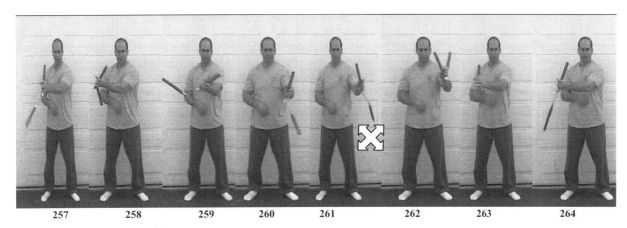

257 258 259 260 261 262 263 264

Pass it across the center in an **X** motion right to left, left to right.

265 266 267 268 269 270 271 272 273

Roll it around the left hand so left handle becomes right handle. Let it swing under the left armpit.

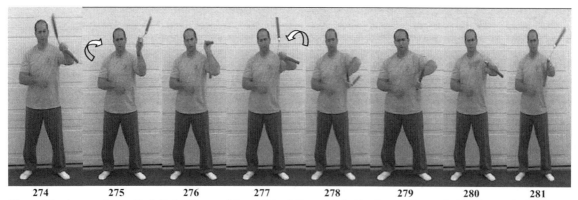

Throw it back up and over the left shoulder, and throw it back forward. As it swings underneath the left armpit throw it back up and over the left hand.

Roll around so that the left becomes right, and throw it over the left shoulder. Grab it from under the left elbow with right hand.

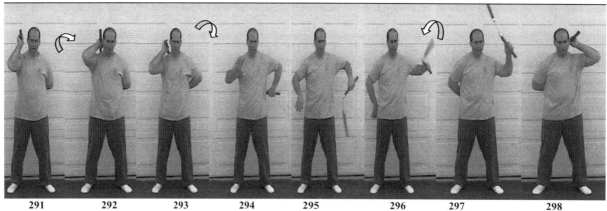

Pull it out with right hand and throw it over the right shoulder as you reach over with left hand, and grab it around the left hip area. Pull it out and throw up over left shoulder as you grab it with right hand around the right hip area in an X motion.

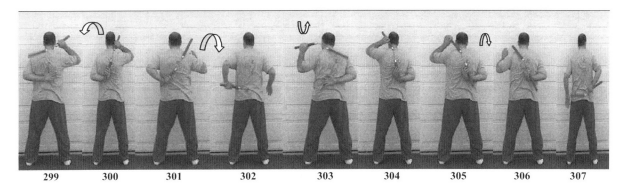

Back view only -------------------- Back view only ------------------- Back view only ------------------ Back view only ---------------Back view only ---------------

As you pull it out, tuck it underneath the right armpit .as you switch to a by-jon fighting stance. Throw it forward in a hammer principle punching motion. Let it swing around and under the right armpit, then tuck it.

Go back to natural stance and throw the other side of the handle across the center passing it to the left hand and grab both handles. Expose the chain with both hands open, keeping both handles of the nunchaku tucked between the thumb and the inside of the hand. Bring both handles together and bow, eyes always forward. Finish.

Sparring & Sport VS. Street Fighting
Inside the Reality of a Street Altercation

When facing a regular person or a skilled fighter on the street for a real fight, no wasted movement or circling footwork is used. We practice the art of simplicity. How can I take out an opponent or assailant with speed and with most effective intercepting without wasting any energy and with the most economical motion possible? By the time you circle around your assailant he would have taken you out before you even had a chance to respond. When Sijo demonstrated his art of intercepting in the TV show Long Street, he intercepted his opponent's emotions without any unnecessary footwork. His reaction was simple and direct to the target, using the straight line applying the (SDA) **SINGLE DIRECT ATTACK**, based on proper timing, correct hip rotation and proper body alignment.

When we are talking about sports or sparring than we are commenting about something totally different then real combat. Circling footwork might be applied, but not at all times. JKD footwork is based on correct distance, so we cannot just apply only one way of intercepting the opponent. Some footwork is required to close the gap between you and your opponent, and some are applied in one motion. You can attack on a straight-line or a curved line depending on the situation. Most attacks happen in a straight line. When facing a skilled fighter attempting an angular attack, no matter how proper your timing is or how fast your intercepting is, a skilled fighter will move fast to evade any oncoming attack whether the attack is in a straight line or curved line. I can try to circle around a kick boxer or TKD Maui Thai but problems may happen when you are trying to intercept. You are facing a long weapon, so some other footwork should be applied such as the side-step to push shuffle footwork attack followed with HIA (hand immobilization attack) to take out any counter attacks that occur when you are attacking. Use the simplest and most direct way without having to circle around your opponent which may give him or her enough time to responded to your intercepting. A good JKD practitioner uses the shortest distance between two points and finishes the fight without having to think or wait for the opponent's attack. You intercept at the opening and use the retreat back shuffle in a straight line with slight circling to only break down and confuse your opponent.

The circling foot work in JKD is the most effective when applied against orthodox opponents. The front foot must pivot in a circular motion as if you have a ball bearing mounted on the bottom of the front foot. The rear foot must rotate counter clockwise with a slight hop back to take advantage of the opponent's center line allowing you to hit him. Your opponent will have to adjust his position to counter attack, but it will be too late, because you should be able to strike him on the outer side, taking away all of his energy by sweeping out the leg knocking him straight down. When applied against a southpaw fighter the same motion is applied except you pivot and circle clock wise with slight step back giving yourself enough distance so that you can attack by using the longest weapon against his knee cap or ribs. If you try to attack with a short weapon like a straight punch or backhand he might attack first and he will reach his target faster and with much more power.

Chris is on guard and delivers a sidekick and lands against Joe's knee as he circles around him for a better angle of attack and better punching range.

Joe counters him by taken advantage of his center line and delivers a devastating hook to Chris's faces causing him to loose focus.

(6)   (7)   (8)

Chris delivers a straight line, simple direct attack against Joe's well -guarded centerline….

Chris and Joe face each other for a sparring match. Chris executes and delivers a sidekick and lands against Joe's knee and circles around Joe in a clockwise circular motion for a better angle of attack and better punching range. Joe counters Chris by stepping to the inside to take advantage of his centerline, and deliverers a solid right hook to the face.
    Chris counter clocks Joe as he lines up with him again and executes a straight lead punch that lands on the target. Joe parries the punch with the rear hand and slips off Chris's attack and follows thru with a rear corkscrew to Chris's head. Don't expect NOT to get hit. During this sparring match both fighters got hit and they both had a good defense and a good offense. No matter how much they both tried, they always found a weak point in each the others defense to hit back and score on the other. If this was a real altercation, the man with the simplest direct attack would have dominated the fight with ease, but do to protective gear and NOT fully delivering of the punches and the kicks, the match will last about 20 minutes, but in reality the fight would have ended in 1 minute due to fast and hard strikes that were being delivered by both fighters. Many things should be taken into consideration when you are practicing with your partners in a sparring match. Both partners should test one another's skills and point out the effectiveness of the hits. You have to train yourself to a level where the mind and body will react as ONE during sparring and real life altercations and with no hesitation. Minimize repetitive movements and use broken rhythm to break his timing of offense and defense. Limit hopping or circling around your opponent. Straight-line attacks are very effective because it allows you to take slight steps to the left or the right and you will be able to deliver more damaging hits. When you strike, hit hard and finish the fight fast by executing very effective blows that will guarantee a knock out.

Jeet Kune Do - Street Combat

Jeet Kune Do is extremely effective as far as street situations are concerned. The way we train in class is the way it's treated on the street. Every technique in Jeet Kune Do is treated as a fight or a self-defense situation.

Lots of classical Martial Artists fail to see that Jeet Kune Do is not just hand trapping or for show. Jeet Kune Do is an offensive and defensive method of fighting. That is why it is called
"SCIENTIFIC STREET FIGHTING," and it lives up to its name.

Lots of the illustrations below are not for teaching purposes. They are only to show the reader or any open minded Martial Artist that Jeet Kune Do can fit in any situation and style of Martial Arts. This is because it is all styles and not bound by any one style. Also I would like to show that Martial Arts is way of life, and I think every one should have some kind of self-defense training no matter what style it is, as long as it helps you in a real life situation.

"IT IS WHAT IT IS, JEET KUNE DO. JUST ACCEPT IT FOR WHAT IT IS."

1)   2)   3)   4)

5)   6)   7)   8)

9)   10)   11)   12)

1) 2) 3) 4) 5)

1) 2) 3)

4) 5) 6) 7)

8) 9) 10) 11)

ITS SHOW TIME

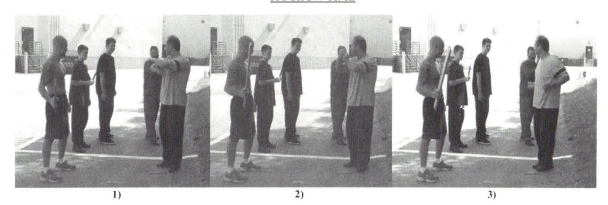

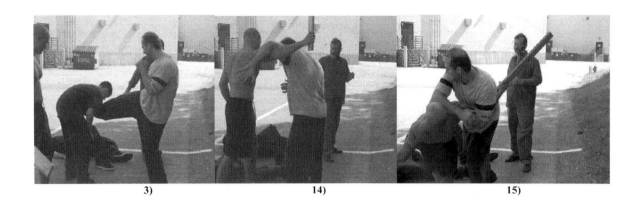

3)   14)   15)

16)   17)

1)   2)   3)   4)   5)

6)   7)   8)   9)

8) 9) 10) 11)

1) 2) 3) 4)

5) 6) 7) 8)

9) 10) 11)

1) 2) 3)

4) 5) 6)

1) 2) 3) 4)

5) 6) 7)

THE END

Jeet Kune Do The System Without A System ®

"The Ultimate In Personal Expression"

PEACE　　　　　　**LOVE**　　　　　　**JKD**

If you think MY JKD is different from yours....**Well, IT IS!**

Jeet Kune Do Terminology
The most used words throughout the book

Cantonese /Phonetics — **Translation**

#	Cantonese /Phonetics	Translation
1	JEET KUNE DO	THE WAY OF THE INTERCEPTING FIST
2	JEET	STOP/INTERCEPT
3	KUNE	FIST
4	DO (DOUGH)	THE WAY
5	YUT JEE CHOON KUNE	CHARACTER "SUN" THRUSTING PUNCH. IT RESEMBLES THE CHINESE CHARACTER SUN
6	CHOON CHOY OR CHOON KUNE (KOON)	VERTICAL PUNCH
6A	LYNN WHY KUNE OR JICK CHUN	CONTINUOUS CHAIN OF PUNCHING STRAIGHT BLAST
7	CHOP CHOY OR CHO KUNE (KOON)	LOW HAMMER PUNCH
8	CHOW KUNE OR JUNE KUNE (KOON)	SHOVEL HOOK. IT RESEMBLES AN UPPERCUT.
9	GOON JEE KUNE (GOON .G. KOON)	GINGER FIST. IT RESEMBLES THE GINGER PLANT
10	CHOP CHOY OR PING CHOY	HORIZONTAL PUNCH
11	FOON NUN KUNE (FOON NONE KOON)	PHOENIX PUNCH
12	LOY AND NOY DOT GOCK KUNE	INSIDE AND OUTSIDE DIAGONAL PUNCH. IT RESEMBLES A HOOK.
13	GWA CHOY	BACK HAND
14	TUN SOW (TON SOW)	SHOWING HAND
15	POCK SOW (POCK SOW)	SLAPPING HAND /PALM BLOCK
16	BONG SOW (BONG SOW)	WING ARM DEFLECTION
17	JEEP SOW (SOW)	BREAKING BLOCK SIMULTANEOUSLY
18	HUEN SOW (HOON SOW)	CIRCLING HAND OR CIRCLE SOMETHING INSIDE SOMETHING ELSE.
19	GUNG SOW (GUNG SOW)	LOW SWEEP BLOCK
20	JOM SOW (JOM SOW)	CHOPPING HAND
21	GUM SOW (GUM SOW)	PRESSING HAND
22	FOOK SOW (FOOK SOW)	BRIDGING HAND
23	CHUM-Q	BRIDGING BLOCK
24	WOO SOW (WOO SOW)	GUARDING HAND /PROTECTIVE HAND
25	LOP SOW (LOP SOW)	GRABBING HAND OR PULLING
26	LON SOW (LON SOW)	L-BAR ARM, IT RESEMBLES THE LETTER (L)
27	LOY	INSIDE
28	NOY	OUTSIDE
29	BIU JEE (Gee) OR SOW (B~U. G OR SOW)	SHOOTING FINGERS OR HAND
30	BIU JON SOW (B~U. JOHN SOW)	FORWARD, THRUSTING HAND
31	COW SOW (COW SOW)	CATCHING HAND
32	DING SOW OR HEY OR TIE (DING SOW)	HAND RAISING HAND
33	FACK SOW (FUC SOW)	HIGH BLOCK
34	HUNG SOW (HUN SOW)	STROLLING HAND
35	GWAT SOW (GWAT SOW)	LOW PASSING BLOCK
36	JING JAN (JIN JAN)	VERTICAL PALM HEEL STRIKE
37	CHUNG JAN (CHUN JAN)	ANGLE SPADE PALM STRIKE
38	CHUNG DIE JAN (CHUN DIE JAN)	LOW ANGLE PALM STRIKE

39	POW JAN	LIFTING PALM OR VERTICAL PALM STRIKE FINGERS POINTING DOWN
40	SOONG (SOONG)	DOUBLE
41	FUN SOW OR WONG JAN	HORIZONTAL CHOP
42	JOW SOW (GOW SOW)	RUNNING HAND
43	HEY JON (HEY JOHN)	UPWARD ELBOW
44	GWY JON (GWHY JOHN)	OVER ARCING ELBOW
45	SONG JON (JOHN)	OUTWARD ELBOW
46	PIE JON (JOHN)	INWARD ELBOW
47	SOW JON (SOW JOHN)	RETRACTING, BACKWARD ELBOW.
48	TIE SUT	RAISING KNEE
49	LOY OR NOY HUEN WONG TECK OR GYEUK (GUKE)	INSIDE OR OUTSIDE CIRCLING CRESCENT KICK (LEG)
50	QUA TECK (QWA TECK) OR BIU GYEUK	INVERTED KICK OR PIERCING LEG
51	SUT	KNEE
52	SOW	HAND
53	TECK	KICK
54	JEET TECK	STOP KICK
55	JICK TECK	FRONT KICK
56	JUCK TECK	SIDE KICK
57	OW TECK	HOOK KICK/ROUND HOUSE KICK
58	HOW TECK	BACK KICK
59	SO TECK	SWEEP KICK
60	JUNE TECK	SPINNING BACK KICK
61	GYEUK (GUKE)	LEG
62	JING GYEUK (GUKE)	FRONT KICK/LEG
62	MOH YIN GYEUK (GUKE)	INVISIBLE KICK
63	CUP YAI SUT (CUP YIE SUT	STOMPING KNEE
64	WONG GYEUK (GUKE)	SIDE KICK
65	TIU GYEUK	PIERCING KICK
66	JUT GYEUK (GUKE)	JERKING LEG
66	GUNG JING GYEUK (GUKE)	FRONT LIFTING LEG
67	SIU LEEM TAU (FIRST FORM)	WING CHUN LITTLE IDEA FORM
68	CHUM-Q (SECOND FORM)	SEARCHING FOR THE BRIDGE FORM
69	BIU JEE (THIRD FORM)	WING CHUN THRUSTING FINGERS FORM
70	MOOK JOANG (JON)	WOODEN DUMMY
71	MOOK YAN JOANG FOT YUT LING BOT	108 WOODEN DUMMY MOTIONS
72	YUT-LING BOT	1-0-8
73	MA	HORSE
74	HOY	OPEN

75	BY-JON	ON GUARD FIGHTING POSITION
76	MA BOO	FOOT WORK
77	JING MA	CENTER NATURAL STANCE
78	CHO MA	STANCE PIVOT OR SIDE PIVOT
79	TOH MA	STEP SLIDE ADVANCE
80	TOY MA	RETREATING STANCE
81	SEEP MA	MOTION INTERCEPTING OR THREE POINT STANCE
82	SOONG MA	ADVANCE STEP THROUGH
83	LOY SEEN WHY	INSIDE STEP AND FACE
84	HOW HUEN JUNE MA	BACK CIRCLE STEP THROUGH
85	HUEN BOO	CIRCLING STEPS
86	YOW MA	RIGHT STANCE
87	JORE MA	LEFT STANCE
88	"YEE" JEE KIM YIN MA	GOAT RESTRAINING STANCE OR CHARACTER "TWO" PIGEON TOE HORSE STANCE
89	JEET SA JAN	IRON PALM TRAINING
90	LEEN GON JOW/ DIT DA JOW	HERBAL LINIMENT (OIL)
91	LOY KWAN SOW	INSIDE ROLLING HANDS
92	NOY KWAN SOW	OUTSIDE ROLLING HAND
93	LOOK SOW	ROLLING HAND
94	CHEE SOW	DOUBLE STICKY HANDS
95	CHEE DON SOW	SINGLE STICKY HAND
96	JEEP SOW	BREAKING HAND
97	TUET SOW (TOOT SOW)	FREEING HAND
98	CHUNG GANG	THROAT SQUEEZE
99	QUACK SOW	SPREADING HAND
100	JOAN SEEN	CENTER LINE
101	SEE GONG SING	TIMING
102	MN	GATE
103	YIN	NEGATIVE ENERGY
104	YANG	POSITIVE ENERGY
105	GING LAI (LIE)	JKD BOW SALUTATION
106	GO	HIGH
107	MIDDLE/CENTER	JOAN
108	LOW	DIE
109	FIE	QUICK
110	CHEEN	FRONT
111	HOW	BACK
112	YOW	RIGHT
113	JORE	LEFT
114	SIFU **IN CHINESE** SENSEI **IN JAPANESE**	MARTIAL ARTS INSTRUCTOR
115	JO- SE OR SIJO	FOUNDER OF THE STYLE
116	CHUNG SE	GRANDMASTER OF A SYSTEM
117	LEE JUN FAN (FUN) NOT A CEILING FAN	BRUCE LEE
118	LEE SEE LUNG	LITTLE DRAGON
119	KWOON (KWAN) DOJO IN JAPANESE	MARTIAL ARTS SCHOOL
120	TODAI (TOE DIE)	STUDENT
121	TOW GIT (TAO GIT)	HEAD BUTT

1	2	3	4	5	6	7	8	9	10	11	12	13	14	15	16	17	18	19
Yut	Yee	Sum	See	Umm	Look	Tit	Bot	Giu	Sup	Sup Yut	Sup Yee	Sup Sum	Sup See	Sup Umm	Sup Look	Sup Tit	Sup Bot	Sup Giu

20	21	22	23	24	25	26	27
Yee sup	Yee sup Yut	Yee sup yee	Yee sup Sum	Yee sup See	Yee sup Umm	Yee sup Look	Yee sup Tit

Wing Chun Gung Fu Glossary
By world renowned Master Augustine Fong
Note- some modification have been made to pronounce better

B

Bruce Lee = Lee Jun Fan/Founder Of Jeet Kune Do
BY-Jon = On Guard Fighting Position
Bak Gek = Sparring
By Ying = Losing Body Structure Or Loss Of Balance
By Ying Chee Sow = Irregular Structure Sticky Hands
By Ying Jing Noy Gyeuk = To Regain Lost Balance By Controlling With A Front Instep Kick
By Ying Loy Ow Gyeuk = To Regain Lost Balance By Controlling With An Inside Instep Kick
Bat Jaam Do = Eight Slash Knives; The Name Of The Wing Chun Butterfly Knives And The Knife Form
Bat Seen Choi Chee Sow = 8 Immortal Table Sticky Hands For Demonstrations
Bow Ja Geng = Whipping Or Explode Energy
Bow Ja Lick = Explode Power
Bik Boo = Jamming Stance In The Knives Form
Bik Ma = Chasing Stance With The Pole
Boo Lay Ying = Glass Technique
Bock = Shoulder
Bong An Chee Sow = Blindfolded Sticky Hands
Bong Do = Wing Arm Block With The Butterfly Knives
Bong Family = A Family Of Wing Chun Techniques That Contact On The Little Finger Side Of The Wrist
Bong Gyeuk = Outer Shin Block With The Knee Turned Outward
Bong Sow = Wing Arm Block Contacting On The Wrist Area
Biu Do = Shooting Or Thrusting With The Knives Also The Stance To Step Forward
Biu Jee = Shooting Fingers
Biu Jee Ma = Outward Circling Stance
Biu Gwan Or Biu Kwan = Shooting Or Thrusting With The Pole
Biu Jong Sow = Centerline Thrusting Block Or Strike With The Thumb Side Up, Contacting On The Thumb Side Of The Wrist
Biu Ma = Shooting Forward Stance With The Pole
Biu Sow = Shooting Fingers Block, Contacting On The Little Finger Side Of The Wrist

C

Chum = To Sink, One Of The Principles Of The Sue Lum Tow
Chum Geng = Sinking Power To Duck Away From Attacks
Chaan Boo = Go Forward And Jam Stance In The Knives Form
Chaan Do = A Upper Slash Or Chop With The Butterfly Knives
Chaan Jan = To "Push Out" With The Palm; An Upper Gate Palm Strike That Drills Out With The Palm
Chop Kune = Low Punch
Chai Gyeuk = Any Kick That Stamps Down; Also A Scraping Kick Contacting With The Blade Edge Of The Foot
Chai Sut = To Stomp Downward With The Knee
Cho Kune = Pulling Punch; The Wing Chun Basic Rotational Punch
Chan Dai Jan Or Dai Chan Jan Also Juk Jan = To "Cut In"; A Low Knife Edge Palm Strike, Contacting With The Little Finger Side And With The Palm Up
Chan Gang = Neck Chop With The Little Finger Side Of The Palm Down Or Palm Up
Chan Jan = "Knife Edge" Palm Strike Contacting With The Little Finger Side Of The Palm
Cheen Chor Ma Or Jing Chor Ma = Forward Bracing Stance
Chee = 1) Internal Energy 2) Sticking
Chee Dan Gyeuk = Single Sticky Legs Exercise
Chee Do = Sticky Knives
Chee Gok Chee Sow Or Jee Gok Chee Sow = Light Sticky Hands
Chee Geng = Sticking Energy
Chee Gung = Internal Energy Exercises
Chee Gyeuk = Sticky Legs Exercise
Chee Gwan Or Chee Kwan = Sticky Pole Exercise
Chee Sow = Sticky Hands Exercises; There Are Many Types Of Chee Sow
Chee Sow Chee Gyeuk = Sticky Hands And Legs Exercise
Chee Soong Gyeuk Or Chee Gyeuk = Double Sticky Legs Exercise
Chee Sun = Body Sticking
Choi Geng = Taking Over Power
Choeng Kiu Jan = Long Bridge Palm That Drills As The Stance Turns, Contacting With The Little Finger Side Of The Palm; From The Biu Jee Form
Choeng Kiu LICK = Long Bridge Power
Chong Jou Si Gan = Creating Timing
Chor Ma = "Sitting" Horse Stance, The Basic Turning Stance
Chor Do = Stomping With The Knife Handle
Chou Gyeuk = Snapping Front Kick
Choung Chee = Aggressive Energy
Choung Geng = Forward, Aggressive Power
Cho Kune Or Cho Tow Kune = Hammer fist
Chui Meen Joi Ying = Follow The Structure; Straight On Facing And Chasing
Chui Ying = Facing Straight-On Structure; Facing The Shadow
Chum Boo = Cat Sinking Stance In The Knife Form
Chum Jong = Sinking Elbow Bock, Immovable Elbow Line
Chum Kiu = 1) Searching For The Bridge 2) The Name Of The Second Form, Sinking The Bridge
Chum Sun = To Evade By Sinking The Body, Ducking
Chun Geng = Short Thrusting Power
Chun Geng Kune = One Inch Punch, A Short Punch
Chuun Lop = Moving Stance Work Between The Poles In The Mui Fa Jong
Chung Kiu LICK = Long Bridge Power
Chung Kune = Straight Punch
Churng Why = Stealing The Line
Churng Why Chee Sow = Stealing The Line Or Regaining The Line In Chee Sow

D

Da = A Strike Or Hit
Da M'jong = 5 Elbows Exercise
Tie Jong = Raising Elbow
Gwy Jong = Diagonal Downward Elbow
Wang Jong = Outward Horizontal Elbow
Pie Jong = Inward Horizontal Elbow
Sow Jong = Retracting Or Rear Elbow
Daai Geng = Directing Energy
Dai = Low Or Lower Level Attack
Dai Bong Sow Or Dai Pong Sow = Low Level Wing Arm Block
Dai Chan Jan = Low Knife Edge Palm Strike
Dai Lim Tow = Big Idea Which Is Built Up From The Little Ideas In The Siu Leem Tau Form
Dai Gyeuk = Low Kick
Dai Ow Gyeuk = Low Roundhouse
Dai Jing Gyeuk = Low Front Kick
Dai Wang Gyeuk = Low Side Kick
Dai Jan Or Haa Jan = Low Level Spade Thrust Palm Strike
Dan Chee Sow = Single Sticky Hands Exercise
Dan Tien = The Center Of Energy In The Body Located Two Inches Below The Navel In Center Of The Trunk
Dang Gyeuk = Nailing Kick
Dang Gwan Or Dang Kwan = Snapping Straight Down With The Pole
Day Har Ow Gyeuk = Roundhouse Kick On The Floor
Day Har Chee Gyeuk = Sticky Legs On The Floor
Day Har Jing Gyeuk = Front Kick On The Floor
Day Har Wang Gyeuk = Side Kick On The Floor
Day Ton Bock Gek = Ground Fighting
Deng Or Tie Gyeuk = Raising Kick
Dim Gwan Or Dim Kwan = Stabbing Pole
Dim Ma = Stamping In The Pole Stance To Give More Energy
Ding Sow = Bent Wrist Block Or Strike Contacting With The Wrist Area
Dit Da = Injuries Such As Bruises, Sprains And Strains
Dit Da Jow Or Dit Da Jow = Herbal Liniment For Bruises, Sprains, And Strains
Doi Gok Gyeuk = Low Diagonal Leg Block Or Strike
Doi Gok Kune Or Wang Kune = Diagonal Punch From Outside Across The Centerline
Dok Gyeuk Siu Leem Tau = Single Leg Form Of Sue Lim Ta
Do = Butterfly Knives
Do (Dough) = Way
Do Boo = Moving Stances With The Knives
Duun Geng = Short Inches Power

F

Fun Dan Chee Sow = Bouncing Sticky Hands
Fun Sow = Continuous Lop Sow Basic Attack To Break Through The Opponent's Structure
Fun Kune = Circling Punch Either Inside Or Outside
Hoi Fun Kune = Outside Whip Punch
Loy Fun Kune = Inside Whip Punch
Fun Kune Or Fun Sow = Continuous Attacking With Controlling While Alternating Punches As In Pock Fun Sow,
Biu Fun Sow And Lop Fun Sow
Fun Sun = To Regain The Body Position
Fun Sun Jing Gyeuk = To Regain The Body Position With A Front Kick
Fak Do = Upward Deflecting Block With The Knives
Fak Sow = Upward Deflecting Block Swinging The Forearm Down And Up, Contacting With The Little Finger Side
Of The Wrist
Fat Do = Right Power In Techniques
Fown Ow Gyeuk Or Fong Noy Gyeuk = Reverse Roundhouse
Fay Jong = Flying Elbows
Fong Sow Seen Why = Blocking Line
Fook Family = A Family Of Wing Chun Techniques Which Use The Palm
Fook Gyeuk = A Downward Leg Block Or Strike Contacting With The Muscle Next To The Shin Boone
Fook Sow = A Palm Controlling Block With The Elbow Down
Fook Sut = An Inward Knee Block Or Strike
Fong Sow Seen Why = Blocking Line
Fung Non Kune Or Fun An Kune = Phoenix Eye Punch With The Index Knuckle Forward
Fun Dough = An Outward Or Sideward Slash With The Butterfly Knives
Fun Sow = An Outward Or Sideward Horizontal Chop

G

Ga Chok = Bouncing Technique Off Of An Opponent's Structure
Gan Jeep Geng = Indirect Power
Gang Da = Simultaneous Low Sweeping Block With A Punch
Gang Gyeuk = 3 Leg Blocking Exercise With The Following Blocks:
Dai Jing Gyeuk = Low Front Kick Blocking With The Calf Muscle
Bong Gyeuk = Shin Block
Jut Gyeuk = Snapping Block
Gang Jaam = Simultaneous Low Sweeping Block With A Forearm Deflecting Block Or Chop
Gang Jaam Do = Simultaneous Low Sweeping Block And Upper Deflecting Block With The Butterfly Knives
Gang Sow = A Low Sweeping Block. There Are Two Kinds Of Gang Sow
Hoi Gang Sow = An Outward Low Sweeping Block
Loy Gang Sow = An Inward Low Sweeping Block
Gang Sow = 5 Blocking Motions
Loy Gang Sow = Inside Low Sweeping Block
Tun Sow = Flat Palm-Up Block Contacting On The Thumb Side Of The Wrist
Hoi Gang Sow = Outside Low Sweeping Block
Jaam Sow = Forearm Deflecting Block
Woo Sow = Guard Hand Block
Jee = Fingers
Jee Gok Chee Sow Or Jee Or Chee Gok Chee Sow = Light Sticky Hands
Jee Gok Geng Or Gum Gok Geng = Feeling Power
Geng Or Ging = Energy; The 8 Types Of Wing Chun Energy Are:

- 1. Bow Ja Geng = Explode Power
- 2. Chee Geng = Sticking Power
- 3. Keng Geng = Listening Power
- 4. Juun Geng = Drilling Power
- 5. Jick Jeep Geng = Direct Power
- Gan Jeep Geng = Indirect Power
- 6. Yan Geng Or Daai Geng = Guiding Power
- 7. Lin Jeep Geng = Connecting Power
- 8. Choong Geng = Aggressive Power

Gin Kune = Moving Side Punch For Pole Exercise
Goiu Ying = Adjusting The Body Structure
Goot Do = Cutting Knife Attack
Goot Gwan = Cutting Down With The Pole
Gor Dan Chee Sow = Attacks In Single Sticky Hands
Gor Lop Sow = Attacks In Lop Sow
Gor Sow Or Guo Sow = Attacks In Sticky Hands
Gour Yung = Guts Or Determination And Self-Confidence To Win
Gu Deng Chee Sow = Sitting Sticky Hands
Gum Gok Geng, Jee Gok Geng Or Jee Gok Geng = Feeling Energy
Gum Jan = Low Palm Edge Strike
Gum Sow = Downward Palm Block Or Strike With The Elbow Turned Outward
Gum Ying = Body Feeling
Gung Gek Seen Why = Attacking Line
Gung Lick Chee Sow = Heavy Sticky Hands To Develop Power
Gyeuk = Leg Or Kick The 8 Positions Of The Kick Are
- 1. Jing Gyeuk =Strike With The Top Of The Heel Just Below The Arch
- 2. Wang Gyeuk = Strike With The Outside Of The Heel On The Little Toe Side
- 3. Soo Gyeuk = Strike With The Inside Of The Arch
- 4. Yai Sut Gyeuk = Strike With The Middle Of The Heel Downward
- 5. Tiu Gyeuk = Strike With The Instep With The Toes Pointed
- 6. Jut Gyeuk = Strike With The Lower Calf And Achilles Tendon
- 7. Tie Sut = Strike With The Top Or Side Of The Knee With The Leg Bent
- 8. Chey Gyeuk = Strike Downward With The Knife Edge Of The Foot

Gyeuk Jong = 8 Kicks To The Mook Jong Or Dummy
Goon Jee Kune = Ginger Fist Punch
Gwy Jong = A Circular Downward Elbow Block Or Strike Contacting With The Forearm
Gwy Sut = A Downward Knee Block Contacting With The Side Of The Knee Or Shin
Gwan Or Kwan = Pole
Gwang Geng = Steel-Bar Power
Gwat Jee Fat LICK = Boone-Joint Power
Gwat Gwan Or Sut Gwan = Opening Up Or Blocking The Inside Or Outside Lower Gate With The Pole
Gwat Sow = A Circular Controlling Technique That Carries The Subject Across The Centerline To Open An Attacking Line

H

Haa Or Chop Kune = Low Punch
Haa Jan Or Dai Jan = Low Palm Strike With The Side Of The Palm
Haan = Economic Motion
Haan Kiu = Walking On The Bridge Or Forearm
Haan Kiu Chee Sow = Walking On The Bridge Chee Sow
Haan Sow = A Long Bridge Block Contacting With The Little Finger Side Of The Wrist
How Chor Ma = Backward Bracing Stance
How Huen June Ma Or How Huen Or How June =- A Turning Stance That Is Executed By Stepping Forward Then Turning 180 Degrees To Face The Opposite Direction
How Jan = A Palm Strike With The Back Of The Palm
Hay Jong Or Tie Jong = Raising Elbow Strike Or Block
Hay Sow Or Tie Sow Or Ding Sow = A Raising Bent Wrist Block Or Strike Contacting On The Little Finger Side Of The Wrist
Hay Sut Or Tie Sut = Raising Knee Block Or Strike Contacting With The Top Or Side Of The Knee
Ho Kam Ming = A Long Time Disciple Of Grandmaster Yip Mun; The Teacher Of Augustine Fong (Fong Chee-Wing)
Hoi Or Oi = Outside
Hoi Bock = Outside Shoulder
Hoi Fun Kune = Outside Whip Punch
Hoi Hurn = Outside Facing Stance
Hoi Jan Or How Jan = Back Palm Strike Or Block
Hoi Joan Seen = Outside Line
Hoi Kwan Sow = Outside Rolling Hands Block
Hoi Ma = To Open The Horse Stance
Hoi Moon Chee Sow Or Hoi Mun Chee Sow = Outside Gate (Position) Chee Sow
Hoi Moon Kune Or Hoi Mun Kune = Outside Gate Diagonal Punch
Hoi Sik = Opening Position
Hoiu = Emptiness, One Of The Major Principles Of Siu Leem Tau
Hoiu Boo = Empty Step Or Cat Stance In The Pole Form
Hoiu Ying = Empty Shadow
Huen Da = Simultaneous Circling With One Hand And Striking With The Other
Huen Fook Sow = Circling One Hand Into The Fook Sow Position
Huen Gyeuk = Any Circle Kick
Huen Jing Gyeuk = Circling Front Kick
Huen Wang Gyeuk = Circling Side Kick
Huen Tiu Gyeuk = Circling Instep Kick
Huen Ma = Circling Stance In The Pole Form
Huen Sow = Circling, Controlling Hand
Huiu Ma = Cat Stance In The Pole Form
Hung Jai = Control Of Power
Hung Jai Chee Sow = Controlling Sticky Hands Motion To Block The Opponent
Hung Jai Geng = Controlling Energy

J

Jeet = Stop Or Intercept
Jam Jong = Stance For Chee Gung
Jaam Do = A Forward Deflecting Block With The Butterfly Knives
Jaam Sow = A Forearm Deflecting Block Contacting With The Little Finger Side Of The Forearm
Hoi Jaam Sow = Outside Woo Sow
Loy Jaam Sow = Inside Jaam Sow
Jow Ma Or Jou Ma = Combining Moving Footwork
Jow Mui Fa Jong = Stance Work On The Plum Blossom
Jow Sow = Changing Lines In Attacks, Going From One Line To Another
Jow Why = Moving Stances While Changing From One Line To Another
Jow Why Chee Sow Or Ngou Sow = Moving Sticky Hands While Changing Lines
Jow Why Yai Sut = Moving Stances To Attack With The Knees
Jick Jeep Geng = Direct Power
Jan = Palm Strike Or Chop; The 8 Palm Strikes Are
- 1. Jing Jan = Front Vertical Palm
- 2. Choon Kiu Jan = Long Bridge Palm
- 3. How Jan = Back Palm
- 4. Die Jan = Low Side Palm
- 5. Pow Jan = Downward Vertical Palm Strike
- 6. Gum Sow = Diagonally Downward Palm Strike
- 7. Chung Jan = Knife Edge Palm Strike To Upper Body And Head With Palm Up
- 8. Wang Jan = Side Of Palm Strike To Upper Body And Head With Palm Down

Jee Gok Chee Sow, Jee Or Chee Gok Chee Sow = Light Sticky Hands
Jee Yow Bak Gek = Free Sparring
Jing = Front Or Center
Jing = Quietness; One Of The Major Principles Of The Siu Leem Tau Form
Jing Bock = Front Shoulder
Jing Chor Ma Or Cheen Chor Ma = Forward Bracing Stance
Jing Dok Lop Ma Or Jing Gyeuk Dok Lop Ma = Front Single Leg Stance
Jing Gyeuk = Front Kick
Jing Jan = Straight Vertical Palm Strike
Jing Joan = Any Strike On The Center
Jing Ma Or Yee Jee Kim Yeung Ma = Front Developmental Stance; It Is Not A Stance To Fight From
Jing Meen = Facing To The Front
Jing Ngour Gyeuk = Toe Up Hooking Kick Or Control
Jing Sun = Wing Chun Front-On Body Structure
Jeen Kune = Punches From The Pole Horse Stance
Jeet Gyeuk = Stopping A Kick With A Kick
Jeep Sow = "Controlling The Bridge"; An Arm Break
Joi Geng = Chasing Power
Joi Yin = Following The Shadow
Joi Yin Chee Sow = Following The Shadow In Chee Sow; A Type Of Chasing Chee Sow
Joi Yin Jong = Following The Shadow On The Floor
Jon Geng Or Juun Geng = Drilling Power

Jong = Elbow
Jong Dai Lick= Elbow Power Produced From Practicing The Punch
Jong Gek = Elbow Pushing From Behind
Jong Sow = 1) A Centerline Block Or Strike Contacting With The Thumb Side Of The Wrist
2) The General Name For The Wing Chun Fighting Position
Joong -Lo = Mid-Level
Joong -Lo Kune = Mid-Section Drilling Punch
Juen Ma = Turning And Circling Stance With The Pole
Juk Dok Lop Ma Or Wang Dok Lop Ma = Side Single Leg Stance
Joan Seen = Centerline Or Centerline Plane
Loy Joan Seen = Inside Line
Hoi Joan Seen = Outside Line
Joan Sum Seen = Vertical Mother line
Juun Geng = Drilling Power
Jut = Snapping Motion
Jut Da = Simultaneous Snapping Control With One Hand And Striking With The Other
Jut Do = Snapping The Knives Sideways
Jut Geng = Snapping Power
Jut Gyeuk = Snapping Kick Or Block
Jut Sow = Snapping Block Contacting With The Thumb Side Of The Wrist

K

Cow Sow Or Cow Sow = Hooking Palm Control
Keng Geng = Listening Power
Kit Gwan Or Kit Kwan = Opening Up Or Blocking The Inside, Upper Gate With The Pole
Kune = Fist Or Punch
8 Families Of Wing Chun Punches Are
- 1. Cho Kune = Pulling Vertical Punch
- 2. Chop Kune = Low Punch
- 3. Loy Fun Kune = Inside Whip Punch
- 4. Hoi Fun Kune = Outside Whip Punch
- 5. Doi Gok Kune = Diagonal Punch
- 6. Cho Kune = Hammer fist
- 7. Jung-Lo Kune = Drilling Punch
- 8. Tie Kune = Raising Punch

Kune Sue Kune = Punch To Punch Exercise
Kune To = Any Hand Form
Kiu = Bridge Or Forearm
Kiu Li = Distance To The Bridge
Kiu Sow = Arm Bridge
Kum La = Joint Locking Techniques
Kum La Chee Sow = Joint Locking Techniques Applied In Chee Sow
Kwack Sow = Double Spreading Huen Sow
Kwan Or Gwan = Pole
Kwan = Rolling
Kwan Do = Rolling Knives
Kwan Ma = Pole Stance
Kwan Sow = Rolling Hands Block

L

La Ma = The Stable, Rooting Stance In The Pole Form
Lon Gwan Or Lon Kwan = Horizontal Long Bridge Pole
Lon Gyeuk = Horizontal Leg Block Contacting With The Shin Boone
Lon Sow = Horizontal Arm Block Contacting With Forearm And Sometimes Palm
Low Do = Twisting The Knives Inward To Block And Strike
Lay Why Chee Sow = Leaving The Gap Sticky Hands
Lick = Muscular Strength
Lick Do = The Correct Power
Lin Jeep Geng = Connecting Power Or Energy
Lin Sue Dai Da = Economy Of Motion
Lin Wan Kune = Continuous Chain Punching
Ling Gung Jow = Muscle Liniment
Lin Why Gyeuk = Flowing Kicks
Look Sow Or Look Sow Or Gung LICK Chee Sow = Heavy Sticky Hands
Lop = Grabbing Or Controlling With The Palm
Lop Da = Simultaneous Controlling And Striking ; Also Refers To A Partner Exercise
Lop Chan Jan = Simultaneous Palm Controlling And Heel Palm Strike
Lop Fook = Grabbing From Fook Sow Position
Lop Sow = Grabbing Hand Control; Also Refers To A Partner Exercise
Lop Sow Chee Sow = Lop Sow In Sticky Hands
Lou Gwan Or Low Gwan = The Half Point Pole Technique; A Short Thrust
Look Dim Bune Gwan Or Look Dim Boon Gwan = Six And Half Point Pole Form
Lut Sow = Attacking Without Initial Contact With The Opponent's Bridge; It Begins With Fighting Position
Lut Sow Chee Sow = Attacking From Mun Sow Position And Immediately Going Into Sticky Hands
Loy = Inside
Loy Bock = Inside Shoulder
Loy Fun Kune = Inside Whip Punch
Loy Geng = Internal Power
Loy Gung = Internal Chee Exercises For Fighting Applications
Loy Seen Why = Inside Facing Stance
Loy Joan Seen = Inside Line
Loy Kwan Sow = Inside Rolling Hands
Loy Moon Kune = Inside Gate Diagonal Punch
Loy Moon Chee Sow = Inside Gate (Position) Chee Sow
Loy Gyeuk = Inside Leg Hook

M

Ma = Stance/Horse
Ma Boo = Moving Stances
Ma Boo Chee Sow = Moving Sticky Hands
Ma Boo Lop Sow = Moving Lop Sow
Mai Jong = The Correct Elbow Position With The Elbow Inward On The Elbow Line
Mai Jong = Closing The Gap
Mun = "To Ask"
Mun Gyeuk = Asking Legs Where The First Motion Sets Up The Second Attack
Mun Sow = Asking Hands Where The First Motions Sets Up The Second Attack
Mun Sow Chee Sow = Asking Hand Within Sticky Hands
Mo Kiu Chee Sow = Walking On The Bridge Sticky Hands
Mo See = Traditional Lion Dance
Mook Lick = Eye Power With Emotion
Mook Jong Or Mook Yan Jong = Wooden Dummy Also The Name For The Wooden Dummy Form
Moon Or Mun = Gate Or Door
Say-I Moon = Dead Gate Which Is Closed
Soung Moon = Live Gate Which Is Open
Mui Fa Jong = Plum Blossom Posts And The Name For The Exercise Of Practicing On The Posts

N

Noy = Outside
Ng Mui = The Buddhist Sue Lum Nun Who Founded Wing Chun
Ng'an Geng Or Ng'on Geng = Elastic Power
Noy Doy Gock Kune = Outward Diagonal Punch
Noy Fun Kune = Outside Whip Punch
Noy Moon = Outside Gate
Noy Seen Why = Outside Facing
Nong Woon = Alternative Snapping Wrist
Noy Gyeuk = Hooking Foot Or Leg
Non Sun = Eye Radiance, Focus And Expression
Noy Jut Sow = Outside Jerking Hand
Noy Lick = Endurance
Noy Kwan Sow = Outside Rolling Hands

P

Pie Jong = Horizontal Inward Elbow Strike
Pock Da = Simultaneous Pushing Palm Block And Punch
Pock Do = Catching Knives Block
Pock Gyeuk = Inside Kick With The Sole Of The Foot With The Knee Bent
Pock Sow = Pushing Palm Block Or Strike
Pock Sut = Inward Knee Block Or Strike
Pow Jan = Flat Palm Strike With The Fingers Pointing Down. This Is Applied To The Lower Body
Pow Sow = Lifting Palm Block
Ping Hen Gong = Balancing Or Equalizing Power
Ping Sun = Side Turning Body Structure Or Position. This Is Not A Wing Chun Position
Por Joan = All Techniques That Control And "Break" The Centerline
Por Si Gan = Breaking Timing
Po By Or Po Pie = Double Butterfly Palm Strike
Poon Sow = Regular Sticky Hand Motion
Pun Doon = Determination In A Fight

S

Sa Bow = The Wall Bag
Sam Gung Ma Or Seep Ma = 3 Angle Stance
San Sow = Slow Attack Exercise
San Sow Chee Sow = Slow Attacks In Sticky Hands
Sat Gwan = Opening The Lower Gate To Inside Or Outside With The Pole
Say Boo = Retreat And Step Back Stance To Deflect In The Knife Form
Say Ping Ma = Low Horse Stance For Pole
Say-I Kune = Shooting Punch
Say-I Moon = Dead Gate
Sow = Hand Or Arm
Sow Gwan = Retreating The Pole
Sow Jong = Retracting Elbow Strike Or Block
Sow Sik Or Sow Sick = Closing Position In The Forms
Sow Woon Geng = Equalizing The Point And Power; Wrist Power
Soong Yum Gang = Sound Power To Emotionally Trap An Opponent
Soong = Double Or Advancing
Soong Bock = Shoulder Attacks
Soong Chee Sow = Double Sticky Hands Exercise
Soong Dai Bong = Double Low Forearm Block
Soong Huen Sow = Double Circling Block
Soong Jut Sow = Double Snapping Block
Soong Kune = Double Punch
Soong Ma = Front Advancing Stance
Soong Pow Sow = Double Upward Palm Block
Soong Yan Chee Sow = Double Sticky Hands With Three People
Soong Yan Dan Chee Sow = Single Sticky Hands With Three People
Soong Yan Jou Why Chee Sow = Moving Sticky Hands With Three People
Soong Yan Lop Sow = Lop Sow With Three People
Soong Yan Mun Sow = Mun Sow With Three People
Soong Tun Sow = Double Palm Up Block
Si Bock = Your Teacher's Si-Hing
Si Dai = A Male Classmate Who Joined A School After You
Si Fu = Your Teacher Can Be Either Male Or Female

See Gan = Timing
- 1. See Gan Seeng = Regular
- 2. Toh Chee See Gan = Delayed
- 3. Poh See Gan = Breaking
- 4. Chong Jou Si Gan = Creating
- 5. See Gan Seeng = Regular Timing

See Gan Pui Hop = The Correct Timing And Power
See Gung = Your Teacher's Teacher
See Hing = A Male Classmate Who Joined The School Before You
See Jay - A Female Classmate Who Joined The School Before You
See Jo = An Ancestor Within The System
See Ma = Deflecting Stance That Braces The Pole
See Mo = Your Teacher's Wife
Si Sook Or Si Suk = Your Teacher's Classmates Who Started After Him
Seen = Line

Joan Seen = Centerline
Loy Joan Seen = Inside Line
Loi Joan Seen = Outside Line
Gung Gek Seen Why = Attacking Line
Fong Sow Seen Why = Blocking Line
Joan Sum Seen = Vertical Mother line
Wang Joan Seen = Horizontal Mother line
Seeng Geng= Raising Power To Destroy The Opponent's Structure
Seep Ma Or Sam Gung Ma = 3 Angle Stance
Sue Geng = Dissolving Power
Siu Leem Tau = "Small Idea Form" The First Wing Chun Form
Soang Jong Or Wang Jong = Outward Horizontal Elbow
Soo Gyeuk = Sweeping Kick
Soor Joan = Seeking Elbow Down To Control The Centerline So The Opponent Cannot Move You
Sor Sow Chee Sow = Trapping Sticky Hands
Soung Moon = Live Gate
Sum Gwang = 3 Joints In The Arm Equivalent To The 3 Gates To Pass
Sun Ying = Body Structure
Sup Jee Sow = Crossed Arm Block In All Hand Forms
Sut = Knee

T

Teck = Kick
Tun Gwan = Snapping The Pole Sideways
Tie = Raising
Tie Gyeuk = Raising Kick
Tie Gwan = Raising Pole
Tie Jong Or Hay Jong = Raising Elbow
Tie Kune = Raising Punch
Tie Or Dang Sut = Raising Knee Block Or Attack
Tiu Gyeuk = Low Instep Kick
Tun Da = Simultaneous Palm Up Block And Punch
Tun Da Gang Da = Simultaneous Blocking And Attacking Exercise
Tun Do = Locking Knife Block
Tun Geng ="Swallowing" Or Sucking Power To Duck Or Control Attacks
Tun Gyeuk = Forward And Upward Leg Block
Tun Ma = Drawing Back Stance From Horse Or Cat In The Pole
Tun Sow = Palm Up Block Contacting On The Thumb Side Of The Wrist
Tun Sut = Outward Knee Block Or Attack
Tung Geng = A Rubber- Band Power
Tutt Sow Or Tut Sow = Freeing Arm Block
Tit Kiu Sow = Iron Bridge
Tik Gwan = Opening The Upper Gate With The Pole
Tiu Do = Snapping Up Knife
Tiu Gwan Or Tiu Kwan = Snapping Up Pole
Tiu Or Tio Gyeuk = Jumping Kick
Tiu Gyeuk = Instep Kick
To Gwan Or To Kwan = Going Forward With The Pole

Toi Dit = Take Downs
Toi Dit Chee Sow = Takedowns In Chee Sow
Toi Ma = Step Back And Turn Stance
Tok Sow Or Pow Sow = Lifting Palm Block
Tong Do = Slicing Knife Attack
Tor Chee Si Gan = Delayed Timing
Tor Ma = Step Slide Stance
Toe Geng= Power That "Spits Out" Or Bounces The Opponent Away
Toe Ma = Advancing Forward Stance In The Pole
Tiu Ma = Jumping Stance
Tun Gwan Or Tun Kwan = Retracting Pole
Tung Ma = Retreating Jumping Stance In The Pole Form

W

Why Jee = A Good Position
Wan Boo = Crossing Step Stance In The Knife Form
Wan Do = Circling Knife Attack
Wan Ma = Step And Circle Into Other Stances In The Pole
Wang Or Wan = Side
Wang Gyeuk = Side Kick
Wang Gyeuk Dok Lop Ma = Side Kick Single Leg Stance
Wang Jan = Side Of Palm Strike With The Palm Down
Wang Jong Or Pie Jong = Inside Horizontal Elbow
Wang Joan Seen = Horizontal Mother line
Wing Chun Tong = Wing Chun School
Won Or Huen Gwan /Kwan = Following Circle With The Pole
Woot Ma = Flexible Pole Stance
Woo Do = A Strike With The Knife Hand Guard
Woo Gyeuk = Blade Edge Of The Foot Block Or Strike
Woo Sow = Guard Hand Block Contacting With The Little Finger Side Of The Wrist
Woo Yi Sun - To Return The Body To A Normal Position
Woo Yi Ying = To Regain The Body Structure
Woo Yi Ying Bong Sow = To Regain The Body Structure With Bong Sow
Woo Yi Ying Gum Sow = To Regain The Body Structure With Gum Sow
Woon Geng, Ngon Geng, Jut Geng = Jerking Power

Y

Yaai = To Attack Stepping Down
Yaai How Gyeuk = To Attack By Stepping Down On The Opponent's Rear Leg
Yaai Sut = To Attack Down With The Knee
Yaan Geng Or Daai Geng = Guiding Power
Yang = Everything That Is Strong, Light, Active Male, Etc.
Yang Chee = The Energy You Inhale From Air; Oxygen
Yap Joan Lou = Closing The Gap
Yow = To Relax; An Essential Principle Of The Siu Leem Tau Form
Yee Jee Kim Yeung Ma = The Mother Of All Stances; The Stationary Front Stance For Developing All Stances Which Means Two Knees Going In Stance
Yee Ma = Transitions Between The Stances In The Pole
Yee Ying Boo Sow = Using Your Structure To Recover Your Position
Yim Wing Chun = The Young Lady That Ng Mui Taught The Wing Chun System To. She Further Refined And Improved The System So It Is Named After Her.
Yin = Everything That Is Weak, Dark, Quiet, Female, Etc.
Yin And Yang = A Pier Of Opposites That Constantly Change. All Things Have Booth Yin And Yang And All Things Change
Yin Chee = Energy You Exhale Or Carbon Dioxide
Ying = Structure
Yip Man = Bruce Lee's Teacher The Late Grandmaster Of Wing Chun Who Taught Publicly Which Spread The System
Yon Geng = Elastic Power
Yuen Geng = Patience Energy Also The Ability To Make The Opponent Move They Way You Want
Yut Boo = Turning Around Stance In The Knife Form With Fak Do And Also Going Through The Legs With The Knives
Yut Gee Choon Kune Or Doi Kou Kune = Vertical Punch

Made in the USA
Middletown, DE
29 November 2015